Customer Service

Career Success Through Customer Satisfaction

THIRD EDITION

PAUL R. TIMM, PH.D.
Marriott School of Management
Brigham Young University

NETEFFECT SERIES

PEARSON

Prentice
Hall

Upper Saddle River, New Jersey

Library of Congress Cataloging-in-Publication Data

Timm, Paul R.
  Customer service : career success through customer satisfaction /
Paul R. Timm.—3rd ed.
      p. cm.
  Includes bibliographical references and index.
  ISBN 0-13-177996-6
  1. Customer services. 2. Consumer satisfaction. 3. Customer
relations. 4. Success in business. I. Title.

  HF5415.5.T513 2005
  658.8'12—dc22

                                                    2004010246

Director of Production and Manufacturing: Bruce Johnson
Executive Editor: Elizabeth Sugg
Editorial Assistant: Cyrenne Bolt de Freitas
Marketing Manager: Leigh Ann Sims
Managing Editor-Production: Mary Carnis
Manufacturing Buyer: Ilene Sanford
Production Liaison: Denise Brown
Full Service Production: Gay Pauley/Holcomb Hathaway
Composition: Carlisle Communications Ltd.
Design Director: Cheryl Asherman
Senior Design Coordinator/Cover Design: Christopher Weigand
Cover Printer: Phoenix Color
Printer/Binder: Phoenix Book Tech Park

Pearson Education Ltd.
Pearson Education Singapore Pte. Ltd.
Pearson Education Canada, Ltd.
Pearson Education–Japan

Pearson Education Australia Pty. Limited
Pearson Education North Asia Ltd.
Pearson Educación de Mexico, S.A. de C.V.
Pearson Education Malaysia Pte. Ltd.

PEARSON
Prentice
Hall

10 9 8 7 6 5 4 3 2
ISBN 0-13-177996-6

Contents

3 Deal with Dissatisfied Customers

Here's an Opportunity for You

4 Exceed Customer Expectations

The Master Key Called A-Plus

5 Use Behaviors that Win Customer Loyalty

It's What You DO

6 Apply Winning Telephone Techniques

Use Phone Responsiveness to Create Customer Loyalty

7 Use Web Sites to Build Customer Loyalty

Tap Into the Miracle of the Internet

8 Use Written Messages to Boost Customer Satisfaction and Loyalty

Writing Can Create Valuable Ties

9 Get Others to Give Great Service

Roles of the Supervisor, Manager, or Leader

10 Understand the Future of Customer Loyalty

Preface

No skills are more important to businesspeople than those skills associated with customer service. Every business, every organization, needs its customers. Building loyal relationships with those customers is a surefire way to succeed as a company or as an individual.

Despite the obvious and tangible advantages to organizations that do so, we see too many companies doing a poor job of building customer loyalty. Too often employees and managers lack a tacit and pragmatic set of foundation skills for effectively serving and satisfying customers. The goal of this book is to provide you with those foundation skills.

This book responds to the need for a different approach to learning the foundation skills essential for career success in the challenging arena of customer service. The other customer service books displayed in bookstores everywhere typically take one of two forms: they either tell the story of one company's efforts at boosting customer service quality, or they reveal a series of tips and ideas. These books are fine as far as they go. I have written several such books myself. People can benefit from such books so long as they can effectively translate the ideas and tips into an applicable strategy for their company. But these books seldom show how to apply these diverse ideas to the reader's organization.

The few textbooks available tend to offer oversimplified suggestions on how to phrase conversations with customers, how to smile and be polite, and the like. Their simplicity defies the real world, where people don't speak from scripts and human relationships are complex and ever-changing. Furthermore, as you will see in this book, customer service involves much more than pleasant interactions.

This book takes a different approach. It ties together the best information from trade books and textbooks—and then adds more. This book offers a clear and usable process for developing the kinds of skills, attitudes, and thinking patterns needed to win customer loyalty. That process includes developing

- a heightened awareness of challenges and opportunities
- the tools for dealing with unhappy customers
- the application of the power of exceeded expectations
- the ability to lead, expand, and empower the service process
- specific skills for professional success
- a clear understanding of the future directions of customer service

This third edition offers a greatly expanded discussion of the roles of technology in today's customer service. I added a chapter on the use of Web sites and other electronic media to meet new customer requirements. Other chapters have been substantially updated based on my more than 14 years of experience as an active customer service consultant and trainer.

Perhaps no set of business skills offers as much opportunity for organizational and professional success as those in the field of customer service. Creating customer loyalty lies at the heart of any organization's reason to exist. The companies that do it well experience enormous profitability, market acceptance, and genuine satisfaction among their employees. The people who make customer service a priority and who excel in the kinds of skills taught in this book achieve unparalleled career success.

Apply the ideas in this book and enjoy the rewards of professional excellence. Then, let me know about your experiences. I can be reached via e-mail at *Paul@DrTimm.com*. For updates and ideas on building customer and employee loyalty, please visit my Web site: *www.DrTimm.com*.

ACKNOWLEDGMENTS

I express my appreciation to the following reviewers and colleagues who helped me with their excellent comments and insights:

Christopher G. Jones, Utah Valley State College
Sherron Bienevenu, Emory University

Foster Positive Attitudes

Recognizing the Role of Customer Service in Your Success

Great service is about attitude. And a service attitude leads to a richer quality of life, not only in the commercial sector.

—Leonard Berry[1]

WHAT YOU'LL LEARN IN THIS CHAPTER

- No business or individual can succeed without developing the skills that create customer loyalty.

- Although customers may be called by many names, all are engaged in an exchange of value. Some customer exchanges are more intimate and complex than others. Service skills allow you to move customers toward deeper relationships and increased loyalty.

- Advertising is a less cost-effective way of getting new customers than is word-of-mouth recommendation from an existing satisfied customer.

- The cost of lost customers can be many times the simple loss of revenue from what they no longer buy. Ripple effects expand the loss dramatically.

- Virtually all companies *say* the customer's satisfaction is paramount, but few successfully translate good intentions into a workable strategy or the systematic application of useful behaviors.

- Service skills provide a master key to career and personal success. A commitment to such skill development pays enormous dividends.

1

THE WAY IT IS . . .
What Happened to the "Service Economy"?

Financial Times columnist Michael Skapinker tells this story:

> If the two characters on my doorstep really had come to install my broadband connection, why did they have the appearance and demeanor of a pair of burglars? I asked if they could identify themselves. One fished around under his sweatshirt and produced a plastic card on a silver necklace. The other chortled that he had lost his identification.
>
> It was not a promising start but I let them in, they wiped their feet on the mat and set to work. They drilled tidily, tacked cables neatly, cleaned up their mess, demonstrated the service and left, promising that my user name and password would arrive shortly. Those first impressions can be so misleading, can't they?
>
> Not really. More than a week later, I can call up websites with exemplary speed. But I cannot send e-mails because that requires a user name and password, which has not arrived. My telephone calls yield a variety of options but not, unfortunately, "if you would like to deliver a sharp blow to the chief executive's solar plexus, press six." Human voices eventually appear and demand a user name. I haven't got one, I tell them. That's why I am calling . . . [2]

The writer goes on to say that he finally gets a user name, but when he tries it the system rejects it. This broadband provider is part of the "service economy," but where is the service?

Every person reading this book could describe similar service fiascoes. We all encounter shabby customer service every day, and much of that poor service can be attributed to poor attitudes among individuals and organizations. We've all come to expect less than optimal service despite the claims that we live in a service economy.

For several decades, enlightened companies have paid a great deal of attention to customer service and methods for improving it. The vast majority of companies have initiated customer service improvement programs or strategies. Yet despite these initiatives, customer satisfaction levels are actually falling. Reports published in major publications such as *Fortune* and the *Harvard Business Review*, among others, show statistical evidence that things are getting worse. *HBR*'s 1998 report revealed that "customer satisfaction rates in the United States are at an all-time low, while complaints, boycotts, and other expressions of consumer disloyalty rise."[3] In the United Kingdom, the National Consumer Council reported a more than 80 percent increase in the number of people making at least one complaint about service levels compared with five years earlier. The British researchers estimate that a 1 percent cut in customer service problems could generate an extra £16 million ($25 million) in profits for a typical medium-size company over five years.[4]

It is tempting to join the chorus of complainers, and no one will criticize you if you do. But we can also look at this state of affairs from another viewpoint: as an opportunity. The upside potential for those who give good service is unlimited. By making the process of satisfying customers a part of our daily lives, we can virtually guarantee our professional success. A key foundation skill needed for this is the ability to foster positive attitudes and an optimistic outlook. Below we discuss some ways of achieving this.

UNDERSTAND THAT NO ONE SUCCEEDS WITHOUT CUSTOMER SATISFACTION

No business or organization can succeed without building customer satisfaction and loyalty. Likewise, no person can make a good living without meeting the needs of customers.

> *Low customer satisfaction levels provide exceptional profit-building opportunities for companies and individuals willing to make the effort to create customer loyalty.*

Those statements may seem to be rather broad generalizations, but let's consider this argument a bit further. Most people would agree that a business needs customers—but not everyone works in business. What about other kinds of organizations? Does a government agency need customer satisfaction to succeed? Does a civic organization, church congregation, political party, family, service club, school, or fraternity need satisfied customers to succeed? To answer these questions, we need first to define what we mean by a customer. The common perception is that a customer is someone who buys something from you. Most people assume that to buy involves the exchange of money. In many cases, that is true enough. But a broader view of "customer" can be useful. In its broadest sense a customer is *someone with whom we exchange value.*

As human beings we are constantly exchanging value with each other. We are, by nature, social beings. When we exchange money for a product or service, we are customers. When we provide work in exchange for a wage, our boss and our company are our customers. When we participate in a civic organization or church group, the people to whom we give support, advice, ideas, information, and the like are our customers. When we give of ourselves to contribute to a strong family, our spouse, parents, kids, and others become our customers. When we build and maintain networks of friends and associates, we become each others' customers.

Exchanging such value involves give and take. We give and accept social support to and from friends and family. We give and take ideas and information to and from teachers or work teams. We give and take buying recommendations to and from trusted associates; we give and take gifts and tokens of appreciation to and from others. In short, much of life involves exchanges of value. As such, many of our interactions are with customers as we have broadly defined that term. The ideas on improving customer service found in this book can be equally applied to all kinds of relationships, not just commercial transactions.

> *Customer service skills provide a master key to success in all areas of one's life.*

By accepting this broader view of what it means to be and have customers, we will see that applying the principles of customer service results in much more than business or financial success. Customer service is a key to career success but, more importantly, it is a master key to success in all phases of one's life. By applying the customer service principles in this book to every aspect of your life, you will gain exceptional levels of success and life satisfaction.

RECOGNIZE ALL THE PLAYERS: CUSTOMERS BY ANY OTHER NAME . . .

> *Different names for customers can imply different kinds of transactions.*

In the world of commerce, we have a lot of names for customers, often varying by the nature of our business or organization. Some examples include clients, patients, passengers, patrons, members, associates, insureds, users, buyers, subscribers, readers, viewers, purchasers, end users, guests, or cases. But, again, the commonality in all these customers is that they engage in some sort of transaction—some exchange of value—with us or with our organization. They give us something (often, but not always, money) in exchange for something else (usually services or goods).

STRIVE TO CREATE CUSTOMER PARTNERSHIPS

> *The customer partnership reflects a high-level relationship.*

Relationships with customers can evolve into rich and fulfilling partnerships. Consultant and author Chip Bell contends that such customer partnerships arise from certain attitudes or orientations. Among these, he says that such partnerships are:

- anchored in an attitude of generosity—a "giver" perspective that finds pleasure in extending the relationship beyond just meeting a need or requirement
- grounded in trust

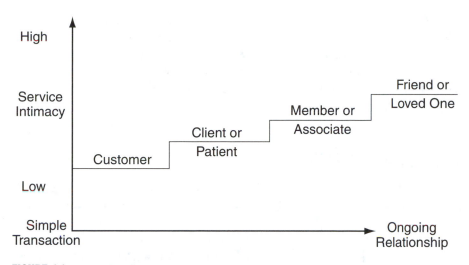

FIGURE 1.1   Levels of "customer" relationships.

- bolstered by a joint purpose
- marked by truth, candor, and straight talk mixed with compassion and care
- based on balance and pursuit of equality (I'll talk more about this in Chapter 4)
- grounded in grace, which Bell describes as "an artistic flow that gives participants a sense of familiarity and ease"[5]

Not every customer relationship becomes a partnership, of course. But such partnerships represent the highest level of customer-provider affiliation. Figure 1.1 represents two dimensions that define levels of customer relationships: the degree of service intimacy and extent of ongoing relationship. When relationships evolve into something ongoing and personally intimate, they can become rich and satisfying.

The earlier description of partnership attributes is echoed by recent research into "social capital." In his book *Achieving Success Through Social Capital*, University of Michigan professor Wayne Baker defines *social capital* as the resources available in and through personal and business networks. Good networks of relationships (including customer relationships, as we have broadly defined "customer") "are vital for good health, emotional well-being, and a meaningful life—even a longer life."[6]

Notwithstanding the semantic distinctions about customers, it remains useful to agree that everyone has customers, or people we interact with who depend on us for information, guidance, services, products, or social support—in short, value. In exchange for value we provide, they will give something back. This exchange system defines, on the most basic level, what it means to be a customer. When this exchange evolves into something more than an isolated transaction, when we move up the stair steps of relationship building, we will enjoy immense levels of career and personal satisfaction.

GET AND KEEP CUSTOMERS

Getting new customers and replacing those lost is an expensive part of any business.

New customers can be tough to get. An oft-quoted statistic says that it costs five or six times as much to get a new customer as it does to keep an existing one. So logically, it makes sense to focus on satisfying customers you already have, thus encouraging repeat business. Without customer retention, you'll spend a lot of time and effort refilling a leaky bucket as you chase an ever-replenishing supply of new customers. (This is the dilemma faced by companies that offer shoddy products or poor service. People may buy from them one time but will not come back.)

Some people think that advertising is a good way to induce people to buy. In fact, U.S. business spends about $11.5 billion a year on advertising. Surveys, however, show that only 25 percent of those polled said that a television ad would induce them to buy a new product. Likewise, only 15 percent and 13 percent respectively said that newspaper or magazine ads would cause them to buy. In short, traditional advertising has little confidence among consumers. Advice or the recommendation from a friend or relative, however, scored 63 percent as a determinant of people's buying a new product.[7] This confirms what people have long known: word of mouth is still the best way to attract customers.

Advertising is less effective at getting customers than positive word of mouth.

Advertising increases awareness of products and services, but personal referrals and recommendations by people who have had a good customer experience lead to actual decisions to purchase those products and services. Over 4,000 empirical studies document the predominant role of social networks—that is, word of mouth—in the diffusion, or spread, of products and services.[8]

To sustain repeat business, generate positive word-of-mouth "advertising" by providing exemplary service. People talk to others about a service experience when it is exceptional, out of the ordinary. You can offer the best products available, but if you fail to supplement them with a positive service experience, few customers will notice the difference between you and your competition. Service success is a matter of setting yourself apart from others through unexpected excellence.

RECOGNIZE THE GOOD NEWS AND BAD NEWS ABOUT CUSTOMER SERVICE

As the old joke setup goes, I have good news and bad news. The bad news is that the typical company will lose 10 percent to 30 percent of its customers per year—mostly because of poor service. When customers have a choice, they'll go to the competition without hesitation. Customer satisfaction is like an election held every day, and the people vote with their feet. If dissatisfied, they walk (sometimes run) to another provider—a competitor. When customers don't have a choice—such as in dealing with public utilities or government agencies—they'll use their feet for something else: they'll kick back. Employees will feel the brunt of customer dissatisfaction, dealing with unhappy customers day after day. The cost to the company comes when frustrated employees get fed up with hearing customer grief and leave. The company then faces the cost and disruption of having to replace employees.

> *Customer service is like a daily election, and customers vote with their feet.*

The good news about the relatively poor state of customer service is that organizations that initiate effective customer retention programs may see profits jump 25 to 100 percent. Nonprofit groups or organizations with no serious competition see reduced turnover, better financial results, and happier staffs. Like it or not, customer service will always be the decisive battleground where winners and losers are quickly sorted out.

CALCULATE THE TERRIBLE COST OF THE LOST CUSTOMER

What happens when poor service causes a customer to quit being a customer? Many people don't understand the real cost of a lost customer. The costs are much greater than we might realize.

To get a clearer view of the cost impact of a lost customer, let's consider a business we are all familiar with: a grocery supermarket. Let me tell you the story of Mrs. Williams:

> Harriet Williams, a 60-something single woman, has been shopping at Happy Jack's Super Market for many years. The store is close to home and its products competitively priced. Last week, Mrs. Williams approached the produce manager and asked, "Sonny, can I get a half head of lettuce?" He looked at her like she was crazy and curtly said, "Sorry, lady. We just sell the whole head." She was a bit embarrassed but accepted his refusal.
>
> Later she had several other small disappointments (she wanted a quart of skim milk and they only had half-gallons), and when she checked out her groceries she was largely ignored by the clerk who was carrying on a conversation with a fellow employee. The clerk made matters worse by abruptly demanding "two forms of ID" with Harriet's check (What do they think I am, a common criminal?) and failing to say thank you.

Mrs. Williams left the store that day and decided that she was no longer going to do business there. Although she had shopped at Happy Jack's for many years, she realized that she had never felt that her business was appreciated. She got the overall feeling that Happy Jack's employees couldn't care less if she shopped there. She spent about 50 hard-earned dollars there every week, but to the store employees she was just another cash cow to be milked without so much as a sincere "thank you." Nobody seemed to care if she was a satisfied customer. But today is different—no more "nice" Mrs. Williams! Today she decided to buy her groceries elsewhere. Maybe—just maybe—there is a store where they'll appreciate her business.[9]

What do the employees think about Mrs. Williams's actions? They're not worried. Life is like that. You win some; you lose some. Happy Jack's is a pretty big chain and doesn't really need Mrs. Williams. Besides, she can be a bit cranky at times and her special requests are stupid. (Who ever heard of buying a half head of lettuce!) Happy Jack's will survive just fine without her $50 a week. Too bad she's unhappy, but a big company like this can't twist itself into contortions just to save one little old lady from going down the street to the competition. Sure, we believe in treating customers well, but we're businesspeople. Let's look at the bottom line. After all, it can hardly be considered a major financial disaster to lose a customer like Mrs. Williams. Or can it?

Appreciate the Cost of the Lost

The employees at Happy Jack's need to understand some economic facts. Successful businesses look long-term. They also look at the "ripple effects" of their service, not just at the immediate profit from an individual purchase.

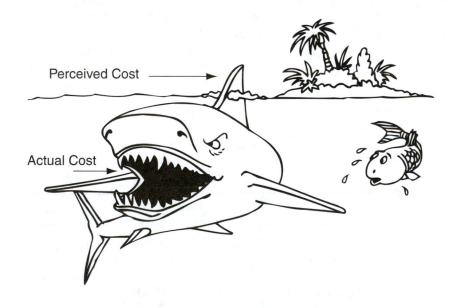

Perceived Cost

Actual Cost

The shortsighted employee sees Mrs. Williams as a small customer dealing with a big company. Let's change that view: look at the situation from another, broader perspective.

Ho Hum, Just the Loss of One Small Customer . . . or Is It?

The loss of Mrs. Williams is not, of course, just a $50 loss. It's much, much more. She was a $50-a-week buyer. That's $2,600 a year or $26,000 over a decade. Perhaps she would shop at Happy Jack's for a lifetime, but we'll use the more conservative 10-year figure for illustration.

But the ripple effects make it much worse. Studies show that *an upset customer tells on average between 10 and 20 other people about an unhappy experience.* Some people will tell many more, but let's stay conservative and assume that Mrs. Williams told 11. The same studies say that these 11 *may tell an average of 5 others each.* This could be getting serious!

> *Ripple effects happen when upset customers tell other people.*

How many people are likely to hear the bad news about Happy Jack's? Look at the math:

Mrs. Williams	1 person
tells 11 others	+11 people
who tell 5 each	+55 people
Total who heard =	67 people

Are all 67 of these people going to rebel against Happy Jack's? Probably not. Let's assume that of these 67 customers or potential customers, only one-quarter of them decide not to shop at Happy Jack's. Twenty-five percent of 67 (rounded) is 17.

Assume that these 17 people would also be $50-a-week shoppers, and Happy Jack's stands to lose $44,200 a year, or $442,000 in a decade, because Mrs. Williams was upset when she left the store. Somehow, giving her that half head of lettuce doesn't sound so stupid.

Although these numbers are starting to get alarming, they are still conservative. In many parts of the country, a typical supermarket customer actually spends about $100 a week, so losing a different customer could quickly double these figures.

How Much Will It Cost to Replace These Customers?

Customer service research says that *it costs about five to six times as much to attract a new customer* (mostly advertising and promotion costs) *as it costs to keep an existing one* (where costs may include giving refunds, offering samples, replacing merchandise, or giving a half head of

> *Replacing lost customers is extremely costly.*

TABLE 1.1   Sales needed to sustain a job.

Salary	Benefits	After-Tax Cost	Sales Needed
$40,000	$18,400	$29,200	$584,000
$25,000	$11,500	$18,250	$365,000
$15,000	$ 6,900	$10,950	$219,000
$10,000	$ 4,600	$ 7,300	$146,000

lettuce). One report put these figures at about $19 to keep a customer happy versus $118 to get a new buyer into the store.

Again, some quick math shows the real cost of the lost Mrs. Williams:

Cost of keeping Mrs. Williams happy $19
Cost of attracting 17 new customers $2,006

Now let's make our economic "facts of life" even more meaningful to each employee.

Understand How Lost Customers Mean Lost Jobs

Table 1.1 shows a simple way to calculate the amount of sales needed to pay employee salaries. Assuming that a company pays 50 percent in taxes and earns a profit of 5 percent after taxes, Table 1.1 shows how much must be sold to pay each employee (in four different salary levels) and maintain current profit levels.

These figures will vary, of course, but no businessperson would disagree that there can be a direct impact on employee jobs. If a $10,000-a-year part-time clerk irritates as few as three or four customers *in a year*, the ripple effects can quickly exceed the amount of sales needed to maintain that job. Unfortunately, many organizations have employees who irritate three or four customers *a day*! Ouch.

Self-Analysis   **Applying the Mrs. Williams Example to Your Company**

Let's take a few moments and go back to the Mrs. Williams example, but instead use your own organization. Suppose that you lose one customer and the other statistics hold true. Take a few moments to calculate the numbers as they apply to your organization. If you work for a non-profit or government agency where the dollar sales is not a relevant measure, calculate the number of people who may be aggravated or upset with you and your organization. Think in terms of the psychological price that must be paid as you deal with frustrated, angry, upset patrons on a day-to-day basis.

Calculating the Cost of Your Lost Customer*

A. Average or typical dollar amount spent
    (per week or month as appropriate): $_____per (customer)

B. Annual dollar amount (weekly figure × 52
    or monthly figure × 12): $_____

C. Decade dollar amount (B × 10): $_____

D. Ripple effect costs (B × 17—people who may
    follow an unhappy customer "out the door"):   + $_____

Annual revenue lost: = $_____

Then,

E. Add customer replacement costs of
    17 customers × $118 (a typical figure):   = $2,006.00

F. Subtract the cost of keeping your present
    customer happy ($19 is a typical figure):   − $ 19.00

G. Replacement" costs (E minus F):   = $1,987.00

Finally,

Total the revenue lost figures (B or C + G)

    A rough cost of your lost: $_____

*Note: These calculations are designed only to get you thinking about the ripple effects of unhappy customers. Their mathematical precision is not guaranteed nor is it that important. The point is, lost customers cost a lot of money.

RECOGNIZE THE CHALLENGE OF TRANSLATING SLOGANS AND GOOD INTENTIONS INTO A STRATEGY

Most people accept, or at least give lip service to, the idea that "the customer is the boss," that he or she is a "king" or "queen" (or at least a prince or princess!). They talk about the customer always being right. They say, ad nauseam, that the customer is "our reason for existing" as an organization. Yet despite these claims, how is the service given? Often, not great.

The real challenge lies in translating such slogans into actions that convey these feelings and beliefs *to the customer*. Even when leaders truly believe in the importance of customer service, they still face the difficulty of

> *One of the greatest challenges lies in translating slogans or good intentions into behaviors customers want.*

getting the customer contact people to do what customers want—especially when a customer's request is a bit unusual. The problem gets trickier when you realize that the lowest-paid and least-trained employees are often those who face the customer every day. For example,

- A multimillion-dollar fast-food restaurant places its success squarely in the hands of the minimum-wage teenager taking the orders and delivering the food.
- A huge financial institution's image is created in the mind of the customer by the entry-level teller who handles the customer's day-to-day transactions.
- A multibillion-dollar government agency is judged largely by the receptionist who answers the phone or greets the customer, thus setting a tone for any transaction. (Many a criticism of the "government bureaucracy" can be traced to a receptionist "getting off on the wrong foot" with a patron.)

When you sincerely buy into the value of a happy, loyal customer and effectively communicate that value to each customer, you virtually guarantee your success. When you supervise others, you need to "infect" them with your same positive attitudes and skills. That can be a challenge for leaders, something we'll talk more about later in this book.

KNOW WHY SERVICE IS IMPORTANT TO YOU—YES, YOU!

> *Service skills are crucial for success at all organizational levels.*

Businesses benefit from good service, but suppose you don't own a business. As "just an employee," what can you gain from developing service skills? The short answer is that customer service skills are the same skills that bring success and satisfaction to all aspects of life. The best reason for learning the processes that create customer loyalty is that *it will make you feel better about your life and yourself.* Sure, there are solid business reasons as we've already discussed. But ultimately, the personal benefits can be even greater.

Based on 30 years of business and professional experience in a variety of organizations, I am absolutely certain that people who utilize the kinds of skills discussed in this book are happier, more productive, more successful, and, yes, wealthier than people who choose to ignore the power of customer loyalty. Take that statement on faith for now, but as you study and apply the ideas in the remaining chapters of this book, you will see what I mean.

We all start out as peons in organizations. Yet from day one we choose how much we want to give to the organizations we work in. Inevitably, the more effort, energy, and commitment we give, the more value we get from

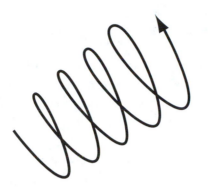

FIGURE 1.2   The customer service helix.

our association with that organization. That's a principle of life that has been proven true throughout time. The flip side—giving the least we can get away with—results in unsatisfying relationships, mind-numbing work, and low levels of satisfaction. Giving average or substandard service will be hazardous to your career health. Undistinguished service leads to unhappy and eventually extinguished careers.

The person who makes a commitment to mastering customer skills will be light-years ahead of one who fails to do so. Betsy Sanders, a Nordstrom retail executive, describes this personal commitment, illustrated in Figure 1.2: "The nature of such a commitment is perhaps best represented by a helix, which curves back around on itself but always moves up as it comes around. Thus, wherever you are in the process, the principles of service leadership provided can be applied to your situation now and will also support your ongoing development."[10]

> *A commitment to using customer service skills ignites a growth process.*

STRIVE FOR THE ULTIMATE GOAL: CUSTOMERS FOR LIFE

The ultimate goal of customer service is to create customer loyalty. Understanding loyalty—what makes your customer loyal and how to measure this—enables a company or person to improve customer-driven service quality. I'll talk more about this later in the book, but for now, it is important to understand what loyalty means.

> *Some customer behaviors may create the image of loyalty but can be a counterfeit.*

To best understand what customer loyalty is, it is useful to first recognize what it is not. Customer loyalty is sometimes mistaken for:

- Customer satisfaction alone. Satisfaction is a necessary component, but a customer may be satisfied today but not necessarily loyal to you in the future.

Service Snapshot	Burgers Supreme

Steve and Debby K. owned an independent fast-food restaurant called Burgers Supreme. For more than six years they built up a loyal clientele, many of whom ate there almost every day. Not only did these customers buy lunch at Burgers Supreme, but they also brought friends and fellow workers. Some of the regulars were teased about owning stock in the restaurant, although none did.

The menu was broad, covering dozens of sandwiches, salads, soups, desserts, and specialty foods like gyros, onion rings, and frozen yogurt. Everything was prepared fresh. But the loyalty went far beyond good food and fair prices.

Almost every regular customer had the unexpected surprise of having Steve, Debby, or one of their employees say, "This meal's on me." Owners, managers, and even employees were authorized to give free lunches to loyal customers. Obviously that didn't happen every time the customer came in, but it did reflect the owners' belief in recognizing customer loyalty. It also reflected their willingness to empower their employees to give something away now and then.

The counter help at Burgers Supreme learned service behaviors from Debby's example. They greeted customers by name, smiled, cheerfully fixed any mistakes, and kept hustling to make sure the restaurant was clean, even during the busiest lunch hour.

Faced with tremendous competition from national chains like Wendy's, McDonald's, and others who serve similar fare, Burgers Supreme ate their lunch, so to speak, with friendly, individual, personalized service. They didn't just talk the talk of customer service. They walked the walk.

- A response to some trial offer or special incentive. You can't buy loyalty; you must earn it.
- Large share of the market. You may have a large percentage of the customers for a particular product or service for reasons other than customer loyalty to you. Perhaps your competitors are poor or your current prices more attractive.
- Repeat buying alone. Some people buy as a result of habit, convenience, or price but would be quick to defect to an alternative.

Recognizing counterfeit loyalty is important. It can lull you into a false sense of security while your competition may be building real customer loyalty.

So, what exactly is customer loyalty? A more reliable definition has evolved in recent years. Considerable empirical research concludes that customer loyalty is best defined as a composite of three important characteristics:

- It is driven by *overall satisfaction*. Low or erratic levels of satisfaction disqualify a company from earning customer loyalty.
- It involves a commitment on the part of the customer to make a sustained *investment in an ongoing relationship* with a company.
- It is reflected by a combination of attitudes and behaviors, including:
  - *repeat buying* (or the intention to do so as needed)
  - *willingness to recommend* the company to others
  - a commitment to the company demonstrated by a *resistance to switch* to a competitor

More recent research by the Gallup polling organization validates these elements and takes the concept a bit further by describing customer "engagement" as a critical variable. In a 2003 article, the *Gallup Management Journal* questions the intuitively obvious link between loyalty and profitability. The researchers conclude that some kinds of customer loyalty may not be profitable. Specifically, they say that "repeated purchase behavior [that] has been motivated—or bribed—by a company's gifts, discounts, or other purchase rewards" may not be profitable. "These customers aren't really loyal; they're just customers who haven't left—yet." The researchers go on to say that "behavioral measures of loyalty are often misleading because they can't differentiate between customers with brand allegiance and those with no commitment. The uncommitted may *appear* to be loyal, but they only remain customers out of habit or because the company continues to bribe them. They're susceptible to the incentives and discounts competitors will offer them to switch."[11]

The Gallup research concludes that if you fail to make an emotional connection with customers, satisfaction is worthless. The study uses a series of measures to define customer *engagement* and concludes that customers who feel a sense of engagement with the organizations they buy from become priceless resources. Several case studies reveal that fully engaged customers—that is, customers who are both satisfied and emotionally connected to a store—visit the store more often and spend more money.

Concepts of engagement, allegiance, and so on offer different ways to express levels of loyalty and commitment a customer may hold toward a company or brand. While the terminology may differ, our earlier definition of the conditions necessary for creating loyalty remains essentially intact. For now, let's agree that customer loyalty is the highest goal of our service efforts.

> *True customer loyalty is a function of overall satisfaction, a commitment to strengthen the relationship, repeat buying, and willingness to recommend you to others.*

Another Look | Why Customer Satisfaction Is Not Enough

Several recent Gallup case studies provide evidence that measures of satisfaction tell us little about customer loyalty. In the case of a leading supermarket chain, proof of the importance of an emotional connection can be found in the frequency of customers' visits and the amount of money they spent during those visits. Shoppers who were less than "extremely satisfied" (those who rated their satisfaction as 1, 2, 3, or 4 on a 5-point scale) visited this chain about 4.3 times per month, spending an average of $166 during that month. Those who were "extremely satisfied" but did not also have a strong emotional connection to the chain actually went to the store less often (4.1 times per month) and spent less ($144). In this case, extreme satisfaction represented no added value to the store.

However, when Gallup looked at customers who were extremely satisfied and emotionally connected to the store ("fully engaged"), a very different customer relationship emerged. These customers visited the store 5.4 times and spent $210 a month. Apparently, not all "extremely satisfied" customers are the same. Those with strong emotional connections visited the grocery chain 32 percent more often and spent 46 percent more money than those without emotional bonds. Satisfaction without engagement? Worthless. Satisfaction with engagement? Priceless.[12]

Probes

1. What does this research suggest about companies that simply measure customer satisfaction?
2. What are the key challenges facing organizations that want to build customer loyalty?
3. How could your business apply this information to build customer loyalty?

A FINAL THOUGHT

Customer service skill development provides the most significant arena for career success. Whether you work for a huge corporation or you run a lemonade stand, the principles of customer service remain the same. You live and die by what your customers think of you.

In fact, your number-one task, regardless of your job title, organizational position, experience, or seniority, will *always* be to attract, satisfy, and preserve loyal customers.

Summary of Key Ideas

- Businesses or individuals cannot succeed without creating customer loyalty.
- Customers may be called by many names, but all are engaged in an exchange of value. Some customer relationships are more intimate

and complex, but the exchange element remains constant. Moving customers toward deeper relationships with you requires service skills.

- Advertising is generally less cost effective in getting new customers than a word-of-mouth recommendation from an existing satisfied customer.
- The cost of lost customers can be many times the simple reduction of their sales. Ripple effects expand the loss dramatically.
- While all companies *say* the customer's satisfaction is paramount, few successfully translate good intentions into a workable strategy or specific behavior.
- Ultimately, service skills provide a master key to career and personal success. A commitment to such skill development pays enormous dividends.
- Customers who feel a positive sense of emotional engagement with you and your company will be your most priceless assets. They make the difference between a successful and an unsuccessful company.

Key Concepts

cost of the lost customer

customer satisfaction versus loyalty

exchanging value

lost customer–lost job relationship

loyalty and engagement

ripple effects

social capital

word-of-mouth advertising

Self-Test Questions

1. What defines a customer (using this term in the broad sense)?
2. What are some attitudes or orientations that define a customer relationship? What factors account for a strengthening of this relationship?
3. How can customer skills be valuable even in nonprofit organizations (or organizations that have no competitors)?
4. Why does word-of-mouth "advertising" work so effectively?
5. How can a person build his or her "social capital"?
6. How do ripple effects escalate the problem of the lost customer?
7. What three key characteristics define real customer loyalty?
8. What do we mean by an "engaged" customer, and how does this relate to customer loyalty?
9. What characteristics are often confused with customer loyalty but do not represent real loyalty?

Application Activity: Interview Service Providers

1. Interview five people about their customer service attitudes. Specifically, ask them to describe their internal and external customers and what they feel about the importance of serving them.

2. Ask two businesspeople to estimate the typical amount customers spend with them. Then calculate the "cost of a lost customer" based on the scenario in this chapter. Ask each businessperson to react to this estimate. Does it seem plausible? Too high? Too low?

3. Describe three businesses that have won your customer loyalty—places you enjoy doing business and are likely to remain a customer. What, specifically, causes you to give them your loyalty? (Note: Often it's subtle little things that win you over.)

4. What major corporations that you've heard of seem to be doing the best job of building customer loyalty? In what ways do they attempt to build long-term relationships with customers?

Notes

1. L. Berry. *On Great Service: A Framework for Action*. Qtd. in *The Seattle Times*, published via America Online, April 3, 1995.

2. M. Skapinker. "Awkward Customers: Companies Still Have Much to Learn About the True Meaning of Service." *Financial Times*, February 12, 2003, p. 8.

3. Cited in D. Freemantle. *What Customers Like About You* (London: Nicholas Brealey Publishing, Ltd., 1998), p. 1.

4. Ibid. p. 2.

5. C. R. Bell. *Customers as Partners* (San Francisco: Berrett-Koehler Publishers, 1994), pp. 5–6.

6. W. Baker. *Achieving Success Through Social Capital* (San Francisco: Josey-Bass, Inc., 2000). Qtd. on dust jacket.

7. K. Goldman. "Study Finds Ads Induce Few People to Buy." *Wall Street Journal*, October 17, 1995, p. B6.

8. E. Rogers. *Diffusion of Innovations*, 4th ed. (New York: Free Press, 1995).

9. P. R. Timm. *50 Powerful Ideas You Can Use to Keep Your Customers*, 3rd ed. (Hawthorne, NJ: Career Press, 2002), pp. 15–19.

10. B. Sanders. *Fabled Service* (San Diego: Pfeiffer & Company, 1995), p. xv.

11. W. J. McEwen and J. H. Flemming. "Customer Satisfaction Doesn't Count." *Gallup Management Journal*. March 13, 2003. [Online]. Available http://gmj.gallup.com/management_articles/customer_engagement/article.

12. Ibid.

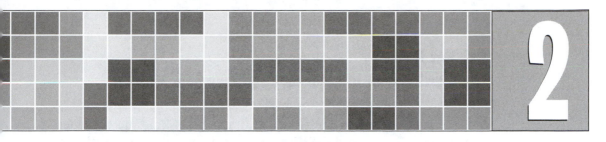

Recognize and Deal with Customer Turnoffs

The Customer Keeps Score

Research by the Forum Corporation suggests that 70% of the customers lost by 13 big service and manufacturing companies [studied] had scooted because of a lack of attention from the front-line employees. It's an emotional tie, not mere satisfaction that brings the customer back.

—Tom Peters[1]

WHAT YOU'LL LEARN IN THIS CHAPTER

- Everyone has pet peeves about poor service they receive. In most cases, these annoyances are little things that may have a negative, cumulative effect.
- The cumulative impact of little customer irritators can dramatically impact a company, as illustrated later by the Kmart versus Wal-Mart example.
- Customer turnoffs can be categorized as stemming from value, systems, or people problems.
- Great value arises from moving people beyond satisfaction and their "zone of indifference" into the category of loyal customer.
- Two major steps are needed to create customer loyalty.
- Five tips are offered for better listening when dealing with customer complaints.
- Systematic observation, active listening, explorer groups, mystery shoppers, focus groups, comment cards, and online feedback can assess customer satisfaction, expectations, and wants.

THE WAY IT IS . . .
The Terrible Cost of Ignoring Customer Concerns[2]

A great way for a business to fall on its face is to assume that it knows exactly what the customer wants—without actually asking the customer. A historic look at a major auto manufacturer in the 1980s and early 1990s shows the impact of the failure to have customer engagement. During that time, Volkswagen Corporation of America saw its U.S. sales drop by 90 percent from its 1970 high of over a half-million cars to about 50,000 automobiles sold in 1993. What happened?

Despite being the virtual inventor of subcompact cars (who can forget the ubiquitous Beetle?), VW's competitive advantage had almost evaporated by the early '90s. Competitors (especially the Japanese manufacturers) engaged in extended conversations with their customers and used feedback received to develop appealing features. VW didn't talk to their customers. Their engineers decided that they knew the *right* way to position a steering wheel, while customers told the Japanese manufacturers they wanted adjustable tilt wheels. VW designers were certain that its radios were just fine, while customers told competitors of desires for high-quality, multi-speaker stereo sound.

The result: Customers came to perceive VW autos as offering less value. By the early 1990s, Volkswagen of America was fighting for its life.

VW has made a dramatic comeback since those days and is one of the premier auto manufacturers today. But the company paid a terrible price— it had to scramble for its life—because it failed to stay current with customer expectations and wants.

Companies and individuals cannot remain competitive if they are insulated from customer input. To stay on top, engage customers in defining value.

BE AWARE THAT EVERYONE HAS PET PEEVES ABOUT SERVICE

Gather a few people together and ask them to describe some pet peeves about their experiences as customers, and you'll get an earful. Everyone can recall situations where they were treated poorly, or where they bought products or services that just didn't measure up.

I often begin customer service training sessions by having the group think about specifically irritating experiences and generate a list of gripes. You may find it useful to articulate some of your own pet peeves. Take a moment to make a list of *specific* things about customer service that turn you off.

Self-Analysis	My Pet Peeves in Customer Service

Quickly list 10 specific turnoffs. What kinds of things irritate you when you are a customer? Think about several customer contexts: retail, repair services, restaurants, government agencies, etc. Be as specific as possible about exactly what irritates you. Perhaps cite an example if that helps you express your idea.

1. _____
2. _____
3. _____
4. _____
5. _____
6. _____
7. _____
8. _____
9. _____
10. _____

Based on my 15 years of consulting and training in customer service, I suspect some of these kinds of turnoffs may be on your list:

- being ignored or receiving rude or indifferent service
- having to wait too long
- poor quality work (especially on repair jobs) or shoddy products
- sale items not in stock
- merchandise prices not marked, forcing a price check at the cashier
- dirty restaurants or rest rooms
- phone calls put on hold or forcing you to select from a long menu of choices
- employees lacking product knowledge
- high-pressure sales tactics
- employees talking down to you or using confusing jargon
- inflexibility when you make a request

Do you see some of your pet peeves on this list? Most people will, although there are many other possibilities, as well.

> *Everyone has examples of irritating experiences as customers.*

RECOGNIZE THAT THE LITTLE THINGS MEAN EVERYTHING

Service turnoffs are, more often than not, little things that irritate us. Problems with shoddy products or poor quality work happen, of course, but it's the little annoyances that are most likely to grind us in everyday customer experiences.

We can typically buy almost any product we want from several different vendors. We can buy a television from an upscale department or furniture store, a discount store, an electronics shop, a catalog merchant, a consumer warehouse, or an Internet retailer. What causes us to choose one over the other?

> *Since most things can be purchased from one of several places, often little factors determine where we shop.*

Price is a consideration for many consumers, of course, but what if the prices are about the same? In those cases (or when the buyer is not price sensitive) people are likely to select a vendor on the basis of a lot of little things. Perhaps they like—or strongly dislike—a store's advertising. Perhaps the location is convenient, the merchandise displays are attractive, the clerks are friendly and knowledgeable, or the selection and warranty offered are good. Maybe the Web site is friendly and easy to use. Possibly the company or service provider supports social causes the buyer likes. The possibilities for differentiation are endless.

Perhaps nowhere is the illustration of little things making big differences more evident than in the competition among the giant discount retailers. In the 1980s, the discount giant Kmart Corporation surpassed Sears to become the world's largest retailer. Kmart's reign at the top was, however, short-lived. In the early 1990s, Wal-Mart passed Kmart for the number-one spot. What's the difference between Kmart and Wal-Mart?

Think about that question. What is the difference between a Kmart and a Wal-Mart store? It may be easier to list the similarities. Kmart and Wal-Mart stores are similar in size, locations, layouts, colors, displays, merchandise variety, prices, and many other characteristics. So, what accounted for the recent devastation of Kmart and the stratospheric rise of Wal-Mart?

> *Little things can account for huge competitive advantages.*

A good case can be made for the little things Wal-Mart has implemented to improve customer service. Over the years I have routinely asked seminar participants to imagine with me that they were to go to a strange city where they had never been before. When they got there, they would be taken to a Kmart store. I then ask, "What is it going to be like—specifically?"

Inevitably, I would get an earful of comments about dirty floors, poorly displayed merchandise, surly checkout clerks, no one to help find things, the smell of popcorn, battered shopping carts with square wheels. Occa-

Greeters can put a human face on a large company. (©1997, Washington Post Writers Group. Reprinted with permission.)

sionally, someone would mention a positive (the Martha Stewart line of home furnishings) or a neutral (the "Blue Light Specials"), but the overwhelming number of comments would be negative.

I would then ask that they visualize visiting another strange city and going to Wal-Mart. When I ask what they expect there, the comments are almost always favorable, with many people mentioning such things as:

- the greeters at the door to welcome customers
- employees wearing vests with name tags to help customers find things
- cleaner floors, tidier parking lots, stores that don't smell like popcorn
- quick checkouts staffed with friendly people who actually seem to like their job

Notice my emphasis in this exercise: identify things they *expect* to be different. As we'll see later in the book, expectations can be more important than the reality. In reality, some Kmart stores do a good job with all the things listed above, and some Wal-Mart stores are not so great. But customers don't typically expect positive things from Kmart.

The results of these kinds of little things are astounding. When Wal-Mart first surpassed Kmart in the early 1990s, both retailers had approximately equal sales. Today, the gap has become huge. Kmart is in bankruptcy as I write this. Its 2003 sales were $28 billion, while Wal-Mart has become the largest company in the world! As of 2004 Wal-Mart had 1.4 million employees with sales of some $258 billion annually—almost 10 times the sales of Kmart.

But here is the salient point: Kmart and Wal-Mart have sold the same kinds of stuff for about the same prices using a similar marketing format via the same number of stores! Little things mean *everything* when it comes to customer loyalty.

Service Snapshot | **Michelle's Attention to Detail Means PR Firm Success**

A story by Robert McGarvey illustrates the importance of paying attention to the little things: Minding details projects an attitude of professionalism that attracts and keeps customers. Michelle, who started a public relations business, was explaining her communications techniques to a prospective client when suddenly the company executive interrupted: could she promise that her work wouldn't be marred with misspellings?

Misspellings? Michelle was stunned. She couldn't imagine why the executive asked. Later client calls revealed a pattern: Inattention to the "little stuff"—not returning phone calls promptly, not itemizing bills, acting before asking for approval—was driving prospective clients wild. The real key for succeeding in business is not always brilliance but competence in day-to-day details, Michelle says. She won an account once because she was the only presenter who followed up her meeting with a letter.[3]

IDENTIFY THREE CATEGORIES OF CUSTOMER TURNOFFS

To better understand customer turnoffs, I've collected thousands of responses about specific things that irritate people. Some categories became clear as I analyzed the responses with researcher Kristen DeTienne. We found that customer turnoffs fall into three categories: value, systems, and people.[4]

Value Turnoffs

A fundamental turnoff for customers is the feeling that they receive poor value from a product or service. In short, shoddy products or sloppy work can put customers through the roof.

Value can be simply defined as *quality relative to price paid.* If you purchase an inexpensive, throwaway item at a discount store—say a 79 cent pen—you may not be upset if it doesn't last very long. But buy a $79 ballpoint fountain pen that leaks in your shirt pocket and you'd be furious. If you make a major purchase of an automobile, appliance, or professional service and it quits working or fails to meet your needs, you will experience a value turnoff.

> *Value is a function of a product's quality relative to its price.*

The major responsibility for providing customers with appropriate value lies with the top leadership of the organization. It's the executive decision makers in a company who determine the products or services that will be sold. In a one-person enterprise, the owner determines the quality/pricing formula which defines value. If you run a lemonade stand, you determine how many lemons and how much sugar you will use. (Ideally, you check with your customers to see how they like it.) If you start an auto dealership, you will need to choose if you want to sell Hyundai or Lexus, Ford or Lincoln. All may be fine cars, but the perception of value (product quality relative to price) may be different in the eyes of your customers. If you offer tax preparation services, you will need to decide whether you hire clerks who input data into software programs or certified accountants who can advise clients on tax planning. Either strategy may be acceptable, but the perception of value will differ. Other people in an organization can affect value, but leadership bears the major responsibility for ensuring it.

Systems Turnoffs

Say the word *systems* and many people think of computers or phones. In the context of customer service, however, the term *systems* is broader than that. The term is used here to describe any *process, procedure, or policy used to "deliver" the product or service to the customer.* Systems are the way we get the value to the customer. When seen like this, systems will include such things as:

> *Systems involve any action or procedure used to get the product or service to a customer. Systems problems are primarily the responsibility of management.*

- company location, layout, parking facilities, phone lines
- employee training and staffing
- record keeping (including computer systems for handling customer transactions)
- policies regarding guarantees and product returns
- delivery or pick-up services
- marketing and sales tactics
- customer follow-up procedures
- billing and accounting processes

The elimination of systems turnoffs is primarily the responsibility of managers in most organizations. This is because systems changes often require spending money (e.g., for new locations, remodeling, additional staffing and training, and added delivery services). Nonmanagement employees can and should be involved in suggesting systems changes, however. Management can get some of its best change ideas from employees at all levels. But ultimately, a manager must initiate a systems change.

How Important Are Systems?

While every organization needs systems for doing business in an orderly manner, some people argue that the majority of customer service problems are caused by systems mistakes or the illogical application of systems. The converse, however, is true as well. Business consultant Michael Gerber believes that systems may well be the most important key to business success. He cites hamburger giant McDonald's as an example. In an excerpt from a brochure advertising Gerber's "The E-Myth Seminar," Gerber describes

Another Look | Don't Let Your Systems Drive Your Customers Crazy![5]

By Ron Kaufman

Customers are often left frustrated by a company's smooth-running and standardized, but in-flexible policies. Does your company "run like clockwork"? Are your accountants pleased with how smoothly everything moves along? Are your managers content with how customers are managed throughout your system? If so, watch out! Your present methods may include policies and procedures that are convenient for the company, but utterly frustrating for your customers. . . .

In recent weeks I have had a series of actual experiences bizarre enough to make me wonder whether anyone is listening at all! For example, there's the case of "The Conference Rate" at Hilton Hotel in Los Angeles:

I was making arrangements to attend the American Society of Training and Development Annual Conference in Los Angeles. As a frequent flyer, I have many award coupons offering a 50 per cent discount from usual hotel rates. I called Hilton Hotels in California to make my reservations. The reservations clerk was infinitely helpful. First, she took my name, then my contact numbers. She confirmed the dates, my room preference and credit card number. She asked if I was a Hilton Honors Club member, which I was not. She signed me up on the spot and then remarked: "Now that you are a Hilton Honors Club member, I can offer you an even lower rate, and an upgraded Towers room on a higher floor. A fruit basket will be waiting for you upon arrival." I was delighted. And my special discount rate was just US$85 per night.

In signing off, I said: "Thank you for your help. I am looking forward to staying at the Hilton during the conference." "The conference?" she shot back quickly. "What conference are you attending?"

I replied that I was attending the American Society for Training and Development's 50th Annual Conference at Disneyland. She said quickly: "Mr. Kaufman, if you are attending a conference during your stay, you must use our special conference rate of US$112." I laughed at her proposal and stated that I was happy with the special rate she had already confirmed on my behalf. "Oh no," she repeated. "If you are coming for a conference, you must use the special conference rate. We have a block of rooms set aside for conference participants on a lower floor. These rooms are specially reserved for the people who are attending the conference."

My protests were to no avail. She checked with her supervisor, who concurred. "I'm sorry, but that's our policy," she said without much concern. I surrendered to her insistence, listened as she cancelled my Hilton Honors Club reservation, declined to have her book me back into the same hotel at the higher conference rate, and hung up the phone in disbelief.

I called right back. I reached a different reservations clerk and made another reservation. I used my frequent flyer award coupon and the new Hilton Honors Club membership number

Another Look	Don't Let Your Systems Drive . . . *continued*

I had received in the previous phone call. This time I kept my mouth shut about attending any conference!

I paid just US$85 when I went to Los Angeles. I enjoyed the Hilton Towers room and enjoyed the complimentary fruit basket upon arrival. No thanks to Hilton's absurd policy and customer unfriendly procedures, though.

Somewhere deep inside the marketing department of Hilton Hotels, yield management professionals have carefully calculated the maximum rate they can, and will, charge participants at an international conference. Meanwhile conference participants are also thinkers, communicators and frequent flyers . . . real-live customers! Hilton Hotels, are you listening?

working with a client named Murray, who was so tied up in the day-to-day work of his business that he failed to grow a successful company. Gerber calls this episode "The Day I Fell in Love with McDonald's." From this, I believe you will better understand the importance of good systems.

When my meeting with Murray ended, I was exhausted. I had pages of notes, hours of conversations swirling in my head, and a long drive home. I needed a few minutes to collect my thoughts. So, I pulled into a McDonald's to grab a bite and sort out my notes.

Talk about being confused. I didn't know where to start with Murray and his company. He loved his product and his dreams for the future. But something was wrong. I just couldn't put my finger on it. . . . Then it hit me.

Maybe it's fate, but that day was the first time I was in a McDonald's twice in the same day. Suddenly, from the corner of my eye, I watched a lady approach the counter, and the young girl who was serving asked if she could take her order. Nothing out of the ordinary. But there was something about what happened that caught my interest. It was both *what* she said and *her manner* of saying it.

I've been to McDonald's restaurants from coast-to-coast. And I've been served by males and females, young and old, and many different ethnic groups. But regardless of where I am, or who is serving me, two very interesting things happen to me each time. First, I feel *comfortable*, because I know what to expect. And second, because I know what to expect, I feel *in control of my experience.*

At that moment I knew the secret of the McDonald's success. Wow! What an amazing discovery. Instantly I could see that this secret can work in any business . . . The essence of the secret is *how* they [sell] that's so wonderful. It's their *system* that makes it a success. The key is that they have a system for *every-thing*. Regardless of who is working on a shift, the entire staff is taught the system. . . . There is no indecision. No confusion. No hesitation. No sour faces. No frustrated looks. Everything works like a well-oiled machine.[6]

Gerber's observations illustrate the importance of effective systems in any business. It is the systems that can create comfort for both employees and customers. Knowing what to do and how to do it comes, of course, from extensive training and careful design of the delivery systems. Failure to design and train on effective systems not only negates the usefulness of systems but can result in many customer service turnoffs.

People Turnoffs

People turnoffs are almost always communication problems. Employees who fail to communicate appropriately, both verbally (with words) and nonverbally (without words), can quickly irritate a customer. Some examples of people turnoffs are:

- employees who fail to greet or even smile at a customer
- people who give inaccurate information or convey a lack of knowledge
- employees chatting among themselves or allowing telephone interruptions while ignoring a customer
- behaviors that project a rude or uncaring attitude

People turnoffs occur when customers feel you don't care.
(ZIGGY ©1995 ZIGGY AND FRIENDS, INC. Dist. by UNIVERSAL PRESS SYNDICATE. Reprinted with permission. All rights reserved.)

- sales tactics that come across as high pressure
- work locations that appear dirty or sloppy
- employees who are dressed inappropriately or have poor grooming
- any communicated message that causes the customer to feel uncomfortable

Employees at all organizational levels can create people turnoffs, often unconsciously. In most cases these turnoffs arise because people fail to understand how they come across to other people. Everyone interested in having a successful career would be wise to become constant students of communication. Even the most subtle or unconscious behaviors can communicate the wrong messages and result in lost customers.

> *Communication turnoffs often result when employees are ignorant of the kinds of "messages" they are sending to customers.*

GET YOUR CUSTOMERS BEYOND THE "ZONE OF INDIFFERENCE"

Thinking about customer turnoffs is particularly important when we consider that the correlation between customer satisfaction and loyalty is rather tenuous. Even satisfied customers may be neutral toward their relationship with a business. They may feel little or no sense of engagement, and the littlest thing can push them over the edge toward dissatisfaction. Service levels may meet their needs adequately but fail to motivate their continuing loyalty. Just as motivation researchers Frederick Herzberg, Bernard Mausner, and Barbara Bloch Snyderman discovered long ago, satisfied workers are not necessarily motivated workers.[7] Likewise, satisfied customers cannot be assumed to be motivated repeat customers. Things are okay but there is little to engage the customer in the long run.

Actually, customers who are satisfied may be *inert*, not motivated. Their satisfaction simply means the *absence of dissatisfaction*, not the motivation to become a loyal customer. A "zone of indifference" lies between the dissatisfied and the motivated (see Figure 2.1).

The challenge, then, is to get customers beyond satisfaction to *motivation*. This is best done by responding to customer perceptions and expectations.

Dissatisfied — Satisfied — Motivated

Zone of Indifference

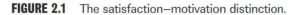

FIGURE 2.1 The satisfaction–motivation distinction.

Let's first consider what we can do if we have a customer who is on the dissatisfied side of the continuum— a customer who needs to be recovered.

VALUE SERVICE RECOVERY

> *Customer problems should be viewed as loyalty-building opportunities.*

Despite the best efforts of customer-savvy people, problems inevitably will arise. Problem situations should not be viewed as tragic, but as opportunities to further solidify customer loyalty. Anyone can give good service when customers don't have particular needs, but it is precisely when a need or problem arises that customer skills are put to the test.

Chapter 3 goes into detail about how to recover the loyalty of unhappy customers. For now, you need to know that the payoff for recovering potentially lost customers is actually an *increased* likelihood that they will be loyal to you—they are more likely to be motivated according to our model.

> *Addressing and attempting to resolve a customer problem earns that customer's loyalty— even if the attempt is not completely successful.*

It sounds strange, but studies have shown that a customer who encounters a problem with a company—and has that problem addressed promptly and effectively— will be even more likely to remain loyal than a customer who never had a problem. Even in cases in which the customer's problem is not resolved 100 percent in his or her favor, the loyalty still increases. Just the fact that the problem was acknowledged and addressed seems to be the key variable in strengthening the customer relationship. This is a powerful argument for opening the communication channels with customers.

An interesting example of customer recovery occurred when Toyota Motors first introduced the Lexus line of luxury cars. With much fanfare, Lexus burst on the scene as *the* standard of excellence in its market. Shortly after the product's introduction, it became necessary to recall the vehicles for a design defect. Toyota was, of course, embarrassed but went through with the recall of thousands of new vehicles. However, someone in the organization (an optimist, no doubt) saw this recall as an opportunity to showcase the excellent vehicle service Lexus customers would be entitled to. One selling point of the new line of cars was that they would be professionally serviced by exceptional dealers. Various dealers took the opportunity to make lemonade out of this lemon by doing things like:

- calling customers and arranging to pick up their cars so they wouldn't have to take them to the dealership
- arranging for loaner cars while the work was done
- giving every service customer's car a thorough wash-and-wax job—free
- apologizing and making recompense by giving customers gifts ranging from a fresh rose to a $50 bill to make up for the inconvenience

In short, Toyota/Lexus turned a potential embarrassment into a watershed opportunity to demonstrate their service excellence. Many Lexus customers cited that experience as the reason they continued to have their car serviced at the dealership even after the warranty expired, generating significant profits for dealerships.

RECOGNIZE THE EMOTIONAL ELEMENT IN SERVICE EXCELLENCE

British consultant David Freemantle emphasizes the important role of emotions in giving customers excellent service and in creating competitive advantage. Turnoffs are far more likely to occur when there is little or no emotional connection between customers and organizations. In his book *What Customers Like About You*, he contends that "**emotional connectivity** is at the center of all relationships and is thus the center of excellent customer service."[8] This connectivity occurs when people in an exchange are tuned in to the genuine feelings people have about the situation and about each other. Many customer turnoffs can be overcome when emotional connectivity is created. Among the personal techniques Freemantle recommends for maximizing such connectivity include:

- creating a climate of warmth before the customer approaches you
- sending out warm and positive signals to each customer
- being sensitive to the customer's emotional state
- encouraging customers to express their feelings
- listening with genuine interest
- finding something you like in each customer
- eliminating any negative feelings you have toward a customer.[9]

An old saying claims that "people don't care how much you know until they know how much you care." A genuine sense of concern for customers must be the bedrock of any organization's customer loyalty efforts.

Pickles by Brian Crane

Express gratitude often. Without customers you have no business, no job.
(©1997, Washington Post Writers Group. Reprinted with permission.)

LOYALTY COMES FROM CUSTOMERS' AWARENESS THAT SERVICE IS YOUR BUSINESS

Customer turnoffs arise when companies make service something less than an integral part of their operating philosophy. Having a "service de-partment" should be seen as a redundancy. Every de-partment exists only to serve its customers, internal and external. Nordstrom executive Betsy Sanders says, "As long as you seek to add an extra dynamic to your busi-ness [like time, energy, and resources to isolate service as some special program] the results will be disappoint-ing. Service begins to be meaningful when it is an internal dynamic. This dynamic develops when you accept service as the underpinning of your en-terprise, believing that without your customers, you would not exist."[10]

> Service must be seen as the very essence of your business, not a side function.

Customers are quick to see the depth of a company's commitment to service. The organization that distinguishes itself in the eyes of its cus-tomers is rare. Most companies have not made enough of an impression one way or another for their customers to even think about them, much less to share these thoughts with others.[11] That element of loyalty—recommending a company to others—is lost because of undistinguished service.

EARN YOUR CUSTOMER'S LOYALTY

How can we help a customer step outside the zone of indifference and be-come a "raving fan" of our company? Two steps can provide the essence of a sound strategy:

1. Reduce or eliminate value, systems, and people turnoffs.
2. Exceed customer expectations to create a positive awareness.

We'll talk a bit about the first of these in this chapter and go into depth about exceeding expectations in later chapters.

RECOGNIZE AND ELIMINATE YOUR CUSTOMER'S TURNOFFS

The first step in reducing or eliminating turnoffs is to recognize their existence. The three kinds of turnoffs de-scribed earlier (value, systems, and people) provide a useful way of categorizing and recognizing who shoul-ders major responsibility for each. But how can we tell if we are turning off customers?

> Nothing can substitute for empathy—putting yourself in your customer's shoes.

The short answer is to put yourself in the shoes of your customers. Ob-jectively assess the way they are treated and compare this with how other companies may be treating them. As Yogi Berra said, "You can observe a lot by just watching." A systematic way of "watching" is particularly useful because it gives objective data. Five major ways of gathering data include listening, explorer groups, mystery shoppers, focus groups, and feedback systems.

Listen with More Than Your Ears

Few people are really good listeners, but those who are gain a lot of good information. Some people mistakenly think that listening is a passive activity—something you "sit back" and do while you are waiting for your next opportunity to talk. Not so. Good listening requires active mental work.

> *Good listening requires active mental effort.*

When you do it well, people will open up and share important ideas with you. Pay attention to your talk-listen ratio. If you talk a lot more than you listen, you could be turning off your customer or failing to get good ideas on how to improve.

To be a better listener, use these ideas:

- *Judge the content of what people are saying, not the way they are saying it.* Customers may not have the "right" words, but they know what they need better than anyone. Look past their tone of voice or their inability to articulate exactly what they want. Fish for clarification.
- *Hold your fire.* Don't jump to make judgments before your customer has finished talking. If he or she is upset, don't respond defensively. Just hear the person out.
- *Work at listening.* Maintain eye contact, and discipline yourself to listen to what is being said. Tune out those thoughts that get you thinking about something else.
- *Resist distractions and interruptions.* Make the customer the center of your attention.
- *Seek clarification from customers so you fully understand their needs.* Do this in a nonthreatening way using sincere, open-ended questions. Don't interrogate, but do ask customers to help you understand what they mean, if you are confused. (Often the words "help me to understand" can be an effective way to show your concern and get clarification.)

Use Explorer Groups

The use of "explorer groups" involves going to or sending employees to other businesses to see how they do things. When you hear about a great idea another business is using, send out an explorer group to scope it out. One supermarket known for exceptional service encourages employees to take a company van to go to the scene of good service given by others. The explorers take notes and discuss possible implementation in their store. Explorer groups need not be sent only to direct competitors; often totally unrelated businesses have great ideas that can be adopted for use.

Another way to gather service data is to "explore" how your own organization is serving customers by being a customer. Call your company and listen to the impression created by the person answering the phone. This is what your customer is hearing. How do you like it? Log onto your company's Web site or call the help desk. Then think carefully about the impressions your customers are getting. Visit company locations or areas in your own organization and look carefully at details your customer may see. Or, if you are well known to the employees, send a new employee or an associate. Ask them to report on how they were treated.

> *Call, go online, or visit your own company the way customers do, and see how you are treated.*

Try Mystery Shopping

A more structured variation on this explorer idea involves "mystery shoppers" who visit company locations posing as customers. Trained shoppers—usually provided by outside shopper services—look for specific behaviors or processes and then report their results to management and the employees who served them.

For example, a friend of mine owned several barbershops. As the owner, he had encouraged his hairstylists to use specific behaviors with all customers. To evaluate how often such behaviors were happening, he developed a checklist of things he wanted each of his hairstylists to do, 12 in all. Some of these behaviors included:

- greeting each customer with a smile
- introducing himself or herself
- asking customers how they'd like their hair cut
- looking directly at the customer as he or she answers
- calling the customer by name
- maintaining a clean work area

The shop owner then recruited customers (often students from the nearby university), giving them money for the haircut and a checklist. Immediately after having his or her hair cut, the customer left the shop, filled out the checklist and then returned to the shop to reward the stylist with a dollar tip for each item checked. The system gave immediate feedback and reinforced what management wanted its employees to do. The stylists were delighted to receive such generous tips!

> *Mystery shopping works best when it is used to reward employees, not to catch them doing things wrong.*

Mystery shopping is best when it is done systematically (that is, at scheduled intervals, not just once in a while) and the results are used to reinforce positive employee behaviors rather than to catch them doing things wrong. A specific checklist is critical so that each employee "shopped" will be measured with the same yardstick.

The activity at the end of this chapter will teach you how to be a mystery shopper.

Use Focus Groups

Focus groups have long been used for marketing research, but they can also play an important role in understanding customer perceptions and expectations. A focus group is a group of customers or potential customers invited to share their impressions and ideas about the business. Although some marketing consultants may disagree with me, there's no great secret to how focus groups work and any intelligent person could run one effectively. Here is the procedure:

> *Keep focus groups diverse, limited to about a dozen people, and comfortable.*

- Select a random sample of your customers or patrons to participate in the focus group session. Don't pick just people you know or customers you like. You may, however, want to be sure they are among your better customers by qualifying them according to how often they buy or how much they spend with you. You can get customer names off their checks, credit cards, or other records you have.

- Formally invite the customers to participate, telling them when and where as well as how long the session will take. I recommend a written invitation. Let them know the reason for the group: that you are attempting to better understand customer needs, identify turnoffs, and gather ideas on how you can improve service to them.

- Limit your focus group to 8 to 12 people. Ask customers to confirm their attendance, but expect that some will not show up. Fifteen confirmed reservations will generally get you 12 actual participants. Follow up with phone calls to confirm attendance. (One supermarket I worked with was so excited about the focus groups that they invited 40 or 50 people every month! The problem, of course, is that a group that large makes it hard for all people to be heard. Some people dominated the group while others, who had equally good ideas but were uncomfortable speaking before so many people, suppressed their opinions.)

- Reward focus group participants. Tell those invited that you will give them something for their participation. Retail stores may give focus group participants a gift certificate, a free dinner, or even cash. In marketing research, it's not uncommon to pay people $50 or more for a one- or two-hour session.

Carefully plan the focus group; don't just throw some people together and expect to get good information. Here are some tips for making the most of this approach:

- Set the stage by having someone from top management welcome the group.

- Create an open atmosphere where participants will feel comfortable giving you all kinds of feedback. Be polite, open, encouraging, and receptive.

- Avoid cutting people off when they're making a critical comment, and do not, above all, be defensive of the way you're doing things now, when in the eyes of the customer it's not working. Your job is to listen, not to defend.

- Keep any follow-up questions open-ended. Don't interrogate. It's fine to ask for clarification when needed, but don't force people to justify every comment. Often, people are simply giving you impressions and they can't always document them with specific evidence.

- When focus group members express compliments, remember to acknowledge and say thank you. Then make a statement such as, "We're happy to hear that we are doing things you like, but our major purpose here is to identify ways that we can do a better job in meeting your needs. How can we do even better?"

- Limit the group to a predetermined amount of time. Typically a one-hour or 90-minute (maximum) session works best. Any longer than that, and you'll lose people's interest.

- Tape-record the entire focus group session, and transcribe key notes for review. As you analyze the results of this group session, look for keywords that might tip you off to what the customers are looking for. If, for example, concerns about the amount of time needed to complete a transaction comes up repeatedly, make a note of how you might meet customer needs more quickly. It can be useful to categorize comments into value, systems, and people turnoffs as discussed earlier in this chapter.

- At the end of the focus group session, be sure to thank the participants for all of their input—and give them their pay.

Probably the most important thing to avoid when receiving negative feedback (in focus groups or any other context) is debating, justifying, or arguing with the customer. They are describing situations as they see them, and their perception is reality.

Implement Customer Feedback Systems

Customer feedback systems take several forms. The commonly used "comment card" is probably better than nothing but has many drawbacks. In a moment I will describe a better version, but first let's look at the disadvantages to feedback via printed cards that customers fill out and send back to management. While such cards can provide an outlet for customers and occasionally some useful data, several drawbacks are evident in many such systems:

> *Traditional feedback card systems may be better than nothing, but they have some serious drawbacks.*

- Cards will often be completed only by people who are very satisfied or very dissatisfied. You get the comments on both extremes but less data from the middle—those customers who are somewhat neutral.

- Some cards are poorly designed and ask the wrong questions. Designing the card calls for research skills to be sure you are getting valid data. I recall a restaurant feedback card that had a long list of yes-no response questions about food portion size, temperature, price, and so on, while I wanted to comment about the server. The card had no such options.

- Occasionally cards require too much of the customer. While questionnaire formats can be too limiting, open-ended cards may ask too much of a customer's ability to express him- or herself. For many people, writing a clear description of a complaint is too laborious. Writing is not a comfortable communication media for some people. Believe it or not, I've also seen cards that require the customer to provide the postage!

- Sometimes the card fails to tell the customer what to do with it. Some can be submitted only in a drop box in the store or restaurant.

Overall, feedback cards are less useful than the other methods of finding out about customer concerns. The apparent ease of having a feedback card system makes it attractive for companies too lazy to go after better data.

A better approach to gaining good feedback is available via Web-based systems. One company, Allegiance Technologies®, for example, has a simple-to-use process for people to give feedback. It is called the Active Listening System™ (ALS). With this system, customers can contact the company to provide a complaint, a compliment, a suggestion, or ask a question using simple menus. The data goes directly to the company and Allegiance keeps track of the time needed to respond. Allegiance provides the company with a running log of comments as well as data about the timeliness of their responses. Customers may give input anonymously, or they can provide their name. The only requirement is that the customer gives an e-mail address, so that the company can respond. (This e-mail address is stored on Allegiance's mainframe computer and is not given to the company unless authorized by the customer.) For a closer look at the Allegiance system, go to www.allegiancetech.com.

While the Allegiance system works best when customers have access to the Internet, it can also be adapted to paper or telephone, by adding personnel who input comments into a database. The results of ALS are more openness to feedback, quicker responsiveness to customers, and the creation of stronger customer-company engagement. Banks, health-care organizations, and other businesses who have adopted ALS rave about its effectiveness.

Service Snapshot | **Monika's Attitude of Service**

Monika works at a medium-size credit union. In her two years there, she has won repeated awards and bonuses for her effectiveness as a teller and member-services representative. Her supervisor consistently ranks Monika's work as outstanding, and her opportunities in the financial service industry look rosy. When I asked her about her customer service "technique," she laughed and said she doesn't really have a technique; she just tries to treat people the way she'd want to be treated.

Monika pays attention to the little things, avoiding people turnoffs as much as possible. When a member approaches her desk, she immediately looks up and says "hello" with a smile. If she's busy helping someone else, she still makes eye contact to acknowledge the customer and let him or her know she'll be available in a moment. She is especially good at handling transactions quickly and efficiently without rushing the customer. When I asked her how she prepared for her career, she told me that when she was a little girl her favorite toy was a cash register. She loved to play store and keep Monopoly money in a special section in the cash drawer. She even used to iron her play money to keep it crisp, she laughed!

Technique aside, Monika projects a friendly, helpful attitude. She works hard to keep current on changes in systems and procedures and gives her employer 110 percent effort every day. She loves her job and her customers. Serving others with professionalism and skill is its own reward, she says.

A FINAL THOUGHT

Repositioning customers from that reasonably satisfied zone of indifference into the category of motivated, loyal fans requires close analysis of what may be turning them off. This analysis must be an ongoing process, not just occasional or haphazard actions. If we have made mistakes that leave the customer unhappy, we need to view these as opportunities for solidifying a relationship with good recovery skills. We also need to continually seek information to implement the kinds of changes that will reduce value, systems, and people turnoffs. This is the first step to earning customer loyalty.

The second step, exceeding customer expectations, is the topic of later chapters. But before we discuss that, we will look in more depth at some ways to deal with dissatisfied customers.

Summary of Key Ideas

- Everyone has pet peeves about the ways they are served (or not served). Often, these are little things that have a cumulative effect in creating a dissatisfied or, minimally, an indifferent customer.
- The impact of a series of little things can have a dramatic effect on organizational or individual success. The little things can work to one's advantage or disadvantage, but they must be attended to.
- Customer turnoffs can be usefully categorized into value, systems, and people problems. Value and systems problems are best addressed by company leaders; everyone can help eliminate people problems primarily through improving interpersonal skills.
- People turnoffs are almost always communication problems. Employees communicate inappropriate "messages" by their words or nonverbal actions.
- Value is a function of a product's or service's apparent quality relative to its cost.
- The term *systems* refers to anything involved with getting the product or service to the customer. Systems involve a wide range of procedures, policies, technology, training, staffing, locations, facilities, and systematic actions.
- Service recovery seeks to win back customers when they have had a disappointing experience. Customers whose problems are addressed by the company will actually be more likely to do repeat business than customers who never have a problem.
- Customer loyalty emerges when service is your business, not just an added dynamic. The term "service department" is redundant. All departments should be in the service business—first.
- We can best reduce customer turnoffs by actively listening to customer concerns, using explorer groups to see what others are doing, using mystery shoppers to test our own service, conducting periodic focus groups to better understand what customers want or need, and gathering feedback data.
- Although feedback cards are widely used, they often present drawbacks that contaminate the data received. These problems can be overcome with other data-gathering approaches such as the Web-based Active Listening System offered by Allegiance Technologies (and similar companies).

Key Concepts

Active Listening System

Allegiance Technologies

customer turnoffs

emotional connectivity

explorer groups

focus groups

people turnoffs

satisfaction versus motivation

systems turnoffs

value turnoffs

zone of indifference

Self-Test Questions

1. Develop a list of examples where little things have made a difference in a buying decision you made. Be specific.
2. Describe in your own words the three categories of customer turnoffs. Give an example of each.
3. Describe three systematic ways companies can get a clearer picture of what may be turning off their customers.
4. Explain the processes of active listening, explorer groups, and mystery shopping.

Application Activity: Let's Go Mystery Shopping

1. Select a minimum of four businesses of the same type (retailers, restaurants, banks, auto dealers, etc.) to visit as a mystery shopper. Your task will be to pose as a potential shopper seeking information. You may want information about account types from banks, details on a particular computer or appliance from electronics stores, information about a particular automobile, and so forth.
2. **Ground rules:** Be yourself during these visits. Don't attempt to act. Respond naturally to the employees. Don't go in with the attitude that you'll catch them doing something wrong. Instead, maintain an open and unbiased attitude. Carefully observe what the company does well or poorly. Don't go in with a chip on your shoulder, and don't overemphasize the negative. If you can't remember whether the employee did or did not do something positive, assume that he/she did.
3. Immediately after each visit, complete an evaluation form. You may design your own form or use one like the sample below. Remember, you can (and probably should) modify this data-gathering form to make it more appropriate for the type of businesses you will be visiting.

Sample Mystery Shopper Form[12]

Name of business: _____ Date & time: _____

Employee's name (if available): _____ Task: [what you are shopping for]

	Did	Did Not
A. When you entered, did the employee		
1. Look up, make eye contact?	_____	_____
2. Smile with a genuine smile?	_____	_____
3. Acknowledge you with an appropriate greeting?	_____	_____
4. Make you wait too long before helping you?	_____	_____
B. While assisting you, did the employee		
5. Project a positive, helpful attitude and willingness to assist?	_____	_____
6. Pay full and undivided attention to you	_____	_____
7. Deliver accurate and speedy, but unhurried, service?	_____	_____
8. Ask you if there is anything else he/she can do for you?	_____	_____
C. Given the opportunity to offer or introduce other products, did the employee		
9. Acknowledge or identify other things that may meet your needs?	_____	_____
10. Offer further information or introduce you to others for more info?	_____	_____
11. Ask you for your business?	_____	_____
D. When the transaction/visit was over, did the employee		
12. Thank you for coming in?	_____	_____
13. Invite you to come again?	_____	_____
14. Offer a friendly goodbye?	_____	_____
E. At any time during the transaction, did the employee		
15. Ask for your name and/or call you by name?	_____	_____
16. Make you feel like a valued customer?	_____	_____

Score one point for each "did" answer.   Total: _____ _____

General comments or observations: What was particularly good or bad about the shopping experience?

4. When you have gathered your data from four or more locations, compile a brief report describing what you found. Identify key turnoffs (by category), if possible. Comment on things done well and opportunities for improvement. If you owned this business, what would you do to reduce possible turnoffs and improve the service? Be specific.

Notes

1. T. Peters. "Service or Perish." *Forbes ASAP*, December 4, 1995, p. 142.

2. This story is covered in detail in "From Beetle to Bedraggled: Behind VW's Stunning U.S. Decline." *Advertising Age*, September 13, 1993.

3. Excerpted from R. McGarvey. "Little Things Do Mean a Lot." *Reader's Digest*, June 1993, p. 33.

4. K. DeTienne and P. R. Timm. "How Well Do Businesses Predict Customer Turnoffs?: A Discrepancy Analysis." *Journal of Marketing Management*, 5(2), 1996.

5. Excerpted from "Don't Let Your Systems Drive Your Customers Crazy!" by consultant/trainer Ron Kaufman, found on his Web site, www.ronkaufman.com, 2003.

6. Excerpted from an advertising piece by Nightingale-Conant Corporation advertising Michael Gerber's "The E-Myth Seminar" audiotape program. Nightingale-Conant, 1996. This tape program can be purchased from N-C at 1–800–525–9000.

7. F. Herzberg, B. Mausner, and B. Snyderman. *The Motivation to Work*, 2nd ed. (New York: Wiley, 1959).

8. D. Freemantle. *What Customers Like About You* (London: Nicholas Brealey Publishing, Ltd., 1998), p. 23.

9. Freemantle, pp. 63–4.

10. B. Sanders. *Fabled Service* (San Diego: Pfeiffer & Company, 1995), p. 9.

11. Sanders, p. 3.

12. This mystery shopper form was developed by the author and is copyrighted. Permission is granted to use this for educational purposes; however, any commercial use requires written approval from the author. Contact Dr. Paul R. Timm via e-mail: Paul@DrTimm.com.

Deal with Dissatisfied Customers

Here's an Opportunity for You

Companies can boost profits by almost 100 percent by retaining just 5 percent more of their customers.

—Frederick Reicheld and W. Earl Sasser[1]

Those who enter to buy, support me. Those who come to flatter, please me. Those who complain, teach me how I may please others so that more will come. Those only hurt me who are displeased but do not complain. They refuse me permission to correct my errors and thus improve my service.

—retailing pioneer Marshall Field

WHAT YOU'LL LEARN IN THIS CHAPTER

- Customer retention requires positive attitudes toward problem solving. This does not necessarily mean that the customer is always right.
- Who is right or who is wrong is not the key issue in customer disputes. How all parties can cooperate to solve the customer's concerns is.
- A customer complaint is an opportunity to cement a relationship and create customer loyalty.
- Recovery skills are necessary to career success and will be regularly used.
- Key skills in recovery involve feeling the customer's "pain," doing all you can to resolve the problem, and then going the extra step via "symbolic atonement."
- Handling chronic complainers can best be done by understanding their motives and then getting them to propose an acceptable solution.
- Effective written communication uses human relations principles such as reader self-interest, reader-centeredness, and individual treatment to deal with customer concerns.
- Abrasiveness is a drawback to customer relations, while assertiveness leads to better problem resolution.

THE WAY IT IS . . .
Customer Complaints May Lead to Repeat Business

Successful handling of customer complaints can be a gold mine of repeat business. Some statistics from surveys reported by the U.S. Office of Consumer Affairs reveal some interesting facts. Among these:

1. One customer in four is dissatisfied with some aspect of a typical transaction.
2. A dissatisfied customer, on average, will complain to 12 other people about the company that provided poor service.
3. Only 5 percent of dissatisfied customers complain to the company. The vast "silent majority" would rather switch than fight. They take their business elsewhere.

But there is good news for companies that learn to effectively handle complaints. Such companies can charge an average of 8% to 15% more than their competitors, even in businesses where competition is keen. (Example: Maytag, the quality home appliance maker with the "lonely repairman" campaign supports a premium-priced product in a highly price-sensitive market.)

The best news of all is that customers who have their complaints handled well are very likely to do business with the company again. While only 9% to 37% of dissatisfied customers who don't complain report a willingness to do business with the same company again, fully 50% to 80% of those whose complaints are fully resolved will consider doing repeat business—even if their complaints were not resolved in their favor![2]

I talked in Chapter 2 about the importance of reducing turnoffs. These efforts are worthwhile, but reality tells us that we cannot predict with certainty every possible customer complaint. In short, dissatisfaction happens.

> Customer recovery isn't always easy, but it is tremendously profitable.

What we choose to do about it can go a long way toward creating customer loyalty. It's not always easy, but saving customers can be enormously profitable. Effective complaint handling begins with the right attitudes coupled with the skills we'll discuss in this chapter.

MAINTAIN A HEALTHY CUSTOMER RETENTION ATTITUDE

Hopefully, the discussion in Chapter 1 about the value of customers is firmly implanted in your mind. The best attitudes for service providers stem from the desire for a win-win relationship with the customer. Both parties want to feel good about the business transacted. This is not necessarily a "customer is always right" attitude. Restaurant owner Jeffery Mount explains:

When I bought my restaurant, I wanted it to become cutting edge: customer-centered, employee empowered, socially responsible. I read the business rags and listened to the gurus for the newest and the greatest teachings. Everywhere I went I heard businesspeople chant the mantra that the customer is always right.

I even proudly hung on my wall that ubiquitous sign, which is plastered on walls of progressive companies throughout the land: *Rule #1: The customer is always right. Rule #2: If the customer is wrong, see rule #1.* I all but insisted that my staff pledge their allegiance to the infallible customer.

My, how times have changed. There's no way you'll hear me say now that the customer is always right. We wouldn't be doing ourselves or our customers a favor by insisting on that.[3]

We'll come back to some examples from Mount's restaurant in a moment, but why do you think he changed his ideas about the customer being right? The answer lies in the fact that customers, just like you or me, at times make mistakes or demand unreasonable things. The oversimplified attitude about the customer's "rightness" is far less productive than one that says "I will do my best to provide the customer with satisfaction (and more) whether the customer is right or wrong. What matters is an attitude of wanting to solve the problem at hand.

> The "rightness" or "wrongness" of a customer isn't the issue. What matters is wanting to solve customer problems.

Jeffery Mount illustrates with a story about a customer who is clearly wrong but who is treated in a manner that solves the problem and builds loyalty:

> Recently, a customer ordered finger sandwiches for a business luncheon. We advised against it. Wrong product, we warned her; too dainty, too small to feed hungry men and women at midday. Serve our hearty deli sandwiches, we suggested. "Oh, no," she replied. She insisted on finger sandwiches. Guess who called up, panicking, because "these sandwiches aren't going to be enough food"? "No problem," we said. We quickly created a bodacious big sandwich platter and delivered it in a New York minute. Even made a little money along the way.[4]

The issue is *not* whether the customer or the company is right. The attitude is one of cooperation and problem solving that won Mount's restaurant a loyal customer.

In addition to a problem-solving rather than blame-setting attitude, service recovery is best handled when seen as an attitude of opportunity rather than a painful chore. Granted, most of us would prefer not to hear about customers' dissatisfaction. That's human nature. But given that dissatisfaction does occur, an attitude of accepting the opportunity and challenge can be useful. Customer complaints are opportunities to cement relationships. The vast majority of such relationships are worth saving, although occasionally—I stress *occasionally*—we need to let go of the chronic complainer, as we'll discuss later in this chapter.

> Complaints are opportunities to cement relationships and create customer loyalty.

| Self-Analysis | What Are Your Feelings About Dealing with Difficult Customers? |

Below is a list of words that may describe the ways you feel about dealing with upset customers. Select the five that best describe your general feelings. When you have finished this chapter, review these words to see if you have some better ideas on how to deal with these emotions. Discuss your results in a small group, asking for their feedback on how to deal with the feelings you have.

afraid	confident	foolish	relieved
angry	confused	frustrated	sad
anxious	contented	glad	silly
apathetic	distraught	hesitant	uncomfortable
bored	eager	humiliated	uneasy
calm	ecstatic	joyful	wishful
cautious	elated	nervous	
comfortable	excited	proud	

My top five:

1. _____
2. _____
3. _____
4. _____
5. _____

DEVELOP YOUR RECOVERY SKILLS

Customer service is easy when nothing goes wrong. However, a study by the Technical Assistance Research Program (TARP) estimates that approximately one in every four purchases results in some form of customer problem experience.[5]

Employees often underestimate the negative ripple effects caused by even one unhappy customer. To reduce the impact of such ripples, we need to develop *recovery skills*. As the name implies, we try to recover the potentially lost customer. We can best do this by remembering the following strategies.

Feel Their Pain

The first step in developing such skills is to recognize that upset customers are likely to be disappointed, angry, frustrated, or even in pain, and they blame you to some extent. Typically they want you to do some or all of the following:

- listen to their concerns and take them seriously
- understand their problem and the reason they are upset
- compensate them or provide restitution for the unsatisfactory product or service
- share their sense of urgency; get their problem handled quickly
- eliminate further inconvenience
- treat them with respect and empathy
- see that someone is punished for the problem (sometimes)
- assure them the problem will not happen again

You may not need to do all of these things in every situation, but typically the upset customer requires several of them.

Do All You Can to Resolve the Problem

When attempting to recover an unhappy customer, the icing on the cake is the "something extra" you give by way of making up for the problem. Jeffery Mount's restaurant recovered the customer who ordered too little food by rushing in with the "bodacious big sandwich platter." No matter that they tried to dissuade the customer from ordering the wrong food in the first place. They fixed it with something extra—a quick rescue.

Suppose you buy a new pair of shoes and the heel falls off. You call the shoe store and the owner says to bring them back and he'll replace them. You take time off work, drive downtown to the store, and battle for a parking space, spending about an hour doing this. He cheerfully gives you a new pair of shoes. Are you satisfied now?

Probably not. Why? Because he really hasn't repaid you for your inconvenience. Sure, he stood behind the product and perhaps even did so in a pleasant manner, but you still came out on the short end.

Go Beyond: Offer "Symbolic Atonement"

What kinds of things can we do to make up for the problem? Much of the remainder of this book will deal with this topic. Meanwhile, here are a few possible ideas that could be seen as going the extra mile in the eyes of a customer:

- *Offer to pick up or deliver the goods to be replaced or repaired.* Lexus got a lot of mileage out of offering to pick up the recalled cars rather than have customers bring them in.
- *Give a gift of merchandise to repay for the inconvenience.* The gift may be small, but the thought will be appreciated. Customer service expert Ron Zemke calls this "symbolic atonement." Things like a free dessert for the restaurant customer who endures slow service or extra copies

of a print job to offset a minor delay are examples. It's the thought that counts.

- *Reimburse for costs of returning merchandise such as parking fees, etc.* (Mail-order retailers often pay all return postage fees to reduce customer annoyance and inconvenience.)

- *Acknowledge the customer's inconvenience and thank him or her for giving you the opportunity to try to make it right.* A sincere apology can go a long way. Make the wording of the apology sincere and personal. Say, "I'm sorry you had to wait," rather than "The company regrets the delay." Empathy can be expressed with statements like, "I know how aggravating it can be to . . . " or "I hate when that happens, and I'm sorry you had to go through . . . "

- *Follow up to see that the problem was handled.* Don't assume the customer's difficulty has been fixed unless you handled it yourself and have checked with the customer to see that the fix held up.

> *If you don't have the authority to do what's needed to save the customer, become his or her advocate. Go to bat for the customer with your boss.*

You may not have the authority to do all of these things (although many of these cost practically nothing), but you can go to bat for the customer with your boss. Just being the customer's advocate can help reduce much of the problem. If all goes well, you should feel a genuine sense of satisfaction after handling an unhappy or irate customer.

UNDERSTAND WHAT HAPPENS IF THE CUSTOMER IS STILL NOT SATISFIED

Often you can creatively recover an unhappy customer, but this is not a perfect world and people are not always rational, so sometimes you too get upset. Professionalism requires that we do everything possible to avoid letting our anger or frustration show to that customer or other customers.

The key things to remember are:

- *If you try your best to satisfy the customer, you have done all that you can do.*

- *Don't take it personally.* Upset people often say things they don't really mean. They are blowing off steam, venting frustration. If the problem was really your fault, resolve to learn from the experience and do better next time. If you had no control over the situation, do what you can, but don't bat your head against the wall.

- *Don't rehash the experience with your coworkers or in your own mind.* What's done is done. Recounting the experience with others probably won't make their day any better, and rehashing it to yourself will just make you mad. You may, however, want to ask another person how they would have handled the situation.

■ *Use every customer contact experience as an opportunity to improve your professionalism.* Even the most unpleasant encounter can teach us useful lessons.

LOOK BACK AND LEARN FROM EACH SITUATION

When the customer situation has cooled, you may want to review it with an eye toward improving your skills. Think where you used your recovery skills, and ask questions like these:

■ What was the nature of the customer's complaint? Was it generated primarily by value, systems, or people?

■ How did the customer see the problem? Who was to blame; what irritated the customer most; why was he or she angry or frustrated?

■ How did you see the problem? Was the customer partially to blame?

■ What did you say to the customer that helped the situation?

■ What did you say that seemed to aggravate the situation?

■ How did you show your concern to the customer?

■ What would you do differently?

■ Do you think this customer will do business with you again? Why or why not?

Making careful notes of your responses to these questions can build your confidence and professionalism.

> *Review how you handled a problem situation with an eye toward improving your skills and professionalism.*

HANDLE THE OCCASIONAL CUSTOMER FROM HELL

"Stubbornness is the energy of fools," says the German proverb. Sometimes we need to draw the line between upset customers with legitimate problems

and chronic complainers who consume our time with unreasonable de-mands—the dreaded "customer from hell."

Be Sure This Really Is a Chronic Complainer

Step one in dealing with such people is to be sure you've got a chronic com-plainer. When you've tried the normal recovery approaches and nothing seems to work, look for the following telltale signs:

- They always look for someone to blame. In their world accidents don't happen: someone is always at fault, and it's probably you.
- They never admit any degree of fault or responsibility. They see themselves as blameless and victims of the incompetence or malice of others.
- They have strong ideas about what others should do. They love to define other people's duties. If you hear a complaint phrased exclusively in terms of what other people always, never, must, or must not do, chances are you're talking to a chronic complainer.
- They complain at length. While normal complainers pause for breath every now and then, chronics seem able to inhale while saying the words, "and another thing . . . "[6]

Know What to Do with This Guy (or Gal)

When faced with that occasional chronic complainer (they really are quite rare, fortunately), try these techniques:

- Actively listen to identify the legitimate grievance beneath the endless griping. Rephrase the complainer's main points in your own words, even if you have to interrupt to do so. Say something like, "Excuse me, but do I understand you to say that the package didn't arrive on time and you feel frustrated and annoyed?"
- Establish the facts to reduce the complainer's tendency to exaggerate or overgeneralize. If he says he "tried calling all day but as usual you tried to avoid me," establish the actual number of times he called and when.
- Resist the temptation to apologize, although that may seem to be the natural thing to do. Since the main thing the complainer is trying to do is fix blame—not solve problems—your apology will be seen as an open invitation to further blaming. Instead, ask questions like, "Would an extended warranty solve your problem?" or "When would be the best time for me to call you back with that information?"
- Force the complainer to pose solutions to the problem, especially if he doesn't seem to like your ideas. Also, try putting a time limit on the

conversation by saying something like, "I have to talk with someone in 10 minutes. What sort of action plan can we work out in that time?" The object of this is to get him away from whining and into a problem-solving mode.

Another Look	Some Useful "Buzz Phrases" When Dealing with Upset Customers:[7]

1. *"Anyone in your position . . . "* The suggestion here is that the customer holds an important job or social rank. Don't be afraid to lard it on. No one ever gets tired of being told how good they look or how important they are.

2. *"I'd sure appreciate it if . . . "* This phrase implicitly asks the customer's permission, suggesting that the customer has the power to grant or refuse.

3. *"You could really help me by . . . "* This suggests that the customer is not only taking a hand in the complaint-resolution process but is also taking something of a parental or "older sibling" role.

4. *"Perhaps you could give me some advice . . . "* This request makes the customer into a veritable fount of wisdom.

5. *"Because of your specialized knowledge . . . "* This opening suggests a high degree of skill or advanced study. People love to think that others view them as highly intelligent.

6. *"Someone of your attainments . . . "* This implies that the customer is a great success in life.

7. *"As you, of course, know . . . "* Such a phrase suggests vast learning on the customer's part. This phrase is especially effective when you are telling customers something you know that they don't know. Most people don't like to admit that they are ignorant, even of things that they have no reason to know.

8. *"You're absolutely right about that . . . "* Use this routine but effective "stroke" to readily concede some minor point the customer makes. The customer will then be more willing to give ground on the major points of contention.

9. *"Someone as busy as you are . . . "* Try this to imply that the customer is one of the world's movers and shakers—and to imply that the problem will be resolved as quickly as possible.

10. *"I'd sure be grateful if . . . "* This suggests an easy way to make someone happy, a natural human drive.

Note that some of these phrases start with "I," a word you should normally avoid in confrontations with customers. You can use it safely here because you are using "I" in a totally non-challenging way. If you are feeling more aggressive, however, and a more confrontational approach seems in order, just start your remarks with the word "You."

Get the chronic complainer to pose possible solutions to the problem rather than just dwell on blaming someone.

We have, of course, no guarantees when dealing with such customers, but the effort may well be worth it. Converting one of these folks into a normal, rational customer can be professionally rewarding. If it doesn't work, so be it. You've given your best and that's all anyone can ask.

A Prentice Hall booklet called *The Customer Service Manager's Handbook of People Power Strategies* includes the following section called "10 'Buzz Phrases' That Help You Disarm Irate Customers." Commit these to memory, use them frequently until they become comfortable and just roll off your tongue, and see how they can dramatically enhance your success with people in conflict situations.

HANDLE A NASTY COMPLAINT LETTER

Today's customers don't write very often, but when they do it reflects a significant effort. Perhaps because they are fairly rare, a letter carries considerable impact. Letters provide a graphic and tangible reminder of a customer's dissatisfaction and have a nasty habit of appearing in your personnel file. So it makes sense to respond to them and to document what you've done.

If you choose to respond to a letter with a phone call, be certain to have the letter in front of you and to refer to the specific points as written. Also, make notes of what the customer says and how you respond. If you answer a letter with a letter of your own, be certain that your letter conveys an attitude of problem solving, projects goodwill, and exhibits professionalism. Apply some of the following tips when writing to customers.

Be an effective writer by applying the same human relations skills you

Apply human relations skills to your writing. A poorly written letter will come back to haunt you.

would use in a face-to-face encounter. Specifically, be especially sensitive to people's feelings, interests, wants, and needs. Failure to do so creates unnecessary strains on a relationship. The fact that a letter is a hard copy of a conversation makes it especially important that it be tactful. A poorly written document will come back to haunt you.[8]

USE THE 3 F'S (FEEL, FELT, FOUND)[9] TO DISARM THE UPSET CUSTOMER

Seminar leader and author Rebecca Morgan teaches people how to express ideas so that upset customers won't become more upset. She describes the "3 F's" technique:

> The 3 F's are a skeleton on which to hang the rest of your response to a customer.

This technique acknowledges the customer's feelings and offers an explanation in a way she can listen to. For example, "I understand how you could *feel* that way. Others have *felt* that way too. And then they *found*, after an explanation, that this policy actually protects them, so it made sense."

Try using the 3 F's approach as Morgan advises. Be careful how you word it. Do not say "I know how you feel" (you really can't know exactly how another person feels) but do say "I can understand how (or why) you'd feel that way."

USE HUMAN RELATIONS SKILLS TO CONVEY APPROPRIATE TONE

Let's consider a few principles of human relations and how these might apply in communication with unhappy customers. The first and perhaps most basic principle concerns people's self-interest.

People Are Strongly Interested in Themselves

It is the nature of the human being—and all other known creatures, for that matter—to be concerned with and motivated by their own personal needs, wants, and interests. This self-centeredness, or egocentricity, is normal and not particularly harmful unless carried to the extreme, when there is *no* caring about others.

> *Our primary motivation is self-interest.*

When people speak or write, they reflect this egocentricity in their language. A study once conducted at a Midwestern university showed that every fifth word written or spoken by a human being is *I* or one of its derivations—*me, mine, my, we, ours, us.*[10]

Even though we are all self-centered to some degree, most of us learn to temper the tendency to focus on and talk about ourselves exclusively. Indeed, the extremely egocentric person is avoided like someone with a contagious disease.

The point here is that business writers can turn this egocentricity into an advantage if they recognize the reader's needs. Effective communicators learn to express concern and appreciation for the views of others in letters, memos, reports, proposals, and other documents.

> *You can turn a person's natural egocentricity into an advantage by recognizing his or her needs.*

People Prefer Receiver-Centered Messages

One important way to reflect consideration for another person is by phrasing your message in terms of that person's viewpoint. Expressing the appropriate viewpoint involves much more than just selecting certain

> *The receiver-oriented communicator thinks of the other person first.*

keywords. A genuine receiver viewpoint causes a document's tone to reflect a sincere interest in the other person. Self-centered writers and talkers think of themselves first. Receiver-oriented writers think of and convey their messages in terms of what the message receiver wants or needs.

One "red flag" that we should look for are the words *I, me, my,* and so forth found in abundance in our messages. Second or third person (you, or the impersonal, one) often conveys more receiver interest and objectivity.

Please don't conclude that you should try to eliminate the use of *I* and its variations. To do so may be impossible in some cases. In other cases, your efforts may result in rather tortured syntax and excessive wordiness. Besides, the use of *I, we,* or *me* does not always indicate a non-reader viewpoint. For example, the person who says, "I hope you will be happy with this decision," is not really violating a receiver viewpoint even though the sentence begins with the word *I.* The overall tone and sense of caring for the other person is far more important than simply avoiding the use of first-person pronouns.

Look at the following sample sentences and see the difference in the tone of the receiver-oriented version compared to the "I-centered" one:

I-Centered	*Receiver Viewpoint*
We require that you sign the sales slip before we charge this purchase to your account.	For your protection, we charge your account only after you have signed the sales slip.
I have been a sales professional for 22 years.	My 22 years' experience as a sales professional provides a strong background in understanding customer concerns.
I am sending your software back to you for an update.	So that you may update this software to the most current version, it is being returned to you.
I'd like to show you this life insurance plan.	As a young father, you'll be interested in a life insurance plan tailored to the couple with small children and a limited budget.

Phrasing ideas in terms of the receiver's viewpoint conveys an interest in the other person and recognizes a principle of good human relations.

People Want to Be Treated as Individuals

We can improve the tone of written documents by phrasing our information as though talking to individuals, rather than groups. A personally addressed business letter singles out a reader for individual attention. Such a letter conveys a more sincere regard for the specific person than one addressed to "Dear Customer" or "Dear Fellow Employee."

> The sweetest sound to most people is the sound of their own name.

Names or other information can be easily inserted while keeping most of the letter the same for all readers. Explore these possibilities when you consider developing form letters to deal with recurrent situations. Avoid the "blanket tone"—attempting to talk to people as a group rather than as individuals.

> The "blanket tone" makes a reader feel lost in the crowd.

When a document makes a reader feel lost in the crowd, the blanket tone is responsible. For example, consider the blanket tone in the excerpts below:

Blanket Tone	*More Personal Tone*
When a thousand requests are received from prospective customers, we feel pleased. These requests show that our product is well received.	A copy of the booklet you requested is being sent to you today. Thank you for requesting it.
The cooperation of our charge customers in paying their accounts is appreciated. By paying on time, they allow us to give better service.	I certainly appreciate your paying the account. Your prompt payment allows us to give you better service and keep prices down.

Strive to express ideas in terms of the individual's benefit. One way to do this is through direct address, or "this means you!" statements. Each day we see examples of this approach in television and radio commercials. The announcer "personally" addresses each of the several million people who may be listening and attempts to make each one feel that he or she is spoken to as an individual. Direct address shows your receivers how your message applies to them and how it can meet their individual needs in some way.

People Want Positive Information

Positive language often conveys more information than negative language. It also tends to be more upbeat with a more pleasant tone. Rather than telling a person what is *not* or what you *cannot* do, focus on the positive— what *is* or what you *can* do. If you say, "I *cannot* give cash refunds on sale merchandise," it conveys only negative information. It does not say what you can do; it only rules out one of the possibilities. On the other hand, the positive statement "I can arrange to have the product exchanged for another model that may better meet your needs" conveys more specific and positive information.

Positive language also has a more pleasant ring to the ear. Yet many common negative phrases still creep up in business writing, such as:

We *regret* to inform you that we cannot . . .
We have received your *claim* . . . [*claim* has a negative connotation for most people]
Your *failure* to comply . . .
We *regret* that we cannot permit . . .

To illustrate the difference in tone between positive and negative word choices, here is an example: A corporate executive wrote to a local civic group denying a request to use the company's meeting facilities. To soften the refusal, however, the executive decided to let the group use a conference room, which might be somewhat small for its purpose, but was probably better than no room at all. Unfortunately, the executive was not sensitive to the effects of negative wording. She wrote:

We regret to inform you that we cannot permit you to use our company training room for your meeting, because the Beardstown Ladies' Investment Club asked for it first. This group has a standing date to use our place the third Thursday of every month. We can however, let you use our conference room; but it seats only 25.

A review of the letter clearly brings out the negative words (*regret, cannot, seats only 25*) first, while the otherwise positive message (you can use the conference room) is drowned out.

A more positive way of addressing the same situation would be this tactful response:

Although the Beardstown Ladies' Investment Club has already reserved our company training room for Thursday, we would like to suggest that you use our conference room, which seats 25.

No negative words appear in this version. Both approaches yield the primary message of denying the request and offering an alternative, but the positive wording does the better job of building and holding goodwill for the company.

Let's look at some examples of negative and positive sentences. Note the tone of each. (The negative words are in italics.)

Negative Wording	Positive Wording
You *failed* to give us the part number of the muffler you ordered.	So that we may get you the muffler you want, will you please check your part number on the enclosed card?
Smoking is *not* permitted anywhere except in the lobby.	Smoking is permitted in the lobby only.
We *regret* to inform you that we must *deny* your request for credit.	For the time being, we can serve you only on a cash basis.
You were *wrong* in your conclusion, for paragraph three of our agreement clearly states . . .	You will agree after reading paragraph three of our agreement that . . .
We *cannot* deliver your order until next Wednesday.	We can deliver your order on Wednesday.

People Don't Like Abrasive People

If you tend to have a somewhat abrasive personality, it can hurt the tone of your messages. Abrasiveness refers to an irritating manner or tone that sounds pushy or critical. To determine if you tend to have an abrasive personality, you might ask yourself questions such as these:

Self-Analysis   Do You Have Abrasive Tendencies?

- Are you often critical of others? When you supervise others, do you speak of "straightening them out" or "whipping them into shape"?

- Do you have a strong need to be in control? Must you have almost everything cleared with you?

- Are you quick to rise to the attack, to challenge, to say no?

- Do you have a strong need to debate with others? Do your discussions often become arguments?

- Do you regard yourself as more competent than your peers? Does your behavior let others know that?

The abrasive personality will tend to communicate in a manner that can be irritating to others. Try to recognize in yourself whether you have a strong need to control or dominate other people or a tendency to have a knee-jerk reaction to things others may say. If you suspect

> *Assertiveness and abrasiveness are different. To be assertive is to be pleasantly direct.*

that you do, it would be important for you to make an extra effort to soften the tone of your communications.

Keep in mind that there is a major difference between being abrasive and being assertive. Assertiveness simply means that you express your feelings and observations in a normally phrased manner that is nonthreatening to other people. For example, instead of saying to someone, "You don't make any sense," the assertive person would say, "I'm having a difficult time understanding what you're saying." Or rather than saying, "Deadbeats like you burn me up," the assertive person might say, "People who consistently make late payments cause us a lot of extra work and lost revenue." Few people get offended by the assertive individual. Indeed, one definition of assertiveness is "being pleasantly direct."

UNDERSTAND THAT ASSERTIVE BEHAVIOR IS NOT AGGRESSIVE BEHAVIOR[11]

Many people confuse assertiveness with aggressiveness. Aggressive behaviors differ in the following ways:

1. *Aggressors communicate from a position of superiority.* Aggressive people feel that they know best or must get their way at almost any cost. They see communication situations as win–lose, meaning that they either get their way or they have lost. And if they lose, someone else won! The idea of compromise or a decision whereby all parties benefit or win is foreign to them.

2. *Aggressors can be indirect, manipulative, or underhanded.* The aggressive communicator may not be the guy or gal with the big mouth. Sometimes aggressive people use tricks and manipulation such as false emotion or acting false roles designed to get their way. (The TV detective Columbo is actually being aggressive in his questioning by playing dumb and getting people to reveal their guilt.)

3. *Aggressors set themselves up for retaliation.* Aggressive communicators eventually face adversaries. By being less than authentic, they spin webs of deception that get more and more confusing. Like habitual liars, they eventually lose track of what they told whom.

4. *Aggressors use a lot of judgmental or emotionally charged terms for emphasis.* The aggressive communicator thinks that strong language is clear but fails to see how it can create barriers to understanding. Emotional language almost always generates emotionally worded responses.

Assertive behaviors avoid these problems by being honest and authentic. They are based on beliefs such as the following:

1. *One should have high self-respect for one's own ideas and abilities.* Assertive communicators know that they are valuable. Their time, talents, and efforts are to be respected. They take a back seat to no one, although they do recognize and respect other people's different abilities.

2. *It is important to respect other people.* They see people as having a wide range of experiences and know that we can all learn something from another person. They know that organizational titles or social status do not guarantee people a right to the best ideas. People need people and can gain much from others.

3. *Win–win solutions can be found for many problems.* The purpose of communication is to create understanding, not to beat out another person. Conflicts or challenges need not be couched in win-lose terms. A fresh perspective or creative twist can often be found to create solutions that leave no one as a loser.

4. *Consensus is best created by direct and honest expression of points of view.* The assertive person wins by influencing, listening, and negotiating, not by manipulating.

5. *Honest, open relationships eliminate the desire for retaliation or distrust.* Communication does not get tangled in a web of game playing. Openness begets openness. People are more comfortable with assertive communicators. They can be trusted.

6. *Emotionally charged language is seldom effective.* Using strong, judgmental words hampers the resolution of problems or the creation of understanding. Neutral, descriptive terms are better. They will not turn listeners off.

Rather than relying on assertive and aggressive communication, some people are simply passive. They communicate ineffectively because they do not really care much—they are *apathetic*. They have chosen to stay out of a particular discussion. Do not confuse passiveness with assertiveness.

Another Look | **Calming Hostile Customers**[12]

A hostile, angry reaction usually follows a certain pattern if it is handled skillfully. This pattern is called the hostility curve, illustrated in Figure 3.1. It is important to thoroughly understand each step of the hostility curve:

1. Most persons are reasonable much of the time. They function at a *rational level.* At this level, you can reason with them about things.

2. When irritations pile up or a specific incident provokes a person, he or she will *take off,* blowing off steam, possibly becoming abusive, and in general expressing a lot of

continued

Another Look   **Calming Hostile Customers**   *continued*

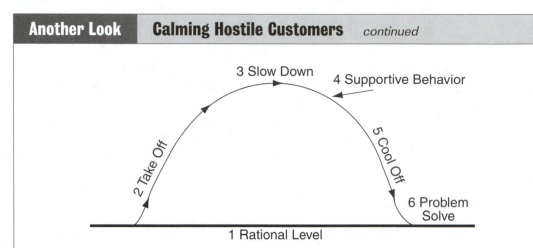

FIGURE 3.1   The hostility curve.

hostility. Once the person leaves the rational level, there is no use trying to get the person to be "reasonable."

3. This taking-off stage cannot last forever. If not provoked any further, the hostile person just runs out of steam and begins to *slow down*. He or she may feel embarrassed for making a scene.

4. At this point, the staff member who has been listening to the hostile customer take off can say something. What you say makes a big difference. Say something *supportive,* such as, "Things can be awfully frustrating when you're under so much pressure" or "I know this has been an upsetting experience for you." In addition, you must be supportive in your nonverbal behavior. Being supportive does not necessarily mean agreeing, but it does mean letting the other person know that you understand his or her feelings.

5. If you do say something supportive, you will usually see the hostile person *cool off.* He or she comes back down to the rational level.

6. Once the person has returned to the rational level, you can begin to *problem solve* with him or her about what caused the anger. Persons are in a mood to problem solve when they are rational, not when they are at the top of the hostility curve.

Probes

1. Why is it important to help an upset customer cool off before trying to solve the problem?

2. How can you best help him or her through the hostility curve? What specific things could you say? What should you avoid saying or doing?

A FINAL THOUGHT

Customer complaints are opportunities for building customer loyalty. Sure, complainers can be annoying, but they can also be your best friends. They can point out ways to improve and strengthen your business like no one else will. That's valuable intelligence for the competitive battlefield. Use it to build customer satisfaction and loyalty.

Summary of Key Ideas

- Customer retention requires positive attitudes toward problem solving but not necessarily an oversimplified "customer is always right" mind-set.
- The key issue in customer disputes is not who is right or wrong, but rather how all parties can cooperate to solve the customer's concerns.
- A customer complaint is an opportunity to cement a relationship and create customer loyalty.
- Recovery skills are necessary to career success and will be regularly used in business.
- The key skills in recovery involve feeling the customer's "pain," doing all you can to resolve the problem, and then going the extra step via "symbolic atonement."
- After doing your best to deal with a customer problem, it is useful to review the episode and learn from it.
- The best way to handle the occasional chronic complainer is to understand his or her motives and then get the person to propose an acceptable solution.
- Effective written communication uses human relations principles such as receiver self-interest, receiver-centeredness, individual treatment, and positive information.
- Abrasiveness is a drawback to customer relations, while assertiveness leads to better problem resolution.

Key Concepts

abrasiveness

aggressive behavior

assertive behavior

blanket tone

chronic complainers

customer retention

hostility curve

positive and negative wording

reader self-interest

receiver-centered and I-centered
messages

recovery skills

symbolic atonement

three F's: feel, felt, found

Self-Test Questions

1. In customer disputes, who is right or wrong is not the key issue. What overriding issue is more important?
2. What are the three important steps needed to recover the potentially lost customer?
3. What are some things you could do to offer symbolic atonement to the dissatisfied customer?
4. What are some of the telltale signs of a chronic complainer?
5. What special customer service techniques can be used when you are faced with a chronic complainer?
6. What are the three F's, and how can they be used to disarm the upset customer?
7. What human relations principles can we apply to improve our written communication?
8. Why should the blanket tone be avoided?
9. Compare and contrast assertive versus aggressive behavior.

Application Activity: Defusing and Recovering the Unhappy Customer[13]

Read the following case. Then get another person to role-play the part of the unhappy customer. Practice responding to his or her concerns in a constructive manner that could lead to recovering this customer. If possible, videotape your role-play and review the tape to identify nonverbal and verbal behaviors.

Before you get into this activity, look carefully at the language used to describe the situation. What problems do you see concerning the tone? How could you express the viewpoints of the two parties in more constructive terms?

A HOT TRAVELER AND A HOT MOTEL MANAGER

The Motel Manager's Story

A fellow from a city several hundred miles away has just checked into your motel. He gives the impression that he is a big-shot government worker. After a short visit to his room, he storms into your office, claiming his air conditioner is faulty. You have recently spent $75 to repair the unit in his room. You are certain that he must have banged it with his fist and that he is responsible for the trouble with the unit. You are not about to let him push you around.

The Traveler's Story

You have just settled into a rather dumpy motel. It is mid-August, and the temperature is 109 degrees. You flip on the switch to the air conditioner; there is a buzz, a hum, and smoke starts to pour out of the vents of the air conditioner. After several bangs with your fist, the smoke vanishes, but the air conditioner will not work. You are hot and tired, and wish you had selected a better motel. At that point, you storm into the motel manager's office and inform him that he runs a cheap, dumpy, and poorly-cared-for motel. You demand that he rush immediately to your room and repair your air conditioner.

Notes

1. F. F. Reichheld and W. E. Sasser. "Zero Defections: Quality Comes to Services." *Harvard Business Review*, September–October 1990.

2. These Office of Consumer Affairs statistics were quoted in *The Customer Service Manager's Handbook of People Power Strategies* (Englewood Cliffs, NJ: Prentice Hall Professional Newsletters, 1989), p 3.

3. J. Mount. "Why Take Sides." *Inc.*, March 1995, 17(3), p. 29.

4. Ibid.

5. TARP research is cited in J. R. Shannon, "The Components Customer Service: A New Taxonomy." *Journal of Customer Service in Marketing & Management*, 2(1), 1996, p. 6.

6. Adapted from "How to Deal with Those Chronic Complainers." *Customer Service Manager's Letter*, September 20, 1989. Published by Prentice Hall Professional Newsletters. The article is based on the work of Dr. Robert Bramson, *Coping With Difficult People* (New York: Dell, 1988).

7. *The Customer Service Manager's Handbook of People Power Strategies*, pp. 9–10.

8. This material is adapted from P. R. Timm and J. Stead, *Communication Skills for Business and Professions* (Upper Saddle River, NJ: Prentice Hall, Inc., 1996), chapter 9.

9. R. L. Morgan. *Calming Upset Customers* (Menlo Park, CA: Crisp Publications, 1989), p. 40.

10. D. Starch. *How to Develop Your Executive Ability* (New York: Harper & Row, 1943), p. 154.

11. From *BASICS of Oral Communication, Skills for Career and Personal Growth*, 1st edition by TIMM. ©1993. Reprinted with permission of South-Western, a division of Thomson Learning: *www.thomsonrights.com*. Fax 800 730-2215.

12. Adapted from ideas presented in *Teaching Patient Relations in Hospitals: The Hows and Whys* (New York: The American Hospital Association, 1983).

13. This case originally appeared in P. R. Timm and B. D. Peterson, *People at Work: Human Behavior in Organizations*, 5th ed. (Cincinnati: South-Western College Publishing, 2000), p. 232.

Exceed Customer Expectations

The Master Key Called A-Plus

Unexpected kindness is the most powerful, least costly and most underrated agent of human change. Kindness that catches us by surprise brings out the best in our natures.

—Sen. Bob Kerrey[1]

WHAT YOU'LL LEARN IN THIS CHAPTER

- Psychological theory supports the importance of exceeding what customers anticipate (creating "A-plus") to pleasantly surprise customers and build their loyalty.

- Consistently exceeding what customers anticipate is a powerful key to career success.

- Expectations change and evolve, forcing intelligent businesspeople to constantly adjust and innovate.

- Encourage and use customer feedback to better assess what they anticipate.

- Six different areas provide the best opportunities for A-plus innovation.

- Use the VISPAC acronym as a reminder of the categories of A-plus opportunities.

- The best A-plus ideas come from alert, innovative people.

THE WAY IT IS (OR WAS) . . .
Walgreen's History of Exceeding Expectations

Writing about retailer Charles R. Walgreen, David Chung says:

Charles R. Walgreen Sr. wanted his small Chicago pharmacy to give patrons fast service that would wow them. Every pharmacy at the turn of the century supplied prescriptions. Every pharmacy delivered. But what if his delivered faster?

He decided to use new technology—the telephone—to boost his business. When a nearby customer telephoned an order for some nonprescription goods, Walgreen (1873–1939) slowly repeated both the order and the caller's address out loud. Then Caleb Danner, the store's handyman, would listen, collect and wrap the items quickly. As Danner darted to the caller's home, Walgreen stretched the conversation for several more minutes, talking about anything under the sun.

This gave Danner time to land at the caller's doorstep, interrupt the phone call and hand the unsuspecting customer the items ordered minutes before on the phone. Soon, she'd spread the word about the extraordinary service.

The "two-minute stunt" and other innovations helped Walgreen change the face of pharmacies and build what now is America's largest drugstore chain, with projections of 7000 stores by 2010.

When Walgreen opened his first shop, on the corner of Cottage Grove and Bowen avenues on Chicago's South Side in 1901, drugstores were drab and dimly lit. Customers stopped to find what they needed and left.

Hidden in the back of the store was the pharmacist, working behind a wooden grillwork partition and surrounded by bottles of compounds, a mortar and pestle, and a jar of leeches.

Walgreen saw an opportunity. Most drugstores had small soda fountains. At first, they sold bottled soda water as a health aid. Later, they added flavors, such as lemon, strawberry and pineapple, and began featuring a small soda fountain apparatus inside their front counter.

Walgreen saw a way to innovate: Why not make the fountains large enough to seat customers at tables and serve treats including ice-cream sodas, phosphates and sundaes?

Walgreen took action after a shop adjacent to his second drugstore became vacant. He rented the space and cut an archway through the common wall. He installed a 16-foot-long marble-top fountain and a 12-foot mirror bordered by intricate woodwork against the far wall. He also added eight small tables and as many booths.

But Walgreen knew that ice-cream parlors weren't entirely new in the Midwest metropolis. He looked for an edge. He knew customers appreciated high quality. So he developed a private-label ice-cream brand for the store that had a higher percentage of butter fat than the ice cream from his suppliers had. His own ice cream was always fresh, because it could be made in minutes in the store's basement.

The soda fountain was a huge success. Customer traffic slumped, however, after summer ended. Walgreen analyzed the situation—he had space to serve ice cream, but people didn't want it when the weather was cold. So he created a new market. Walgreen persuaded his wife, Myrtle, to cook. She fed customers through the winter with a different hot soup, sandwich and dessert menu every day from Monday to Saturday. It worked, and the fountain stayed busy year-round.

The Rio, Ill., native encouraged his employees to innovate, too. In fact, one of the store's fountain managers in 1922 came up with the fountain's greatest hit—the milkshake. He'd seen how much people liked ice cream, so he created a double-rich chocolate malted milk thickened with three scoops of vanilla ice cream and topped by whipped cream and a cherry. It came with a complimentary package of vanilla cookies. It didn't take long before customers began standing three and four deep at the counter to get their taste of what is now an American classic.

Walgreen came up with new ways and expanded product offerings to boost sales to customers attracted to the store. The Perfume Bar allowed female customers to sample many famous brands while men inspected the cases of cigars and pipe tobaccos. "Concentrations," or striking displays of a specific product, were placed in highly visible areas of the store.

Walgreen also poured energy and time into developing other private-label products—from Sure Death Bug Pizen for killing bedbugs to freshly roasted coffee beans to cold cream. To make sure customers were confident in the house products, the store guaranteed in writing that no item would carry the Walgreen name if it didn't meet high quality standards.

Walgreen also knew customers flocked to sales, but felt that too many sales made a store look cheap. Why not offer everyday discounts on some items? The strategy could work if he bought in bulk. So he persuaded other neighborhood pharmacy owners to pool their purchases of the same products. Walgreen became president of the "Velvet Club" and successfully negotiated with suppliers for lower wholesale prices.

Back then, the concept was so radical that people questioned whether the $1 Gillette razors that sold for 69 cents at Walgreen's were indeed genuine. "Don't be afraid of anything sold at a Walgreen store, for quantity buying permits low prices, and we often sell the equal of gold dollars for less than 100 cents," Walgreen said in the chain's newsletter, The Pepper Pod.

Realizing that customers shopped where they felt most comfortable, Walgreen launched The Pepper Pod in December 1919 to interact more closely with patrons. He made sure the 12-page newsletter included something for everyone. Articles included "Beauty Hints," "Christmas Suggestions" and "Constipation and How to Prevent It."

Customers were thrilled. Walgreen encouraged them to contribute to the publication, thus deepening their loyalty. One article by a customer carried the headline "Germany of Today" in heavy block letters and gave a firsthand account of post-World War I Berlin.

Walgreen never stuck to the tried and true. He wanted his customers to come into a Walgreen store and actually experience the service. To assure it would be good, Walgreen wrote employee manuals on cleanliness, the importance of smiling, and good sales skills.

He even listed ways to handle a preoccupied or worried customer: "Express a real sympathy and understanding in your dealings. . . . Don't try to distract his attention from his worries by talking unnecessarily."

Walgreen always wanted employees to make that extra effort. In a book called "Set Your Sales for Bigger Earnings," Walgreen provided more tips on how to give the best service.

One illustration showed a smiling, clean-cut salesclerk tying up a stack of items in a neat bundle. The explanation said, "Little extra services are the cheapest kind of advertising that merely takes thought and a few seconds of time!" "Success," Walgreen wrote in the same book, "is doing a thousand little things the right way—doing many of them over and over again."

Exceeding expectations has become a cliché in customer service, yet the principle is sound. As the opening quote by Senator Kerrey notes, the "unexpected kindness," or, for that matter, any unexpectedly pleasant experience, can change human behavior. In the context of customer relationships, the change may well result in creating a more loyal customer. This chapter looks at the principle of exceeding what customers anticipate as an impetus for strengthening relationships. In order to exceed what customers anticipate, we must first understand something about the expectations customers bring to a transaction. To do so, we must make serious efforts to truly understand our customers.

STAY CLOSE TO YOUR CUSTOMERS

Innovations that keep the customer constantly in mind has been a critical key to many a successful company. As the Walgreens story shows, people's needs, wants, and expectations change, and businesses need to be vigilant in recognizing the opportunities in such changes. Reacting to customer changes is good, but being proactive in anticipating changes is better.

How can you best anticipate changing customer needs? Staying close to the customer and maintaining an ongoing dialogue are important keys. But just what can you do with the input received from customers? You can use it to better understand their current expectations and, more importantly, to plan approaches that will exceed those expectations. Ultimately, today's customer service success arises from a central theme that is simple to state yet challenging to implement. The underlying theme is: *You achieve customer satisfaction, retention, and loyalty by exceeding, in positive ways, what customers anticipate.*

I call this process of exceeding the anticipated "A-plus." Creating A-plus experiences for your customers may well be the master key to building customer loyalty. Before we look at the A-plus formula and suggest some ways to successfully implement this approach, let's consider the psychology behind A-plus.

> *A-plus is an approach supported by basic psychological theories. It utilizes human nature to create stronger relationships.*

UNDERSTAND WHY CUSTOMERS DO WHAT THEY DO

At a basic psychological level, people are motivated to act in a particular way because their action will either result in a gain (reward) or avoid a loss (punishment). Customers are rational people. If a buying experience is positive, they will see it as a gain and probably come back; if it's negative, they'll regard it as a loss and try to avoid returning. If it's so-so, they'll stay in that zone of indifference we discussed in Chapter 2.

Customers Anticipate the Future Based on Past Experience

Customers entering into a transaction anticipate (albeit perhaps unconsciously) being treated a particular way. What they expect is often based on their past associations with this business, person, or organization or ones they see as similar. If they had a good experience in the past, they'll probably anticipate something satisfactory. If

> *As people enter into a transaction, they harbor certain expectations of how it will be.*

the last transaction wasn't so positive, they might assume the next one won't be better.

What customers anticipate is *perceptual*. Their expectations exist in their own minds. Sometimes they are accurate and rational; sometimes they aren't. And to make matters more complicated, their expectations are ever-changing. They present moving, hard-to-define targets.

Customers Hold Expectations About Products, Services, and Their Experience

When going into a transaction, customers anticipate some things about both the products or services they may buy and the experience of buying. For example, they may be quite excited about buying a new car but expect the interactions with the dealer to be a hassle. Or, they may hate buying the product (say, paying an electric bill) but know that the interaction with the people at the electric company is generally pleasant and efficient.

When people judge the quality of a tangible product, they use fairly objective and somewhat predictable criteria. For example, if a person buys a new automobile, he or she will be likely to judge its quality by such things as:

- driving and handling characteristics
- low frequency of repair (it seldom has to be fixed)
- appropriate size (it holds a family comfortably)
- good price relative to its quality
- workmanship (it seems to be well built with a nice paint job)

Likewise, when we judge the quality of a service (say, a house painter's job), we measure it by such standards as:

- the timeliness of the work (he met the deadline)
- careful preparation of the surfaces to be painted
- neat mixture and application of the paints
- cleanup after the job

These kinds of standards are pretty predictable; they're much the same for each customer.

But evaluating the degree of customer satisfaction goes beyond the core product or service bought. It involves the entire buying *experience*. The standards by which customers measure satisfaction with an experience are more ambiguous.

> *Customer satisfaction goes beyond the core product. Customers evaluate the entire buying experience.*

Another Look | **Independents Stake Out Niches to Combat Large Chains[3]**

By Judith Nemes

Fran Pryor had good reason to be jittery when she took over Arbor Vitae Java & Juice coffee-house five years ago. A Starbucks Corp. coffee store was right around the corner. Soon, a second location opened nearby and a third popped up just three blocks away. "We needed a strong draw to get our customers here because they have to drive by three Starbucks to get to us," says Ms. Pryor, adding that previous owners had a tough time staying afloat. She calls the Seattle-based coffee giant "a tough competitor."

Arbor Vitae saw an immediate dip in coffee sales each time a new Starbucks opened, but after a couple of weeks, the regulars returned. Indeed, since taking over the business with her daughter Theresa, Ms. Pryor reports that Arbor Vitae has posted a steady 10% increase in revenues each year, though she's quick to add, "We can't ever be overconfident."

continued

Another Look   **Independents Stake Out Niches**   *continued*

One tactic Ms. Pryor employs to maintain a loyal customer base is a blend of potent coffee she created called "Wild Ass," which has developed a following. Roasting fresh coffee beans on the premises and whipping up natural juice drinks also bring in patrons thirsting for the freshest beverages, she says.

Another draw is the personalized look of Arbor Vitae: The bright space boasts tables of hand-inlaid mosaic tiles, a game table and walls showcasing the work of local artists. Many independent coffeehouses are struggling to survive or closing their doors in the face of formidable competition from the national chains. Yet, some owners are finding ways to appeal to Chicago-area java drinkers, particularly those who seek out alternatives to the predictable lattes and corporate-designed atmosphere offered by Starbucks, Caribou Coffee or Seattle's Best Coffee.

Successful entrepreneurs are those serving up consistently great coffee and other specialty drinks, offering excellent customer service and creating a unique environment that draws on the local character of the neighborhood or the personality of the owner. Increasingly, cafes are hosting poetry readings and musical entertainment. Many encourage area residents to hold book club gatherings and other low-key meetings at their establishments. The majority of profitable coffeehouses have been compelled to offer light food items to jolt revenues.

Meanwhile, the personal touch is an effective counter to the corporate cafes. The owners of independent coffeehouses are often the baristas behind the counter, who, along with other longtime employees, may know what the regular patrons are drinking before they order. At Beans & Bagels, a block away from another Starbucks store, staffers have been working there anywhere from three to five years. They rattle off the orders of regulars with uncanny recall. "My staff is the reason we have such a loyal following," says owner Darren Brown.

For many Chicago and suburban residents, the local independent coffeehouse has replaced the neighborhood tavern as a place to gather with friends or stop for a drink after work. "People love to patronize small independents, so if a coffeehouse owner does everything right, they can realistically expect to pull in 20% profit margins," he adds.

Responding quickly to the arrival of a well-known coffee chain can make the difference between failure and success. Mason Green, owner of the Bourgeois Pig Café, wasn't hurt by the proximity of several Starbucks within walking distance of his Old World-style coffeehouse. But when the chain set up a coffee cart inside Children's Memorial Hospital directly across the street, Mr. Green watched morning coffee sales plummet by 50%.

In response, he moved his business two doors east to a bigger space, where he could serve food to bolster morning sales. He also bought a convection oven and began baking goods

continued

Another Look   Independents Stake Out Niches   *continued*

himself to cut overhead costs. The new location also enabled Mr. Green to expand the ambiance his café was known for, with more interesting antiques, stacks of old books lining the walls and comfortable couches that beckon customers to stay awhile.

The cafe also features live jazz on weekend nights and groups often meet there for discussions. A recent Sunday evening at Bourgeois Pig drew 50 people who came to listen to a Holocaust survivor's tales from World War II.

Probes

1. Do the coffee shops described in this sidebar beat larger competitors on the basis of product quality alone? If not, what accounts for their ability to compete with Starbucks?

2. Describe some of the ways these coffee shops use A-plus tactics to compete with larger chains?

Self-Analysis   Identifying Core Expectations

Identify your core expectations for the following products or services. What must happen for you to maintain a basic level of customer satisfaction?

Purchase of:

a satellite radio system

a laptop computer

repair of your automobile's transmission

lawn service for your home

copy service for an important report

a new bicycle

a dental checkup

a complete physical

carpet cleaning

Be specific about what you'd consider to be *basic* expectations.

Customers will be unhappy if their basic expectations are not met. (GEECH ©
1993 UNIVERSAL PRESS SYNDICATE. Reprinted with permission. All rights reserved.)

To further complicate matters, expectations will not remain the same
among different organizations or under different circumstances. When purchasing a tangible product, people expect different treatment from a "high-
touch," full-service retailer than they do from a warehouse store. They expect
service from a prestigious law firm to be different than that from a state auto
license bureau.

For that matter, people probably expect something different from the
same store at different times, such as less personal attention during busy periods (like Christmas at a retail store or the end of the month at the state
auto license bureau).

Different Expectations from Different Businesses

Suppose you intend to shop at a low-cost, self-service discount store, like Wal-Mart, Kmart, or Target. Going into
the store, you anticipate a certain type of experience.
You probably don't assume that the clerk in the clothing department (if you can find one) will be an expert
in fitting clothing. Nor would you be likely to expect that person to be particularly helpful in choosing or color coordinating items you may want to
purchase. This is not to say that some people who work there would not
have these skills, but you probably wouldn't *expect* them as a general rule.

| What we anticipate differs with different types of businesses. |

If we simply select some clothing items from a rack and take them to a
checkout for purchase, we are neither surprised nor particularly disappointed. That's about what we expected from such a retailer, and if other aspects of the store are okay (it seems clean and well stocked, for instance) we
could be perfectly satisfied.

By contrast, if we were to go to a full-service department store like Nordstrom, Macy's, Bloomingdale's, or an exclusive boutique, we would expect a
different kind of transaction. We would probably expect to have a salesperson

> *When a customer finds his or her expectations exceeded, the likelihood of becoming a repeat customer increases sharply.*

with considerable expertise in clothing fit, color, and materials. We would realistically expect that service person to assist us as we make our purchases.

When we find situations like these just described, our expectations are met. Dissatisfaction is probably avoided; we are in that zone of indifference. The key to A-plus customer service and a corresponding motivation to return (loyalty), however, lies not in meeting what customers anticipate, but in *exceeding* their expectations.

One of three situations may arise as we compare our expectations with the service received:

1. Positive expectations were not fulfilled (experience *not as good* as expected)	2. Expectations met	3. Negative expectations were not fulfilled (experience was *not as bad* as expected)
or		or
Experience was more negative than expected		Experience was more positive than expected

In the condition described in the column on the left, the customer's experience was as bad as, or worse than, expected. She's dissatisfied and likely to defect to another provider, if she has a rational alternative. The customer in the middle column is neither dissatisfied nor particularly motivated to return. This is the zone of indifference described earlier. This customer may or may not return.

In the situation represented in the right column, the transaction was better than expected. Either the customer thought it would be pretty good and it was very good, or the customer thought it would not be good but it wasn't as bad as anticipated. Because positive expectations were sufficiently exceeded (or negative ones shown to be unfounded), this customer is quite likely to be motivated to become a loyal (repeat) customer.

The situation in the right column is what we'll call an A-plus experience. What the customer anticipated was exceeded in positive ways.

UNDERSTAND WHY A-PLUS LEADS TO CUSTOMER RETENTION

> *A-plus is based on a theory from social psychology called equity theory.*

A solid theoretical basis for predicting that the A-plus (right-column) customer will become a repeat customer exists in a theory from social psychology called *equity theory*. Psychologist J. Stacy Adams first articulated this theory in the mid-1960s.[4] It has stood the test of time to be widely accepted as a predictor of some kinds of human behavior.

Equity theory starts with the premise that human beings constantly go into and out of various kinds of relationships, ranging from the intimate to the cursory. Long-term relationships like best friendships and families are on one end of the continuum. Brief, even momentary relationships, like interacting with a clerk at a convenience store on a cross-country trip or chatting with someone in an airport, are on the other end of the continuum. The buyer-seller relationship has a place along this continuum as well.

> *We all constantly go into and out of relationships with other people. Some relationships are lasting, some only momentary.*

Once in a relationship, even a brief one, people immediately and regularly assess the *relative equity or fairness of their involvement* compared to other people. They check to see if what they give to the relationship balances with what they are getting out of it. For a very simple example of a relationship that is out of balance (inequitable), imagine if you pass another person on a sidewalk and say "hello" to him but he ignores your greeting and walks on. You've given something and received nothing in return. You'll feel some awkwardness and may wonder what's wrong with him. Is he angry at me? Didn't he hear me? Is he worried about something?

A higher-level experience might occur if you invite a new friend and her family to your home for dinner and she never even thanks you, let alone invites you to her place for a meal. Common courtesy demands that she do something to "rebalance" the relationship. Perhaps she could bring a gift, something to share at the meal, or the like.

> *People in relationships constantly monitor the relative fairness of the relationship. Are they getting as much from it as they are giving to it?*

Initially, much testing of this theory focused on the workplace where workers' perceptions of fairness (equity) were correlated with certain behaviors. Not surprisingly, studies found that people who were paid less for doing the same work as others, for example, felt a sense of inequity. In my own doctoral dissertation, I looked at the impact of supervisory communication on workers. I found that employees who sensed that their supervisor communicated more often and more positively with other employees than with them felt a clear sense of inequity.[5]

But the theory goes beyond simply citing situations where people may feel inequitably treated. It also predicts what people would do about it. When people sense inequity, they will respond with one or some combination of the following behaviors:

- *Ignore or rationalize the inequity.*   ("He deserves to be treated better than I," "The world isn't fair but I'm not going to fight it," or "I guess he didn't hear me say hello.")
- *Demand restitution.*   (The offended person goes to the boss to demand fairer pay, or the customer wants her money back when product quality is poor.)

- *Seek retaliation.* (This can range from telling others about how bad the organization is to doing harm to the person seen as the cause of the inequity or committing outright sabotage.)
- *Withdraw from the relationship.* (Quit and don't come back.)

So far, this theory seems to bear out common sense. If we feel we are being unfairly treated, we get upset and usually do something about it. Hence, the unsatisfied participant in a relationship (the customer in our case) is likely to do one of these things. The first two alternatives may give the company a chance to patch things up and recover the customer using techniques such as those learned in Chapter 3. But the last two—retaliation or withdrawal—can be devastating. Mrs. Williams, the former Happy Jack's Super Market customer in our Chapter 1 story, did both. She withdrew—quit shopping there—and retaliated by telling her friends, thus starting the negative ripple effects that may have resulted in scores or even hundreds of lost customers or potential customers.

RECOGNIZE THE POSITIVE SIDE OF EQUITY THEORY

> *People who feel they are getting more from the relationship than they put in may also feel psychological pressure to restore a balance.*

Another finding of equity theory predicts this: people who feel that they are receiving *more than they "deserve"* from a transaction also experience a psychological need to restore the balance of fairness. A simple illustration of this is the social pressure you may feel to reciprocate when someone gives you an unexpected gift or invites you to her home for dinner. The relationship will remain unbalanced until you rebalance it with a similar kindness: giving a similar gift, bringing wine or flowers to dinner, or at least sending a thank-you note.

Herein lies the theoretical basis for exceeding customer expectations. By going beyond the expected—by giving customers an A-plus experience—you create an imbalance that, for many people, will require action on their part to rebalance. The logical options for customers are the opposite of what the victim of a negative imbalance feels: they could rationalize or ignore it, of course, but attempts to restore the balance could also take the form of telling others of the positive experience, paying a premium for the goods received, or, in short, becoming a loyal customer. Review the story of the independent coffee shops earlier in this chapter, and think about how the shops create a positive imbalance with their customers. What kinds of things are they doing to give more than is expected?

The challenge for any business is to *create positive imbalances by going beyond what customers anticipate—by exceeding expectations.* This is the master key called A-plus. Applying this master key requires two kinds of ongoing actions:

1. Continually work to anticipate customer expectations, and then
2. Exceed these expectations.

LEARN TO UNDERSTAND WHAT CUSTOMERS ANTICIPATE

Customer expectations can be a moving target. These expectations can change based on experiences with the company or with other businesses seen as similar. Two ways to get a sharper picture of the customer's ever-changing expectations are by fishing for feedback and being receptive to customer input.

Fish for Feedback

Two of the best tools for the feedback fisher are "naive" listening and focus groups. Naive listening is more of an attitude than a strategy. As its name implies, this kind of listening conveys that you are not absolutely sure—are naive—about what the customer wants. Your task is to get them to explain it to you. Create an atmosphere where you and your people are cheerfully receptive to customer comments, even—no, *especially*—comments that might not be so pleasant to hear.

> The best way to get useful feedback is to create an atmosphere where your customers can comfortably give suggestions or complain.

Be Receptive to Customer Complaints and Input

The best way to get feedback is to make it easy for people to complain. Let customers know that you are receptive to their comments and concerns. Then provide ways for them to tell you what's on their minds. The use of *open-ended* questions is particularly important. An open-ended question is one that cannot be answered with a simple yes, no, or one-word response. As such, they invariably elicit much more information. Restaurant servers who ask, "How else can I make your dinner enjoyable?" will get a broader range of responses than one who asks the more common, "Do you need anything else?" or "Is everything okay?"

Of course, questions aren't just for the complainer. We also need to know what changes we must make to maintain our customers' ever-changing expectations. Here is where focus groups (discussed in Chapter 2) can come in.

Use of online feedback or call centers that welcome customer input and process it effectively can dramatically improve the ability to anticipate customer needs. The Allegiance Technologies Active Listening System mentioned earlier (page 37) allows customers to provide complaints, comments, suggestions, and questions and is an example of such a system.

Go fishing for feedback regularly. Open the communication channels, and give your customer an opportunity to comment and complain. Remember that at least 63 percent of unhappy customers will not complain but will defect to another source of products or services. Of those who do complain *and have their problems addressed—even if not fully resolved—*only 5 percent will abandon your business. In a sense, your complaining customer is your best customer. Meeting his or her needs provides an opportunity to solidify a business relationship.

> *Your complaining customer is often your most valuable customer.*

STRIVE TO EXCEED CUSTOMER EXPECTATIONS

Understanding customer expectations will do little good unless you take the second step in the A-plus process: regularly develop ways to exceed expectations.

Take a look at your responses to the exercise on page 72, where you identified some core expectations about several products or services. Now that you've identified the basics needed to keep you satisfied, what unexpected surprises might an enlightened business also offer that would go beyond what you anticipate? What kinds of little things could make you much more likely to become a loyal customer?

Now let's go back to our fictitious scenario involving a discount store Kmart or Target variety. How can these retailers exceed your expectations—provide some level of service above and beyond what you'd normally expect from such a company?

Suppose, for example, you found a person greeting you at the door as you entered the store. Suppose that person welcomed you to the store and asked if they could help you find anything in particular. Would that be just a little more than you expected? Perhaps so, but that is, of course, precisely what Wal-Mart stores have done. By hiring people, often senior citizens on a part-time basis, who serve as greeters, Wal-Mart is surpassing the expectations of many discount store shoppers and, in the process, attracting a lot of customers.

But wait. That idea has been done. Are there ways we can take this a step further? Why not get someone to roam around the store wearing a special vest that says, "Can I Help You Find Something?" printed on it and simply have that individual look for customers who appear to be confused or questioning a particular purchase. This individual would have to be exceptionally personable and knowledgeable about the products in the store. (Home Depot uses this strategy.) Wouldn't that exceed the expectations of most customers in a self-service store? That's an example of an A-plus strategy: consistently doing little things that surprise the customer.

INNOVATE WITH THE SIX A-PLUS OPPORTUNITIES: VISPAC

In my work with clients, I've found that people quickly grasp the concept of A-plus but have some difficulty in translating this conceptual knowledge into specific actions. While people nod in agreement about exceeding expectations, they often don't know how.

For this reason, I take this A-plus idea a step further by targeting categories of opportunity for exceeding what customers anticipate. To help remember these categories of opportunity, I use the acronym VISPAC (as in *vi*sible *pac*kaging).

VISPAC encompasses six categories of A-plus opportunities: value, information, speed, personality, add-ons, and convenience. When a customer feels he or she is getting more than expected in any or all of these six areas, the likelihood of customer loyalty increases dramatically. For the next part of this chapter, we will discuss examples of VISPAC.

Value Opportunities That Create A-Plus Experiences

How can we exceed customer expectations regarding the value—the valuable-ness—of the products we sell? When people think of value, they think of some exceptional products they've owned. Perhaps it's a 15- or 20-year-old Kirby vacuum cleaner, a Ford pickup truck, a Western Auto freezer, or an always accurate and totally reliable tax preparation service. Maybe you have a sweater that dates back a quarter century (I do!), a set of Craftsman tools that never break, or a Timex watch that "takes a lickin' and keeps on tickin'." Each of these products may exceed expectations of value. Buyers of the products feel they got more for their money than they would have ever expected when they purchased the items.

Keep in mind two characteristics of value expectations. The first characteristic is that value may *not be obvious* in the short run. Customers may not fully appreciate the value of something until its long-term quality becomes evident. Conveying A-plus value to customers may take an extended time.

The second characteristic of value is that it is always *relative to the price.* Indeed, a useful definition of value is *the quality of a product or service relative to its price.* Some items we buy are throwaways—inexpensive items we don't expect to last. Yet even these can exceed expectations if they last a bit longer than we thought they would, or if they cost even less than we would expect.

> Value is defined as quality relative to cost. Sometimes value does not become apparent until customers become aware of the product's longevity.

Sometimes customers need simply to be reminded of the value they are receiving. A city government may, for example, send information about how tax dollars are being used in the community to show the tax system's value. Some discount stores program their computers to display the list prices of products bought alongside their discount prices, thus reinforcing what a good deal the customer is receiving.

Given that value is not always immediately obvious to customers, providing A-plus value can be tricky. To create an A-plus situation, customers need to perceive an enhanced *sense* of value. We can do a number of things to create that sense of value.

An enhanced sense of value can be produced via *packaging* (e.g., a product seems better if it's nicely wrapped or presented in an attractive box), by *personalizing* the product (e.g., writing a thoughtful note inside a book you give someone), by offering an exceptional *guarantee* (e.g., Craftsman tools are guaranteed for life), or some combination of these.

In addition, the sense of value can be conveyed by *goodness of fit*, meaning the right product for the customer. Financial products that meet the customer's retirement planning goals, electronic equipment that offers the right features (but avoids features the customer will not use), and custom-tailored Levi's jeans ordered online and manufactured to the exact measurement of customers are examples of companies giving an enhanced sense of value.

Information Opportunities That Create A-Plus Experiences

Virtually every product has an informational component. Something as simple as a can of soup comes with information such as nutritional data, ingredients, directions for cooking, and recipes. A service we buy, such as lawn spraying for insects and weeds, is likely to come with cautions about the chemicals being used, instructions to avoid mowing for a period of time, and the like.

How can we exceed customer expectations by providing more, better, or clearer information than the customer expects? One of my children had knee surgery a few years ago. Following the surgery, he was assigned a physical therapist who was to teach him how to regain strength in his knees. We expected the therapist to basically tell him what exercises to do and let it go at that. But the therapist not only explained what exercises he should do but also gave him paper copies illustrating exactly how to do them, provided a thorough demonstration of each workout, and followed up with a phone call a few days later to see how my son was doing. These were little things, of course, but still an A-plus experience for me and my child.

Today's most effective automobile salespeople no longer tell you that the car has an owner's manual in the glove box. Instead, they often spend considerable time with customers explaining all the bells and whistles on the new car. This is giving A-plus information.

Here are other examples: A hospital client I worked with changed the signs in the hospital when it became evident that the old signs provided too little information. Patients and guests were getting lost. The hospital also installed color stripes on the corridor floors to direct people to various departments. A cellular phone dealer regularly calls customers to see if they understand how to use all the phone's features. He offers to meet customers to explain the features in person, if necessary.

Often the best opportunities for A-plus in the area of information involve using different *media* than is customary. Often, we need to go beyond just offering written instructions. Computer software products, for example, are often accompanied by a learning CD or videotape program. Some exercise equipment manufacturers like NordicTrack use videos to both sell and demonstrate their products. Some products or services are sold with free classes, chat groups, or consulting. How can your business give customers more useful information?

Another Look — Companies Chatting Up Customers[6]

By Mary Ellen Podmolik

Some companies offer A-plus information by encouraging online chat, as Podmolik's article illustrates:

Online chats have become more than a social exercise, as businesses like optionsXpress Inc. use them to help customers navigate their Web sites and complete transactions. Every page of optionsXpress' Web site includes a green icon that offers live assistance—not just e-mail or a toll-free number. Customers who click on it open a window to talk in real time to an agent who answers queries and can even send them Web pages containing more information. Such help is immediate and just a few keystrokes away, so tapping it is faster than waiting for an e-mail response, finding a salesperson in a store or working through automated telephone options.

optionsXpress opened its Web site doors in January 2001 with four online customer service agents, backed by another 30 workers with different specialties. The company's CEO hasn't tracked how much the service is contributing to higher revenues or volume, but says the many repeat customers he sees in the chat area indicate growing customer loyalty.

The need to improve online customer service is leading to several breakthrough technologies akin to instant messaging, and early adopters say they're seeing a more-loyal customer base, although some haven't quantified the financial impact. Some retailers, however, report that customers buy more merchandise when they chat.

Live chat technology works with special software or an application service provider (ASP) and customer service agents who sit at computers waiting for questions. An automated version simulates a person but actually provides "canned" online responses.

Lands' End Inc., an early adopter of the Internet, launched a live chat function in fall 1999 after training its most experienced telephone customer service agents on the Internet and making sure they could type. The agents answer questions from one customer at a time, and

continued

can call up Web pages on the consumer's browser based on the questions asked. The Dodgeville, Wis.—based apparel retailer found that its online shoppers, who account for 25% of revenues, like asking questions without interrupting their shopping. People who engage in chat are spending an average 6% more on orders, says Anna Schryver, Lands' End e-marketing project manager.

Dallas-based Neiman Marcus Group Inc. recently decided to offer live chat for its online retail division, NeimanMarcus.com, in time for holiday shopping.

Harrisdirect, a unit of Chicago-based Harris Bankcorp Inc., has offered live chat to its clients for almost a year, using the same investor services representatives who answer e-mails and telephone calls. "You're dealing with someone's money," [a manager] says. "You want to provide all the things that can make that client feel comfortable about that experience."

Cost-conscious companies are using a cheaper chat variation by providing prepared answers to frequently asked questions. They archive questions that arrive by e-mail as well as the answers and continually update the database. Then, when customers ask questions while navigating the companies' Web sites, word-recognition software pulls appropriate responses from the database and sends them immediately to the user through the Web site.

Some analysts see more promise in this lower-cost, self-service alternative. "From a consumer perspective, live chat is fantastic because you're getting service right away," says David Spindel, technology analyst at Datamonitor.

Retailer Eddie Bauer, part of Spiegel Inc. of Downers Grove, offers "Ask Eddie," an online program that searches the company database for answers that correspond to words in a consumer's query.

Keebler Co. launched an initiative Oct. 1 [2002] that aims to build brand awareness and loyalty, and indirectly increase sales. RecipeBuddie is an interactive instant messaging robot with the persona of Becky, a 35-year-old suburban mother of two. Consumers who use instant messaging applications from America Online Inc. or Microsoft Corp. can have Becky answer their questions or search for recipes based on specific ingredients. The replies are conversational. The Elmhurst-based cookie and cracker company hasn't tracked the number of hits for the first month, but executives think the reaction has been positive. "One of the keys of this kind of online program is we're getting instant feedback in terms of how long people are on the site and how much they're diving through it," says Jeff Johansen, vice-president of marketing.

Whether chats are live or canned, the main benefit is the immediacy of the communication, analysts say. "Any merchandiser will tell you that the heat of the moment is the best time to sell," says Dana Gardner, research director at Aberdeen Group Inc., a Boston-based information technology consultancy. "You don't want to let someone off the hook just because they need a little information."

Sometimes information and the display of products work together. One example comes from marketing researcher Paco Underhill, writing about Wal-Mart:

> Pharmacies have changed a lot in the past two decades, but one thing remains constant: the large burden on staff to stock all those little bottles, jars, and boxes in perfectly straight rows in aisle after aisle. Every time a customer picks something up to read the label, you're guaranteed that the thing needs to be straightened or turned so it faces front. It's a lot of work. Not long ago Wal-Mart tried an experiment: it began replacing traditional shelves with a system of bins. Instead of facing a shelf of aspirin bottles, say, the shopper saw a blowup of the aspirin bottle's label. Under that blowup was the bin, into which the aspirin bottles had been dumped. That made an enormous difference. First, it solved the problem of stocking—a clerk could just roll a trolley of merchandise to the aisle, open the bin, dump in the goods, and move on. No more straight lines. The shoppers liked it better, too—instead of facing a row of bottles with tiny print, they saw a large, easy-to-read version of the label. It was much easier on the eyes, especially for elderly shoppers. Wal-Mart's main concern in making the change was whether shoppers would perceive the bins as being somehow cheaper and lower in quality than the shelves. In fact, just the opposite was true— shoppers said they thought the bins were an upgraded display system—a very elegant solution.[7]

Speed Opportunities That Create A-Plus Experiences

The third letter in our VISPAC acronym stands for *speed*. How can you exceed your customers' expectations with regard to the speed of service? Research of customer turnoffs repeatedly shows that customers dislike having to wait too long for products or services.[8] Across all types of businesses, people want timely response. My research shows that even when engaged in leisurely dining at an upscale restaurant, people still value timely service. They may plan to stay a while, but they want their water glass refilled quickly, for example.

Federal Express and the other air freight companies say they'll deliver your package by 10 the next morning, but they often arrive by 9 or 9:30. The repair department for a major office equipment company makes it a policy to tell customers precisely when the repair person can be there (thus setting an expectation) and then to see that the service person arrives earlier than promised (A-plus). The reason speed is such a powerful way of exceeding expectations is that, in our culture, people often fail to be time-conscious. Repair people and delivery services are often notorious for showing up late—or not at all! It's a major pet peeve of customers, yet one that can be easily fixed.

> *Offering service faster than expected—even when you originally set the expectation—is a powerful form of A-plus.*

Staffing decisions affect speed. At a progressive supermarket, additional cashiers open when more than two customers are in line. Good fast-food restaurants serve your lunch almost before you can order it because they hire enough staff and train extensively. Are there ways you can give customers a little faster service than they expect?

Paco Underhill believes that waiting time may be the single most important factor in customer satisfaction. When shoppers are required to wait in line (or anywhere else) for too long, the impression of overall service plunges. The problem of perceived slow service is widespread. One speed-conscious bank was about to institute a policy of giving away $5 to any customer who had to wait five minutes or more. After studying the teller lines over the course of two days, Underhill's consulting firm informed the client that this policy would cost it about triple what it had set aside. The bank dropped the plan and went to work on other ways of shortening its customers' wait.[9]

Personality Opportunities That Create A-Plus Experiences

The P in our VISPAC acronym is for *personality*. How can you exceed customer expectations with the personality of your people? Every company or organization conveys a personality to its customers. This personality is a composite of countless behaviors exhibited by the people who work there. Friendliness, courtesy, efficiency, professionalism, and quality are all conveyed via both verbal and nonverbal behaviors.

The A-plus opportunity we call personality is so important that Chapter 5 will deal with it at length. For now, the question is, "How can you or your company project positive personality characteristics that exceed customer expectations?"

Add-on Opportunities That Create A-Plus Experiences

How can you exceed customer expectations by adding on—by giving or selling customers something else they will need or appreciate? When shoe store clerks give a shoehorn with a pair of new shoes or when they ask if you'd like to try padded inserts or a pair of lifetime-guarantee socks, they are using this A-plus approach. Sometimes add-ons are sold; sometimes they are given away. Both can be effective. A clerk at a supermarket hands customers a few candy kisses with the receipt as an unexpected thank you. The hotel check-in desk has a basket of complimentary apples. The paint store salesperson checks to be sure buyers have caulking and sandpaper.

HERMAN®

9-14 © 1981 Jim Unger

**"If you buy a goldfish,
I'll throw in the aardvark."**

Add-ons can encourage customer loyalty—if they have perceived value.
(HERMAN® is reprinted with permission of Laughingstock Licensing Inc. All rights reserved.)

The best kinds of free add-ons are those with high perceived value and low cost to the business. For example, gas stations that give away a free car wash with fill-up find that such washes cost them about 7 cents (for soap and water—not, of course, the cost of the auto-wash machine) but have a perceived value of $3 to $5 (which is the price printed on the coupon).* Free popcorn or drinks given away with video rentals cost 3 or 4 cents but have a much higher perceived value. Generous soft drink or coffee refills at restaurants cost little but can be important add-ons.

> *Give away something of perceived value, and you tip the equity scale in your favor.*

---

*The few cents it costs to wash the car can be made up by increasing the cost of gas by a penny or two. The business wins in several ways.

Convenience is a great way to A-plus customers.

Obviously, this A-plus opportunity area ties in closely with its marketing counterpart, add-on sales. Marketers have long recognized the value of trying to sell current customers something else while you already have their attention. This can backfire if salespeople are too pushy, but most customers will not resent low-key inquiries about other products. What add-on product or service can you give your customers?

Convenience Opportunities That Create A-Plus Experiences

Convenience may be the A-plus area with the greatest potential in today's efficiency-obsessed culture. How can you exceed customer expectations by making your product or service more convenient than expected?

Too many companies offer a typical response to a customer with a faulty product: "Bring it in and we'll replace it." But recall our example in Chapter 2 of how Toyota Motors handled a recall shortly after coming into the U.S. market with their new Lexus car line. Dealers called customers for an appointment to *pick up* the car, and they left a loaner car for the customer. If a customer has to go through the trouble of bringing back a faulty product, you might achieve A-plus by offering to deliver a replacement.

Quick-lube auto services have flourished as a response to the need for customer convenience.

Twenty years ago, if you needed an oil change on your car you'd take it to a service station, leave it for the day, get a ride to work, and so on. Today we go to quick-lube shops, drive in, step out of the car, have a cup of coffee in the waiting room, and 10 minutes later we are back on the road. A team of technicians pounces on your car and checks fluids, tire pressure, wiper blades, and more while you relax. That's convenience.

The number-one restaurant food in America is pizza. But if you had to go to a pizza restaurant, order your food, and wait 20 minutes for it to be

**"Don't bother undressing.
I'll turn up the power."**

Convenience is a powerful A-plus opportunity area. (HERMAN® is reprinted with
permission of Laughingstock Licensing Inc. All rights reserved.)

served, I doubt that it would be so popular. It's the widespread availability
of take-out and pizza-delivery services that built the industry.

Customers face a lot of inconveniences daily. If you
come up with great ideas for A-plus service in the area
of convenience, you'll have a strong competitive advantage. Technology, especially shopping via the Internet,
is one obvious resource that is being tapped. I'll talk
more about technology and customer loyalty in
Chapter 7. How can you make things more convenient
for your customers?

> *Convenience is one of the most
> promising A-plus opportunity
> areas because so much of what
> customers face today is
> inconvenient.*

RECOGNIZE WHERE GOOD A-PLUS IDEAS COME FROM

The ideas above are, of course, simply illustrative. The possibilities for A-
plus are quite literally unlimited. A-plus organizations constantly seek out
new "little things" that can and will make huge differences. A-plus requires

constant incremental improvements. Minor improvements and innovations can lead to a payoff that is enormous. A-plus really is the master key for building customer satisfaction, retention, and loyalty. If you're not thinking about A-plus, your competition may be.

To get a constant flow of new A-plus ideas, ask employees at all levels of the organization to apply creativity. Work to create an environment where new ideas are tried and innocent mistakes are not punished. Have supervisors or team leaders get together regularly to brainstorm new ideas. Then reward the best ideas with recognition and possibly prizes. The result of this process (which is described in more detail in Chapter 9) is a lively, vibrant, evolving organization with a strong and competitive advantage that cannot be duplicated by your competition.

A FINAL THOUGHT

Exceeding people's expectations—even in small, almost insignificant ways—can have a dramatic impact on building and strengthening relationships. People with good customer service skills consistently look for ways to provide something unexpected, something that may increase the customer's desire to reciprocate by strengthening loyalty. A-plus service becomes a reality as we pleasantly surprise customers in six categories: value, information, speed, personality, add-ons, and convenience (VISPAC).

Summary of Key Ideas

- Consistently exceeding customer expectations is a powerful key to career success.
- A theory from social psychology called equity theory supports the importance of exceeding customer expectations (creating "A-plus") to keep customers and build their loyalty.
- When people believe they are getting more than they "deserve" from a relationship, they feel subtle pressures to rebalance the relationship by giving more to it.
- Ever-changing expectations force intelligent businesspeople to constantly adjust and innovate.
- Fishing for customer feedback helps us better assess expectations.
- Six areas provide the best opportunities for exceeding expectations: value, information, speed, personality, add-ons, and convenience (VISPAC).
- The best A-plus ideas emerge from alert, innovative people at any level in the organization.

Key Concepts

add-ons

A-plus

convenience-enhancing
  opportunities

core expectations

customer expectations

equity theory

exceeding the anticipated

inequity

informational component (of
  products)

open-ended questions

perceptions of value

VISPAC

Self-Test Questions

1. How does social psychology's equity theory apply to customer loyalty? What are the common responses to perceived inequities?

2. What are some ways managers can train employees to fish for customer feedback?

3. What affects a customer's perception of value, and how can companies enhance this to create an A-plus situation?

4. What are examples of add-ons? What kinds of things are the best add-ons?

5. Describe two ways companies can systematically anticipate customers' ever-changing expectations.

6. How do the "Another Look" sidebars in this chapter illustrate value, systems, and people turnoffs as discussed in Chapter 2?

Application Activity: A-Plus Brainstorming

1. Working in teams of 5 to 10 people, imagine yourself in a business you are familiar with (retail, health care, insurance office, hotel/restaurant, public utility, repair shop, etc.). Using the worksheets found on pages 90 through 96, brainstorm A-plus ideas that might be useful. Be careful not to be overly judgmental as you come up with ideas. The more creative, the better in many cases. Initially, encourage a free flow of ideas, withholding judgment. You can then go back and refine the group's best ideas.

2. If you decide to generate ideas in the personality category, read Chapter 5 before completing this assignment.

VISPAC Worksheet   #1: Value

A-plus your customers by creating a perception of value that exceeds their expectations. List ideas for clarifying or presenting an enhanced sense of value in your product or service. Consider such things as various payment options, clarity of billing so that the customer understands costs of different services, and highlighting any discounts given. Remember that value is a relationship of *quality compared to cost.* Consider such things as guarantees, packaging, etc.

After brainstorming possible ideas, put a check in the box next to ideas for further consideration.

☐

☐

☐

☐

☐

☐

☐

☐

The best idea for implementation now is:

VISPAC Worksheet   #2: Information

A-plus your customers with more, better, or different information than they ex-pect. Consider the possibility of using different media. List ideas for clarifying, improving, or presenting additional information customers may find useful as they use the product or service.

After brainstorming possible ideas, put a check in the box next to ideas for further consideration.

☐

☐

☐

☐

☐

☐

☐

☐

The best idea for implementation now is:

VISPAC Worksheet   #3: Speed

A-plus your customers by exceeding customer expectations about your efficiency or response times. List ideas for reducing delays or providing faster service than customers might anticipate. Remember that slow service is the number-one complaint of customers in almost every type of business. Your task is to be faster and/or to clarify realistic expectations for customers.

After brainstorming possible ideas, put a check in the box next to ideas for further consideration.

☐

☐

☐

☐

☐

☐

☐

☐

The best idea for implementation now is:

VISPAC Worksheet   #4: Personality

A-plus your customers by conveying pleasant, attentive, personable service that exceeds what they may expect. Consider any small verbal or nonverbal "message" you may be sending out. Include possible dialogue ideas for telephone or personal visitors.

After brainstorming possible ideas, put a check in the box next to ideas for further consideration.

☐

☐

☐

☐

☐

☐

☐

☐

The best idea for implementation now is:

VISPAC Worksheet   **#5: Add-Ons**

A-plus your customers by giving or selling them something additional. List ideas for surprising them with a small gift or premium. Consider add-on products they may benefit from or need to make the best use of something they've already purchased.

After brainstorming possible ideas, put a check in the box next to ideas for further consideration.

☐

☐

☐

☐

☐

☐

☐

☐

The best idea for implementation now is:

VISPAC Worksheet   #6: Convenience

A-plus your customers by making life easier for them than they expected. List ideas for enhancing their experience with your product or service. Consider such things as free delivery, in-home or in-office services, your handling follow-up details, etc.

After brainstorming possible ideas, put a check in the box next to ideas for further consideration.

☐

☐

☐

☐

☐

☐

☐

☐

The best idea for implementation now is:

Notes

1. Qtd. in *Parade*, May 12, 2002, p. 17.

2. D. Chung. "Retailer Charles R. Walgreen Sr. His Innovations Helped Build Nation's Biggest Drugstore Chain." Copyright © 1998 *Investors Business Daily*, used with permission of IBD. Transmitted July 22, 1999, on AOL.

3. J. Nemes. "Independents Stake Out Niches to Combat Large Chains." *Crain's Chicago Business*, November 11, 2002, 25 (45), p. SB4.

4. The basic premises of equity theory can be found in J. S. Adams, "Toward an Understanding of Inequity," *Journal of Abnormal and Social Psychology*, 1963, 67, pp. 422–36. Later studies are summarized in L. Berkowitz and E. Walster (eds.), *Advances in Experimental Social Psychology*, vol. 9 (New York: Academic Press, 1976).

5. P. R. Timm. "Effects of Inequity in Supervisory Communication Behavior on Subordinates in Clerical Workgroups." Unpublished doctoral dissertation, Florida State University, 1977.

6. M. E. Podmolik. "Companies Chatting Up Customers." *Crain's Chicago Business*, November 18, 2002, 25 (46), p. SR4. Used with permission.

7. P. Underhill. "What Shoppers Want." *Inc.*, July 1999, p. 78.

8. Ibid.

9. Ibid.

Use Behaviors That Win Customer Loyalty

It's What You Do

Sometimes the smallest, unintended behavior can create relationship turnoffs. Subtle facial expressions, gestures, vocal intonation, or appearance can make the difference between winning customer loyalty or losing it.

WHAT YOU'LL LEARN IN THIS CHAPTER

- Behavior is what people do, and much of it is conveyed via verbal or nonverbal communication.
- Individual actions as well as organizational behaviors convey messages to customers which may be productive or counterproductive to their perception of service received.
- Any behaviors (or lack of behaviors) can communicate; the receiver of the message (e.g., the customer) determines what the message means.
- Exceeding expectations in the area of personality depends on both individual actions and the organization's behaviors or culture.
- It is important to recognize the role of communication in projecting behavior; there are two critical rules of communicating.
- Fifteen specific behaviors can exceed customer expectations in the area of individual personality.
- Seven actions convey the organization's personality (culture) to customers.

THE WAY IT IS . . .
The Power of Personality

"G'morning, Hon," "Hi, there!" and a chorus of other greetings ring out whenever I enter a Waffle House. The ubiquitous southern restaurants are famous for a cheery hello, especially at breakfast time. I never feel like a stranger at Waffle House.

More than 20 years ago, I opened a bank account near my office. Being new to town, I needed the checking account and the branch office was close by. A week after opening the account, I walked in to make a deposit. I'd barely cleared the door when a teller called across the lobby, "Good morning, Mr. Timm." I was stunned. She had remembered my name after only one transaction. I remained a loyal customer of that bank for decades, based largely on the personality of the employees.

The Disney organization builds incredible loyalty by providing a "happiest-place-on-Earth" atmosphere in their theme parks. People enjoy themselves in large part because the employees (whom Disney calls "cast members") seem to be enjoying themselves. Smiles and greetings are exchanged freely and convey the personality of the organization.

Every organization, like every person, has a personality. This personality is conveyed by countless "little things," mostly verbal and nonverbal communication cues. Some people are unaware of how these cues work—how subtle behaviors send "messages" to others. In this chapter we will talk about conveying an A-plus personality—exceeding customer expectations by projecting an exceptionally positive personality.

RECOGNIZE THAT ANYTHING CAN CONVEY A MESSAGE

Behavior is, of course, what people do. It is conveyed to others via both verbal (using words or language) and nonverbal communication. Even when no words are exchanged, personality can still communicate loud and clear. A salesperson who fails to greet a customer, an employee who routinely shows up late, and a repair person who leaves a mess all communicate something. Likewise, the friendly greeter at a store or restaurant, the cheerful voice from a call center, or the associate who always speaks to you communicates something as well.

> *Any behaviors can, and often will, communicate messages to our customers. The receiver of these messages determines what they mean.*

Two important rules of communication must be kept in mind: *anything can and will communicate,* and *the receiver of the message determines what it "means."*

The remainder of this chapter looks at some of the kinds of behaviors—of individuals and organizations—

that convey messages to customers. This is by no means an exhaustive list of all possible behaviors, but it does reflect some of the more common ones that associate closely with customer loyalty.

UNDERSTAND BEHAVIOR AND PERSONALITY FACTORS THAT A-PLUS CUSTOMERS

In Chapter 4 we discussed the importance of exceeding what customers anticipate (we called it A-plus), and we identified six opportunity areas for A-plus: value, information, speed, *personality*, add-ons, and convenience. Because personality is such a significant and complex area of A-plus opportunity, I have set aside a separate chapter to explore it. Personality is a powerful way to create A-plus experiences for customers.

Each customer encounters two interrelated personalities: the personality of the individual who serves the customer and the overall personality of the organization. This organizational personality reflects the company's "culture." Culture is a composite of many factors that strengthen and reinforce individual behavior. If a company is an enjoyable, fun-loving place to work, its people will convey a sense of enjoyment to customers. If the culture is more formal (say, at a law firm or medical facility), this personality may be reinforced by employee behaviors that convey competence and professionalism. Of course, lawyers and medical-office employees may also be fun-loving and personable.

Wal-Mart founder Sam Walton understood organizational behavior when he taught his managers that "People will treat your customers the way you treat your people." Enthusiasm, comradeship, a sense of enjoyment, and humor quickly become evident to Wal-Mart's customers. Southwest Airlines, which has a culture of informality and fun at work, projects an organizational personality very different from that of many of its competitors. This personality has been useful both in attracting customers and in enlisting employees who enjoy working in such an atmosphere. Indeed, research studies of the best companies to work for consistently identify "having fun" as a critically important criterion.

KNOW WHICH INDIVIDUAL BEHAVIORS CAN CONVEY PERSONALITY

Often the subtlest behaviors can send the most powerful messages to customers. It's the little things that mean everything. This chapter looks at 15 individual behaviors that, taken together, project personality. As you become aware of these, you'll quickly recognize A-plus opportunities in each. Awareness alone can improve service, yet many employees are essentially clueless about the impact of these kinds of behaviors.[1]

1. Greet Customers Like Guests

Woody Allen once said that 80 percent of success is just showing up. In customer service, 80 percent of success is just treating the customer like a guest who just showed up. When guests come to your home, you greet them, right? Yet we've all had the experience of being totally ignored by service people in some businesses. Friendly greetings, like those offered routinely at Waffle House, are some of those little things that mean a lot.

> The failure to be greeted creates stress for a customer.

Initiate conversation promptly. Studies have clocked the number of seconds people had to wait to be greeted in several businesses. Researchers then asked customers how long they'd been waiting. In every case, the customer's estimate of the time elapsed was much longer than the actual time. A customer waiting 30 or 40 seconds often feels like it's been three or four minutes. Time drags when you're being ignored.

A prompt, friendly greeting can help people feel comfortable and reduce stress customers may experience. Why would customers feel stress? Because they are on unfamiliar turf. While employees work there every day, customers are just visiting. A prompt, friendly greeting can help everyone relax and grease the wheels of comfortable interaction.

Speak up. Employees should verbally greet customers within a few seconds of their entrance into the business or their approach to a work location. Even if busy with another customer or on the phone, workers should pause to say "hello" and let the customer know that they will be ready to help him or her soon.

Get the customer committed. Did you ever wonder why some fast-food restaurants send a clerk out to write your order on a sheet of paper while you are waiting in line? Think about it. You tell the person what you want, and she marks it on a slip of paper which she then gives back to you to present at the cash register where the order is called out. Why do they do this? It is a way of getting the customer committed. If no one greeted you or wrote your order, you might be more likely to leave before reaching the register. But psychologically, this strategy makes you feel as if you've "ordered," so you stay in line and follow through with your lunch purchase.

Some years ago, I did some research on behaviors of effective personal computer salespeople. PCs were just gaining widespread popularity, and the behavior differences between the successful and unsuccessful salespeople were striking. The unsuccessful ones rattled off a lot of techno-jargon, apparently intended to impress customers, while their successful counterparts quickly invited the novice computer user to sit down and *do* something on the computer. Similarly, my observations of auto salespeople showed similar patterns. The best car sales reps quickly invited prospects to test-drive the car, rather than standing around talking about the car.

Employees should greet each customer promptly, verbally if possible, and try to commit them to doing something as soon as feasible when they come into the business or work area.

2. Break the Ice

The best way to start a conversation depends on what the customer needs. In many cases, especially in retail stores, customers need first to be reassured that this is a nice, friendly place to do business. They need to overcome worries about being high-pressured into buying. To dispel those worries, use a nonthreatening icebreaker. Often customers want to browse, get the feel of the place before they commit to doing business.

The best icebreaker for the browser can be an off-topic, friendly comment. Some good ones might be:

- a compliment ("That's a great-looking tie you're wearing" or "Your children are sure cute. How old are they?")
- weather-related or local-interest comments ("Isn't this sunshine just beautiful?" or "Some snowfall, isn't it?" or "How about those Bulls last night?")
- small talk (Look for cues about the customer's interest in sports, jobs, mutual acquaintances, past experiences, etc. Then initiate a relevant comment.)

If a browsing customer seems to be focusing attention on a product (say he or she is holding several shirts or is looking at a particular item), the person can be reclassified as a "focused shopper."

The best icebreaker for the focused shopper is one that is more specific to the buying decision. It may:

- anticipate the customer's questions ("What size are you looking for, sir?" or "Can I help you select a . . . ?")
- provide additional information ("Those widgits are all 25 percent off today" or "We have additional of those in the stockroom")
- offer a suggestion or recommendation ("Those striped suits are really popular this season" or "If you need help with measurements, our estimators can figure out what you'll need")

Be attentive to customers' needs. Give them time to browse if that's what they need, but be responsive in helping them make a buying decision when they are ready. Retail-industry research shows that 60 to 80 percent of all shopping decisions are made in the store at the point of sale.[2] This is precisely the point where customers come face-to-face with the employee's and the organization's personality. Reassure the customer that you can help them. Ask questions to identify their needs, concerns, or problems.

> *Learn which "icebreaker" comments work best for different kinds of customers.*

3. Compliment Freely and Sincerely

It only takes a second to say something nice to a person. Such comments can add enormous goodwill and move people toward an A-plus experience. Employees should look for opportunities to say something complimentary to their customers and coworkers. Safe ground for sincere compliments includes:

- some article of clothing or accessories they are wearing ("I like that tie!" or "That's a beautiful sweater you have on" or "Those shoes look really comfortable. I've been shopping for some like that" or "What a beautiful necklace")
- their children ("Your little boy is really cute" or "How old is your daughter? She's beautiful" or "He looks like a bright young man")
- their behavior ("Thanks for waiting. You've been very patient" or "I noticed you checking those items. You're a careful shopper" or "Thanks for your friendly smile")
- something they own ("I like your car. What year is it?" or "I noticed your championship ring. Did you play on that team?")

> *Many people are too hesitant to give compliments, yet everyone loves to receive a sincere compliment. Make it a habit to do so.*

To get into the habit of complimenting, try this: set a goal to give 10 sincere compliments each day. Make it a habit, and you'll see a sharp increase in your personal popularity. People love to be complimented. And, of course, complimenting internal customers (e.g., coworkers) can help create a supportive and pleasant work climate.

4. Call People by Name

A person's name is his or her favorite sound. We appreciate it when people make the effort to use our name in addressing us. Just as in my earlier example about the bank teller calling me by name, this action can create A-plus service for customers and build loyalty.

When appropriate, employees should introduce themselves to customers and ask their names. If this isn't appropriate (such as when there is a line of waiting customers), they can often get customers' names from checks, credit cards, order forms, or other paperwork.

> *Use your customer's name if given the opportunity. It builds the relationship.*

Be careful not to become overly familiar too quickly as some customers may feel it's disrespectful. We are generally safe calling people "Mr. Smith" or "Ms. Jones," but we may be seen as rude calling them "Homer" and "Marge." (This is especially true when younger employees are dealing with older customers.) It's better to err on the side of being too formal. If people prefer being addressed by their first name, they'll tell you so.

5. Talk to Customers with Your Eyes

Even in situations where you may not be able to say "hello" out loud or give undivided attention to a customer right away, you can make eye contact. Simply looking at your customer tells him or her much about your willingness to serve. Eye contact creates a bond between you and the customer. It conveys your interest in communicating further. Here is a personal example in which the wrong message was conveyed:

> *Establishing eye contact can convey a message that you are willing to serve customers.*

> I went into a very small watch-repair shop. The shop was no more than 10 feet square. The proprietor was a real expert at repairing timepieces, and his prices were good. As I squeezed into his tiny shop he was serving another customer. I stood not more than 5 feet away from him for several minutes without his ever acknowledging me. It got pretty uncomfortable. Once he finished with the customer ahead of me, he was attentive and effective, but he ran a real risk of losing me before he got a chance to show me what he could do—simply because it felt awkward standing there without being acknowledged. All he would have needed to do is say "hello" and let me know that he would be with me momentarily.

As with your greeting, the timing of eye contact is important. Employees should make eye contact with the customer as soon as possible—within a few seconds—even if they are busy with another person. It's not necessary that they interrupt what they are doing with the customer at hand. Just a pause and a quick look capture new customers and reduce the chance they'll feel ignored and leave.

When working with customers, be sensitive to *how* you look at them. Communication expert Bert Decker says that the three I's of eye communication are intimacy, intimidation, and involvement. Intimacy (as when we're expressing love) and intimidation (when we want to exert power) are both communicated by looking at another person for a long period—from 10 seconds to a minute or more.[3]

But most communication in business settings calls for Decker's third "I": involvement. In our culture, people create involvement by looking at the other person for 5- to 10-second periods before glancing away briefly. This is generally comfortable for people. If you look away more often than that, you may be seen as shifty or suspicious; if you lock in eye contact for longer, it feels like intimidation or intimacy.

> *Eye contact, or lack of it, conveys powerful messages to customers.*

6. Ask Often "How Am I Doing?"

Legendary politician and former New York City mayor Ed Koch would constantly ask his constituents, "How'm I doing?" The phrase became his tag line. There is some evidence that he even listened to their answers. After all, he survived as mayor of the Big Apple for many years. We can learn something from the Koch question.

Businesses need to ask that question in as many ways as possible. In addition to using more formalized measurement and feedback systems (as discussed in Chapter 2), employees should demonstrate an ongoing attitude of receptiveness. Being receptive to people's comments and criticisms can be challenging and at times frustrating. It takes a lot of courage not only to accept criticism but to actually request it. Nevertheless, getting a constant flow of "how am I doing" information is a critical key to providing A-plus personality.

> *An attitude of receptiveness is revealed by a willingness to ask questions—and listen to the answers.*

7. Listen with More Than Your Ears

Since so few people are really good listeners, this skill provides an excellent A-plus opportunity. There is no such thing as an unpopular listener. Almost everyone becomes more interesting when they stop talking and start listening. Be sure that employees pay attention to their talk-listen ratio. Are they giving the customer at least equal time?

The most effective listeners do the following things:

- *Focus on the content of what people are saying, not the way they are saying it.* Customers may not have the "right" words, but they know what they need better than anyone.
- *Hold their fire.* They don't jump to make judgments or finish a customer's thought before he or she has finished talking.
- *Work at listening.* They maintain eye contact and discipline themselves to listen to what is being said. They tune out those thoughts that get them sidetracked, or thinking about something else.
- *Resist distractions.* They make the customer the center of their attention.
- *Seek clarification from customers to fully understand their needs.* Good listeners do this in a nonthreatening way using sincere, open-ended questions.

8. Say "Please," "Thank You," and "You're Welcome"

At the risk of sounding like one of those books about "things learned in kindergarten," *be polite*. It may seem old-fashioned and some customers may not be as polite to you, but that's not *their* job. In a "Dear Abby" advice column, a writer complained about salespeople who said "There you go" to conclude a transaction, instead of "thank you." That kind of comment is not an appropriate substitute for thanking the customer. When someone thanks us, we should respond with "You're welcome," although the popular favorite seems to be "No problem." "No problem" seems to imply that the other person was seen as a potential problem, but they somehow avoided becoming such.

Please, thank you, and *you're welcome* are powerful words for building customer rapport and creating customer loyalty. Attention to such wording can exceed customer expectations and produce an A-plus experience.

9. Reassure Customers in Their Decision to Do Business with You

Buyer's remorse can set in pretty quickly, especially when people make a large purchase. At the time of sale, service providers can inoculate against remorse by reassuring customers that they've made a good purchasing decision.

Phrases like "I'm sure you'll get many hours of enjoyment out of this" or "Your family will love it" can help reassure and strengthen the buyer's resolve to follow through with the purchase and, as importantly, feel good about it. A government agency employee might say, "I'll bet you're glad that's over with for another year" or "I'll handle the renewal—you've done all that is necessary." Such reassurance can help create an A-plus experience.

10. Smile

As the old adage goes, "You are not dressed for work until you put on a smile." Or, as a more cynical person might say, "Smile. It'll make people wonder what you've been up to." But more importantly, it'll tell customers that they came to the right place and are on friendly ground. Personality is rarely projected without a smile.

Keep in mind that a smile originates in two places, the mouth and the eyes. A lips-only version looks pasted on, insincere. It's like saying "cheese" when being photographed. It doesn't fool anyone. In fact, it might scare them away!

The eyes, however, are the windows to the soul and tell the truth about your feelings toward people. So smile with your eyes and your mouth. Let your face show that you're glad your guest arrived.

> *A genuine smile originates in the eyes, not the mouth.*

Now, in fairness, some people smile more readily than others, and in some business contexts smiling may be inappropriate (at a funeral home, for example). For some people a more serious facial expression is comfortable and natural. But in American culture, a smile is generally both expected and appreciated when meeting people. If people don't smile spontaneously, they can practice it. This need not be a Cheshire cat, ear-to-ear grin (in fact, that may *really* get people wondering) but just a pleasant, natural smile. Employees can work on their facial expression as an actor might.

11. Use Good Telephone Techniques

In today's business world, many customers make their initial contact with a company via the phone. Telephone use requires some special behaviors, especially if it is the only contact with customers. A key to successful phone use is to simply *remember that your customer cannot see you*. The personality challenge is to make up for all that lost nonverbal communication by using the voice effectively. Chapter 6 talks in more depth about telephone techniques, but for now, let's review a few key behaviors that can help build an A-plus personality:

> *Remember that your telephone customer can't see you, and adjust your behaviors accordingly.*

- *Give the caller your name.* Let the caller know who you are just as you would in a face-to-face situation (via a name tag or desk plaque). Answer the phone with your name.

- *Smile into the phone.* Somehow people can hear a smile over the phone. Some telephone pros place a mirror in front of them while they're on the phone to remind them that facial expressions can transmit through the wires.

- *Keep the caller informed.* If you need to look up information, tell the customer what you are doing. Don't leave a caller holding a dead phone with no clue as to whether you are still with them.

- *Invite the caller to get to the point.* Use questions such as "How can I assist you today?" or "What can I do for you?"

- *Commit to requests of the caller.* Tell the caller specifically what you will do and when you will get back to them. ("I'll check on this billing problem and get back to you by 5 this afternoon, okay?")

- *Thank the caller.* This lets him or her know when the conversation is over.

- *Let your voice fluctuate in tone, rate, and loudness.* You hold people's attention by putting a little life into your voice. Convey honest reactions in expressive ways. Let your voice tones be natural and friendly.

- *Use hold carefully.* People hate being put on hold. When it's necessary, explain why and break in periodically to let the person know he or she hasn't been forgotten. If what you're doing will take longer than a few minutes, ask if you can call the caller back. Write down your commitment to call back, and don't miss it.

- *Use friendly, tactful words.* Never accuse the customer of anything; never convey that the person's request is an imposition.[4]

12. Watch Your Timing

Nothing impresses so significantly as immediate follow-through. The best customer-oriented people always follow up on commitments to customers.

A simple form can help you follow up with customers and avoid commitments from dropping through the cracks. Have a follow-up form nearby in a notebook or on separate sheets. Include these four columns:

CUSTOMER FOLLOW-UP FORM

Date/Time	Commitment (Name, phone #, what you promised)	Due	Done

13. Reach Out and Touch Them

Physical touch is a powerful form of communication that can impact customer perceptions of personality. Successful employees often take an opportunity to shake hands with a customer or even pat him or her on the back, if appropriate.

A study of bank tellers shows the power of touch. Tellers were taught to place change in the hand of the customer rather than on the counter. Researchers found that customer perceptions of the bank rose sharply among customers who had been touched. In a similar study, servers who touched their restaurant customers when serving the food or while handing the customer something found that their tips increased dramatically.

Among internal customers and coworkers, a literal pat on the back can build instant rapport. But don't overdo it; some people resent people who seem too touchy-feely. Recognize different preferences; try touching behavior but be willing to adjust if the person seems uncomfortable or ill at ease. And, of course, the key word here is appropriateness. Never touch a person in a manner that could be interpreted as being overly intimate or having sexual overtones.

> *Appropriate touching can be a powerful form of communication. But be sure it is socially and personally acceptable.*

14. Enjoy People and Their Diversity

J. D. Salinger said, "I am a kind of paranoid in reverse. I suspect people of plotting to make me happy." If everyone had an attitude like that, as employees we'd look forward to every meeting with every customer. Of course, we quickly learn that some customers do not seem to be plotting to make us happy. Most are very pleasant. Some are unusual. A few are downright difficult.

> *Try to keep your mind free of excessive criticism or cynicism.*

Every person is different; each has a unique personality. But the kind of people who tend to bug us the most are the ones who are *not like us.* Accept this diversity, and learn to enjoy it. Know that people's needs are basically the same at some level and that treating them as guests will create the most goodwill, most of the time.

Work on verbal discipline. To be more accepting of others, focus your "self-talk"—those internal conversations in your mind—and your comments to others on the positive, and avoid being judgmental. Instead of saying, "Can you believe that ugly dress on that lady?" avoid comment or say in a nonjudgmental way, "She dresses interestingly." Instead of saying, "This guy will nickel-and-dime me to death," say, "This customer is very cost-conscious."

At times you'll have to force yourself to avoid the negative and judgmental, but accept the challenge and you can make a game out of it. Sincerely try for one full day to avoid saying anything negative or judgmental about another person. If you make it through the day, shoot for another day. Verbal discipline can become a habit that pays off. You'll find yourself enjoying people more.

15. Maintain a Positive Attitude About Selling

> *Everyone is in sales, regardless of job title.*

Many people hold some imagined negative stereotype about selling. Customer contact people sometimes refuse to call themselves salespeople, preferring terms like associate or even consultant. Yet everyone is in sales to some degree. We constantly sell (convince, persuade, or whatever term you prefer) other people on ourselves, our products or services, and our company.

Like any profession, selling requires professional skills and attitudes. But often these skills and attitudes are different than one might think. For example, it surprises some people to find that you do not need to be an extrovert to be successful at selling. Quiet, thoughtful people often are very successful. A quiet self-confidence is more important than "techniques." Elwood Chapman, who has trained thousands of salespeople, says that you will likely be good at sales if you agree with statements like these:[5]

- I can convert strangers into friends quickly and easily.
- I can attract and hold the attention of others even when I have not met them.
- I love new situations.
- I'm intrigued with the psychology of meeting and building a good relationship with someone I do not know.

Self-Analysis   How Do You Measure Up?

Below is a list of the 15 individual behaviors we've discussed thus far in this chapter. Using the following scale, evaluate how well you do with each behavior:

N = never; O = occasionally; S = sometimes; M = most of the time; A = always.

Be completely honest, there is nothing wrong with admitting shortcomings. Indeed, it is far more damaging to deny them. After rating yourself on the scale, go back through the list and circle the plus (+) or minus (−) to indicate how you *feel* about your response. If you are comfortable with your answer, circle the plus. If you wish you could honestly answer otherwise, circle the minus.

Behaviors		SCALE							Goal
1. I promptly greet all customers.		N	O	S	M	A	+	−	
2. I use appropriate icebreakers.		N	O	S	M	A	+	−	
3. I compliment people freely and often.		N	O	S	M	A	+	−	
4. I call customers by their name.		N	O	S	M	A	+	−	
5. I make and maintain eye contact with customers.		N	O	S	M	A	+	−	
6. I often ask for feedback to find out how I'm doing.		N	O	S	M	A	+	−	
7. I listen well.		N	O	S	M	A	+	−	
8. I always say "please," "thank you," and "you're welcome."		N	O	S	M	A	+	−	
9. I reassure customers in their decisions to do business with me.		N	O	S	M	A	+	−	
10. I smile freely and often.		N	O	S	M	A	+	−	
11. I know and use good telephone techniques.		N	O	S	M	A	+	−	
12. I am always sensitive to timing, and I follow up with customers.		N	O	S	M	A	+	−	
13. I appropriately touch customers when possible.		N	O	S	M	A	+	−	
14. I enjoy people and their diversity.		N	O	S	M	A	+	−	
15. I have good attitudes about "selling" to customers.		N	O	S	M	A	+	−	

For each item where you circled a minus sign, write a goal for improvement on a separate sheet of paper. Make this specific and measurable if possible.

- I would enjoy making a sales presentation to a group of executives.
- When dressed for the occasion, I have great confidence in myself.
- I do not mind using the telephone to make appointments with people I don't know.
- I enjoy solving problems.
- Most of the time, I feel secure.

There is certainly nothing demeaning about selling a product or service. Employees' fear that they are behaving "too much like salespeople" may inhibit them from giving that little extra A-plus attention.

RECOGNIZE ORGANIZATIONAL BEHAVIORS THAT CONVEY THE CULTURE

In addition to the individual behaviors described above, a customer also assesses the personality of the entire organization by looking at group behaviors and attitudes. The communication rule that anything can and will communicate still applies to these behaviors, of course. The composite result of group and individual behaviors conveys much about the culture of the organization. If the customer likes a company's culture, it is well on the way to building satisfaction and loyalty. Here are some organizational behaviors to consider.

1. Consider Your Company's Appearance and Grooming

From the moment we meet people, we begin to size them up. We start to draw conclusions about them almost immediately. What we decide about their trustworthiness and ability is largely a factor of first impressions, and, as the old saying goes, you only get one chance to make that first impression.

The appearance of an organization's employees is one of the first things seen by customers. Dress standards can set a company apart from the competition and create an A-plus experience for the customer. One way this can be done is by looking at what other *successful* companies are doing. You need not be a copycat or wear an outfit you hate, but do consider what other role models do. And then meet or exceed their appearance.

An owner of an auto-repair shop tried an experiment. Each of his repair people was paid on commission for the amount of repair work they brought in. He invited the mechanics to volunteer to change their dress and grooming. Several agreed to cut their hair shorter, shave daily, and wear clean uniforms. The outcome was a good example of A-plus: those who improved their grooming generated far more repeat business than the others. The customers would ask for the better dressed mechanics, and those who chose to dress and groom themselves in the "old way" found themselves getting less work.

> *Employee appearance can have a dramatic effect on business success, especially if it exceeds the expectations of customers.*

Remember, of course, that the key word in dress and grooming is *appropriate*. Salespeople in a surf shop would look foolish in three-piece suits; an undertaker would look ludicrous in overalls or cutoffs. To avoid problems of individual differences in dress that may be inappropriate, some organizations issue uniforms. These may take the form of coveralls, full uniforms, or partial uniforms such as blazers, vests, or work shirts. Some employees like these (they save on the costs of a work wardrobe), while others resist the sameness of the uniformed look. Nevertheless, uniforms can provide an A-plus opportunity.

Determine what level of professionalism you want to exhibit to your customers; then create a look that projects your competence. Your customers notice these things.

Another Look   Edgy JetBlue in the Pink[6]

By Tom Fredrickson

Amy Curtis-McIntyre rakes a finger down a sketch of a flight attendant's uniform that JetBlue Airways Corp. is preparing to unveil. "There is my hip-hop request," says Ms. Curtis-McIntyre, JetBlue's vice president of marketing, admiring the slightly baggy pants crafted by noted designer Stan Herman.

The offhand remark in a meeting with marketing colleagues hints at why JetBlue is one of the only airlines today that's not merely making money, but also thriving: employees pay attention to the details, and they do it with style. What's more, though the airline is but 3 years old, it's already looking for ways to update and refresh its image.

Getting the details just so is vital for any business. . . . When customers see little things like satellite TVs and leather seats, they assume that the big stuff, like keeping the planes in the air, is being handled properly.

Probes

1. How do the "little things," like those described in this example, help project organizational personality?

2. What is your initial reaction to JetBlue as a place to work? Would this be an attractive employer for you? Why or why not?

2. Check the Appearance of Your Work Area

"A cluttered desk is the sign of a cluttered mind," says the desk plaque. Likewise, a cluttered work area conveys a sense of disorganization and low professionalism. Look around you, and see what your customer sees. Is merchandise displayed attractively? Is the customer or employee lounge area clean and tidy? Does the work space look like an organized, efficient place?

Check, too, for barriers. Often people arrange their work space with a desk, counter, or table between them and the customer. While sometimes this is necessary, it can create a barrier—both physical and psychological—between the customer and the one serving. Companies may establish a better personality by doing the following:

- Invite customers to sit beside a desk with the employee instead of across from him or her.
- Offer a comfortable living room–type atmosphere as a place to meet customers or as a waiting area. (I had an A-plus experience when an auto body shop I visited surprised me. It had a waiting room that looked like a living room in a nice home, complete with easy chairs, a TV, a coffee table with recent magazines, and even fresh flowers.)
- Do as some auto dealerships have done: remove all sales office desks and replace them with small round tables. Now the customer and salesperson sit around the table and work together to make a deal. When the table is round, they don't feel as if they are on opposite sides, engaged in "combat" with each other.

> *Round tables rather than imposing desks can convey a sense of cooperation rather than opposition between customers and salespeople.*

Finally, look for customer comfort. Are your customers invited to sit in a comfortable chair? Does your office or store encourage them to relax? Are waiting areas furnished with reading materials, and perhaps a TV? Are vending machines available? Is the vending area kept clean?

Recently, auto dealers have begun to emphasize ways to make their car lots and showrooms, many of which are decades old, more attractive and customer friendly. Some now feature landscaped settings with benches and pathways, different display areas for each auto brand, and interactive systems with screens that show how elements like paint colors and upholstery coordinate together. Take a look at your work areas from the customer's viewpoint.

3. Get Customers to Interact with Your Organization

Just as it is important to get people interacting with employees (as discussed on p. 100), it is also important that they sample the culture—the organizational personality. We talked earlier about getting customers to promptly order their food, try a new computer, or test-drive a car. Other, perhaps less obvious ways to involve customers may include:

- personally handing them a shopping cart or basket
- asking them to begin filling out paperwork
- inviting them to touch or sample the product
- offering a piece of candy or fruit while they wait
- offering a product flyer, information packet, video presentation, or sample to review

If the organizational culture enables such activities, the customer is increasingly likely to have an A-plus impression of the company's personality. It doesn't matter so much *what* they do, so long as they begin to do *something*.

> *Get customers doing something with your company to expose them to your culture.*

Some retailers arrange merchandise so that customers can easily pick it up. Marketing expert Paco Underhill says,

> A trademark of the Gap clothing stores, for example, is that customers can easily touch, stroke, unfold, and otherwise examine at close range anything on the selling floor. A lot of sweaters and shirts are sold thanks to the decision to foster intimate contact between shopper and goods. That merchandising policy dictates the display scheme (wide, flat tabletops, which are easier to shop than racks or shelves). That display scheme in turn determines how and where employees will spend their time; all that customer touching means *that* sweaters and shirts constantly need to be refolded and straightened. That translates into the need for lots of clerks roaming the floor rather than standing behind the counter ringing up sales. Which is a big expense, but for Gap and others, it's a sound investment—a cost of doing business.[7]

This is also a way of giving customers A-plus organizational personality.

4. Correspond Regularly

An athletic shoe store and a rental car agency are good examples of the simple idea of correspondence. A week after purchasing some running shoes, customers receive a handwritten note from the store owner simply thanking them for buying. In no fancy prose, it expresses appreciation for their business and invites them to return via a one- or two-sentence message. A small city airport car-rental desk has employees write thank-you notes to customers when the desk is not busy. The notes are handwritten on the company letterhead and personalized to mention the type of car rented. They thank the customer and invite them to rent again the next time they are in town. The cost of doing this is practically nil since the desk is busy when flights come in but then has slow periods in between. Why have employees waste time when it's slow?

Maintain an open channel of communication with customers via mail-outs.

Don't let your customer forget you. Another way to make customers remember your company is to send them information about upcoming sales, changes in policies, new promotions, and the like. Keep the customer tied in. Likewise, discount coupons or special hours for preferred customers are often appreciated.

A print shop sends all customers a monthly package of coupons, flyers, and samples, including a motivational quote printed on parchment paper suitable for framing. Additional copies of the quote are available free for the asking. The mailing acts as a reminder of the quality of work the shop can do as well as a promotion.

5. Use Hoopla and Fun

People enjoy working in an organization that has fun. Successful companies have regular rituals, whether it be Friday afternoon popcorn, birthday parties, or employee-of-the-month celebrations, that everyone gets involved in. Excellent organizations are fun places to work; they create rituals of their own.

As a manager at a telephone company, I initiated frequent sales contests, complete with skits and prizes. Each time a particular product was sold, the service representative could pop a balloon and find inside a prize ranging from a $10 bill to a coupon good for a piece of pie in the company cafeteria. Employees loved it and got involved.

Other ideas to promote fun in the workplace include:

- employee (or hero) of the week/month recognition
- awards luncheons (include some tongue-in-cheek "awards")
- win a day off with pay
- casual dress days
- halloween costume day
- family picnics

Don't fall into the trap of thinking these things are hokey. Employees at all levels enjoy celebrations and hoopla, and their effects spread to the customer. The rewards need not be large or costly. The fact that employees are being recognized, even with little things, can be very motivating for them.

Rewards can take many forms—some obvious, some more subtle. A few frequently used rewards include the following:

- salary and cash bonuses
- prizes and tangible gifts
- promotions and job enrichment
- preferred work locations, better offices, larger desks
- work schedule flexibility

- pins, badges, uniforms
- reserved parking spaces
- employee of the week (or month) recognition
- compliments, spoken or in writing
- surprise recognition parties or celebrations
- lunches or banquets
- newsletter write-ups

Management is limited only by its imagination when it comes to rewarding employees. But the most important point is that *managers reward the right actions and results.*

6. Reward the Right Actions

Fairly often, organizations inadvertently reward one behavior while hoping for something else. In all too many cases, an organization *hopes* something will happen but actually rewards an opposite behavior. For example, a company rewards individuals and departments for never receiving complaints. The hope is that by receiving no complaints it means the company is doing a good job. The reality, however, may well be that no complaints are heard because the complaints are simply being suppressed. Customers have no effective way to voice their dissatisfaction. Instead, they just quit doing business with the company.

As discussed earlier, it's not bad news to receive a complaint; it *is* bad news to suppress a complaint. Some percentage of customers will always be less than satisfied, and ignoring them does no good. Quite the contrary. Wise companies draw out those customer concerns so that they can be addressed and corrected. As someone once said, "Even the ostrich leaves one end exposed."

Here are some other examples of possible reward conflicts where the wrong behaviors may be rewarded and the right behaviors ignored:

> *Companies sometimes reward the wrong things. For example, rewarding a department for receiving no complaints may simply serve to suppress complaints that could make the company better.*

- Rewarding employees for fast transaction handling when the customer may be left uninformed or may resent being rushed along. For instance, the restaurant that encourages employees to get the customer fed and out may make people who prefer to eat more slowly unhappy. Or, the buyer of electronic equipment who is rushed may leave the store not understanding how to work the features of his or her DVD player.
- Encouraging salespeople to "cooperate with each other to best meet the customer needs" while paying a straight commission. For instance, salespeople practically trip over each other to approach the new customer before the other guy gets him. So much for cooperation.

- Encouraging employees to send thank-you notes to customers but never allowing on-the-job time to do so. This creates the impression that it really isn't that important.
- Constantly stressing the need to reduce the amount of return merchandise by docking the pay of clerks who accept too many returns. The result: customers encounter employees' reluctance to take back unsatisfactory products.
- Paying people by the hour instead of by the task accomplished. Hourly wages are simpler to administer, but they basically pay people for using up time!

The organization's reward system needs to be tilted to the advantage of the employee who provides excellent service. Any rewards should be given in direct relationship to the employee's contribution to customer service that is consistent with the company's mission and service theme.

Stay Close After the Sale

Customers hate a love-'em-and-leave-'em relationship. Yet many companies offer just that. Once the sale is made, the customer goes back to feeling like a stranger. Look for opportunities to contact the customer after the sale. Establish an ongoing friendship, and they'll keep coming back.

Some ideas for contacting the customer after the sale might be:

- mail thank-you notes
- call to be sure the product/service met their needs
- send out new-product information
- send clippings of interest or newsworthy information that may reassure customers of their good purchasing decisions
- send birthday and holiday cards
- invite people to participate in a focus group
- call to thank customers for referrals

Another Look   Blowout on the Ohio Turnpike[8]

On a recent cross-country trip while on the Ohio Turnpike just south of Toledo, my tire blew out. It was 6 p.m. on a Friday, the temperature hovered in the upper nineties, and the traffic was heavy. The right rear tire blew like a bomb and I limped onto the median to dodge the constant flow of rumbling semis. I called the American Automobile Association's hot line on my cell phone. I was greeted by an unsympathetic monotone that mechanically sought my

continued

Another Look	**Blowout on the Ohio Turnpike** *continued*

membership card number, expiration date, address, home phone, complete description of my car, my mother's maiden name, the name of my oldest grandchild and some such stuff. The voice expressed no concern for my situation, nor did it seem to care whether I did business with AAA or not. All the while I am attempting to explain to this voice the imminent danger of being crushed by a big rig roaring by just a few feet from me at 80 miles per hour.

"Exactly where are you?" the flat voice asked. I tried to explain my general location, but that wasn't good enough. I'd need to give an exact mileage marker. So I trekked several hundred yards up the median in 96 degree heat screaming into my cell phone over the roar of the trucks until I could see a mileage marker. Flat voice then told me that a tow truck would be there "in forty-five minutes or less" and that I was to jump out of the car when I saw him coming and flag him down. This, apparently, was necessary so that the truck driver would know *which* white Lexus with the blown-out tire in the median of the Ohio Turnpike at mileage marker 68 was mine.

Fifty minutes later I called for an update to see if there was any possibility the tow truck would actually get here today. A different and more sympathetic service rep answered this time and, after going through all the membership information again, told me he would *"check to see if they'd received my call!"* After waiting on hold for four minutes, I was not encouraged. Then, to his credit, he at least apologized ("I'm sorry about the wait, the truck was called to an accident up the road") and promised me the truck would be there "in twenty-five minutes or less." I waited.

This story has a happier ending. The truck driver—Paul it said on his shirt—was a very nice man. He parked his truck behind mine with emergency lights flashing to block my car from the onrushing traffic, climbed down and immediately apologized in a sincere manner. We chatted about the weather and cars. He told me about the accident he had been called away to handle and told me he was fifty miles away when he got the call. As we chatted, he quickly changed my tire (while explaining about the special tool needed for the locking lug nuts) and I was on the road again in minutes. Paul called to me to say he hoped the rest of my visit to Ohio would be better and wished me happy trails. I tipped him ten bucks. And Paul was instrumental in saving a long-term Triple-A customer.

Probes

1. What are some of the specific personality behaviors cited in this mini case that caused the customer's dissatisfaction? What helped to restore satisfaction?
2. To what extent did this customer's turnoffs arise from value, systems, and people?
3. What actions would you, as a manager, take to remedy the customer problems described in this article?

A FINAL THOUGHT

Individual and organizational behaviors are conveyed to customers via little things. Often people are unaware of how they are coming across and, as such, are at a distinct disadvantage. Broadening our awareness of how other people read our verbal and nonverbal messages is a useful step in improving customer service.

Likewise, just as individuals project their behaviors to customers, so do organizations. The company's collective behavior patterns constitute its culture and may be perceived as favorable or unfavorable by customers (internal and external). The ways managers and leaders interact with subordinates and associates will have considerable impact on the way all employees behave toward customers.

Summary of Key Ideas

- Behavior is what people do. It is conveyed via verbal or nonverbal communication.
- Individual actions as well as organizational behaviors convey messages to customers which may be productive or counterproductive to the customers' perception of service received.
- Any behaviors (or lack of behaviors) can communicate; the receiver of the message (e.g., the customer) determines what the message means.
- Exceeding expectations in the area of personality depends on both individual actions and the organization's behaviors or culture.
- Individual behaviors that impact customer service include greeting customers, breaking the ice by initiating conversation, complimenting, calling people by name, establishing and maintaining eye contact, asking for feedback, listening skillfully, reassuring customers in their buying decisions, smiling, using good telephone techniques, being sensitive to timing, using appropriate touching behaviors, enjoying people, and being positive about selling.
- Organizational behaviors that tell the customer about your culture include the appearance and grooming of employees, the appearance of work areas, the frequency and quality of correspondence with customers, the propensity to get customers doing something relevant to the buying decision, the use of hoopla and fun to celebrate company successes, reward systems that motivate appropriate employee behaviors, and staying close to the customer after the sale.

Key Concepts

appropriate touching

behaviors, individual and
  organizational

getting the customer committed

hoopla and fun

icebreakers

organizational culture

personality

rewarding right actions

three I's of eye contact

verbal discipline

Self-Test Questions

1. What constitutes behavior, and how is it conveyed?
2. How can an organization's culture impact customer loyalty?
3. What are some specific behaviors that project individual personality?
4. What are icebreakers? How can they best be used with different types of customers?
5. What are the three I's of eye communication?
6. What are some specific actions you can take to be a better listener?
7. How can physical touch be used to exceed customer expectations?
8. What are some factors that project a company's culture? List several examples.
9. What are some examples of reward systems that encourage the wrong kinds of behaviors?
10. What actions would you take as a manager to encourage behaviors that could create an A-plus experience for your customers?

Application Activity: Does Behavior Influence Customer Loyalty?

1. This chapter implies a strong relationship between behaviors (of individuals and organizations) and the likelihood of customer loyalty. Let's test that idea.
2. Below are two simple data-gathering forms. The first lists the behaviors discussed in the chapter and invites customers to rate these. The second form asks three simple questions about customer loyalty. We call this the Customer Loyalty Index (CLI).

3. Your task is to gather input by interviewing 10 or more customers of a business or organization. Use the same business for all responses. Follow the interview guide word for word. On the first form, have each respondent answer "yes," "no," or "unsure/not applicable."

Interview Guide

Part I Behavior Questionnaire

When you last did business with [name of company or organization], did the employees there

	Yes	No	Unsure or NA
1. greet you promptly?			
2. use opening comments to help you feel at ease?			
3. compliment you in any way?			
4. call you by your name?			
5. make and maintain eye contact with you?			
6. ask for feedback from you in any way?			
7. listen carefully to your needs or wants?			
8. say "please" and "thank you"?			
9. reassure your decisions to do business with them?			
10. smile freely and often?			
11. use good telephone techniques?			
12. act sensitive to timing and follow up with you?			
13. appropriately touch you (with a handshake, pat on the back, etc.)?			
14. seem to enjoy people and their diversity?			
15. seem to have good attitudes about selling?			
16. keep the workplace clean and attractive?			
17. dress and groom themselves appropriately?			
18. seem to enjoy working for this company?			

Part II Customer Loyalty Index

1. Overall, how satisfied were you with [name of company or organization]?

   Extremely unsatisfied / Unsatisfied / Neutral / Satisfied / Extremely satisfied

2. How likely would you be to recommend [name of company or organization] to a friend or associate?

   Very unlikely / Not likely / Maybe / Very likely / Certain

3. How likely are you to do business with [name of company or organization] again?

   Very unlikely / Not likely / Maybe / Very likely / Certain

Scoring

- For Part I of the interview, score 1 point for each "yes" response. The total possible is 18.

- For the CLI, score each item on a 5-point scale from left to right (e.g., the most negative response is a 1, the most positive is a 5, and those in between are 2, 3, or 4).

- After you have tallied scores for your entire sample of customers (minimum of 10), write a brief analysis of the results. Comment especially on the behaviors that most seem to relate to customer loyalty, as your customers see them.

Notes

1. Many of the ideas in this section are adapted from P. R. Timm, *50 Powerful Ideas You Can Use to Keep Your Customers*, 3rd ed. (Hawthorne, NJ: Career Press, 2001). Copyright Paul R. Timm.

2. Cited in "Yamaha Merchandising Training," Yamaha Corp. Also found in S. Geist, *Why Should Someone Do Business with You Rather Than Someone Else?* (Bonita Springs, FL: Addington & Wentworth, 1997), p. 98.

3. B. Decker. *The Art of Communication* (Menlo Park, CA: Crisp Publications, Inc., 1988), p. 17.

4. An excellent 30-minute videotape training program featuring the author is *Winning Telephone Techniques* produced by JWA Video in Chicago. For information, call 312–829–5100.

5. These ideas are found in E. N. Chapman, *The Fifty Minute Sales Training Program* (Menlo Park, CA: Crisp Publications, Inc., 1992).

6. T. Fredrickson. "Edgy JetBlue in the Pink." *Crain's New York Business*, February 24, 2003, p. 28.

7. P. Underhill. "What Shoppers Want." *Inc.*, July 1999, p. 76.

8. This story originally appeared in Paul R. Timm, *Seven Power Strategies for Building Customer Loyalty* (New York: AMACOM, 2001), pp. 25–26.

Apply Winning Telephone Techniques

Use Phone Responsiveness to Create Customer Loyalty

*Call-center representatives **are** the company to the customer because they are the only employees your customers have contact with.*

—Richard Gerson, Gerson Goodson, Inc.[1]

WHAT YOU'LL LEARN IN THIS CHAPTER

- A better understanding of your own attitudes toward telephone courtesy will result in more effective relationships with customers.

- You should recognize and correct the kinds of telephone mannerisms that can lead to customer dissatisfaction.

- Apply more than 20 techniques to improve your overall telephone effectiveness.

- Ineffective Web page and Internet communication can have many pitfalls in business.

THE WAY IT IS . . .
The Frustrations of Unresponsive Telephone Use

Hearing a radio commercial for a concert, I called the number to buy tickets. The number was an easy-to-remember 888 toll-free number that had the word *ARTS* as the last four digits. So far, so good. On the first try, the phone rang eight times before I gave up and decided to try again later. My second attempt rang nine times, and then a recorded message gave me another number to call. When I dialed that number an electronic voice put me on hold, after which another recorded voice told me to call the first number I had tried!

Hotel reservation lines, airlines, credit card companies, banks . . . virtually all companies run their customers through an electronic maze of choices that supposedly make the call more efficient but often annoy the caller who simply wants to talk to a human being. I have decided to stay more at Holiday Inns because when I call the reservation line I immediately get a person. I have vowed to avoid companies whose phone service is unresponsive or laborious.

Likewise, shoppers on the Internet will stay with you only a few moments. If your company's Web pages load too slowly or if the customer gets caught in a loop, he or she may be lost forever. On numerous occasions, I have filled out all the forms to purchase a product on the Net only to have the system lock up or require me to redo something I've already done. That's when I decide that I don't really need that product. The aggravation isn't worth the potential savings or shopping convenience.

Wise companies are constantly improving phone and Net services, but many are succeeding only at angering or annoying their customers when the customer is ready to buy!

KNOW THE BENEFITS AND DRAWBACKS OF TELEPHONE COMMUNICATION

The telephone certainly can be, as the ads used to say, "the next best thing to being there." In fact, no business can long survive without a phone because, in many cases, a large percentage of their customers make first contact with the company via phone. Likewise, a company without a Web home page is rapidly becoming an anachronism. (I'll talk in detail about Web site customer service in Chapter 7.) Two significant drawbacks to these electronic communicators can almost cancel out their benefits:

1. *Many people have never learned the basics of telephone courtesy and effectiveness.* They've been using the phone since childhood and have never polished their business telephone techniques. What may be everyday casual telephone usage at home may be totally inappropriate for business. The re-

sult can be customer dissatisfaction and a severe loss of organizational image and effectiveness.

2. *People cannot see the person they are dealing with.*   Thus, the phone does not permit most nonverbal communication. Without nonverbal cues to reinforce or clarify a message, the listener or Web page viewer may be easily misled or confused.

Phrased another way, each telephone call or Web site "hit" creates interactions where people are operating blind—without the visual feedback that helps assign meaning to spoken messages.

To compensate for this lack of visual feedback, we as telephone callers create our own conclusions from what we experience—every nuance conveys subtle messages through timing, tone of voice, word choice, and interruptions. For many people, this ambiguity makes telephone use uncomfortable and even threatening. Although it is a great piece of technology, the telephone can also be frustrating. As Web page customers, we likewise draw conclusions from the graphic appearance of a company's site, its speed, and its ease of use.

Here is a story about one incident in which a company lost a customer because it forgot (or never stopped to think about) the drawbacks to telephone communication:

Garth enjoys working on old cars. A few years ago as he drove to work, he noticed a vintage sports car in an auto dealership's lot. Sensing that such a car would do a lot for his image, Garth decided to inquire about it. He telephoned the dealership, and here is how the conversation went.

A receptionist briskly identified the name of the dealership and, just as quickly, commanded, "Hold a minute, please." Fifteen seconds later, the receptionist came back on the line and asked, "Can I help ya?" Garth asked to "speak to someone in used cars, please."

"Just a minute," the receptionist replied.

After a pause, a man's voice said, "Hello?"

"I'd like a little information about the Triumph TR-6 you have on your lot," Garth said.

"Ya mean the red one?"

"Yes. Could you give me some information on that car?"

The male voice hesitated for a moment and said, "I think that's the owner's daughter's car. She's been driving it around. Let me check and see what the deal is on it."

There was a long pause and while Garth waited on hold, another male voice came on the line saying, "Hello? Hello?" to which Garth replied, "I'm already being helped." There was a click as the interrupter hung up without acknowledging Garth's comment.

After a few more minutes, the original salesman came back on the line and said, "Yeah, I think that's the car the boss's daughter has been driving around. If they sell it, they'll want an arm and a leg for it. I think it's a '75 model."

"Well, would you check and let me know if it's for sale?" Garth asked again, getting exasperated.

"Just a minute; I'll ask the owner," he said as he put Garth on hold again. After a few moments, the salesperson again picked up the telephone and abruptly said, "The owner says it's not for sale."

As Garth began to say, "Thanks for the information," he was cut off in mid-sentence by the click of the telephone as the man hung up.

Although this sales representative was probably not intentionally being rude, he sure came across that way. Garth was irritated to the point that he would definitely not do business with this dealership.

Another Look   Online Brokerages Flunk Service Test[2]

The CBS Market Watch online journal, *Internet Daily* summarizes some pitfalls of poor communication in the following excerpt:

> Online brokers have a lot of work to do to improve customer service. Researchers at Jupiter Communications tested 25 web sites' rates of response to customers' messages. Among financial-services sites, 39 percent responded in one day, while the balance took up to three days or, in the case of 25 percent, never responded. By comparison, 64 percent of retail shopping sites answered e-mails in one day. While businesses are concerned with technology costs, researchers conclude that customer service must get greater priority because new online financial service customers "are mainstream, risk-averse consumers who have far less tolerance for technology issues."

Probes

1. What experience have you had with e-mailing and getting responses from companies?

2. If you were running a company, what e-mail standards would you like to see in place? How realistic would this be?

APPLY THESE ACTION TIPS FOR BETTER TELEPHONE USAGE

As we saw in the car dealer example above, behaviors that come across as discourteous, disjointed, or intrusive can quickly sour a caller's impression of a company. The remainder of this chapter offers 23 specific tips for improving telephone and Web page effectiveness.[3]

Action Tip 1: Check Your Phone Attitudes

The telephone is a powerful tool for sales, information gathering, and relationship building. By receiving and initiating calls, we can accomplish a lot.

Yet some people are phone shy. They are hesitant to call others and some-times hesitant about answering incoming calls.

Check your telephone attitudes using the self-evaluation below. It can help you understand some of your feelings about using the telephone. It can also help you improve your telephone techniques by showing what you may be doing wrong.

Your attitudes can impact your telephone effectiveness.

Self-Analysis   How Are Your Phone Usage Skills and Attitudes?

Circle the appropriate letter for each item: N = Never, SL = Seldom, SM = Sometimes, O = Often, A = Always. Then read the instructions at the end of the form.

How often do you . . .

1. Delay calling someone or fail to return a call?	N	SL	SM	O	A
2. Answer the telephone with a curt or mechanical greeting?	N	SL	SM	O	A
3. Let the phone ring, hoping the caller will give up?	N	SL	SM	O	A
4. Save travel time by calling for information ("let your fingers do the walking")?	A	O	SM	SL	N
5. End the conversation by summarizing what was agreed upon?	A	O	SM	SL	N
6. Solicit feedback about your customer service by phone call?	A	O	SM	SL	N
7. Put people on hold for more than a few seconds?	N	SL	SM	O	A
8. Have someone else place your calls for you?	N	SL	SM	O	A
9. Smile as you speak?	A	O	SM	SL	N
10. Speak clearly and in pleasant, conversational tones (no "stage voice")?	A	O	SM	SL	N

If you circled a letter in the two right columns for any of the items, your telephone techniques can use improvement. On a separate sheet, list specific goals for improvement in each area needed.

Action Tip 2: Contact Your Own Company

A telephone call or Web page visit is often the first point of contact a person has with an organization. And as the old saying goes, you never get a second chance to make a first impression. Callers create first impressions and draw immediate conclusions about a person's and company's

Many customers get their first impression of you and your company from an electronic visit.

efficiency, communication skills, friendliness, and expertise, all in the first few moments of electronic communication. In short, your courtesy and effectiveness quickly convey unspoken but important messages to calling customers.

Managers should check on the phone skills of their organization regularly. Have people who know how the phones should be handled call periodically and then prepare a brief report. Likewise, invite inexperienced customers to visit your Web site and let you know what they liked or disliked about it. As always, feedback is the breakfast of champions.

Action Tip 3: Answer Promptly and Be Prepared to Handle Calls

An answer after two rings or less conveys efficiency and a willingness to serve. When the telephone rings longer, callers get the feeling that you are unavailable and that their call is an intrusion. What is worse is that unanswered callers get the message that you think they are not important.

Be sure that your work area is set up for comfortable and efficient telephone use. Place the telephone at a convenient spot on your desk or worktable. Keep current your list of frequently called numbers, and have material you may need to refer to within reach.

Have notepaper, message slips, and pens handy. Use a planner system or desk calendar that has space for you to jot down notes about conversations you have. Get each caller's name and number as soon as possible, and summarize the conversation briefly at the end—especially mentioning any commitments you will need to follow up on.

Always have note-taking materials handy by the phone.

If you agree to do something for a caller, be sure to write it down and then check it off when completed.

Action Tip 4: Avoid Unnecessary Call Screening

Each person should be encouraged to answer his or her own telephone unless they are busy in a face-to-face conversation with a customer. Routine screening of calls by a secretary or receptionist often creates resentment in the caller. The constant use of "May I say who is calling?" is recognized as a dodge—an opportunity for the person to decide if he or she wants to talk or not. Customers get annoyed when there are too many gatekeepers—people who screen calls for others.

The appropriate way to answer a business call is to simply state your name or your department and your name, for example, "Customer support. This is Nancy Chin." Calling yourself *Mrs.*, *Ms.*, *Mr.*, or a title may sound a bit self-important: "Accounting office, Mr. Silvia speaking." Some people use just their last name, although this can sometimes confuse callers. (A manager friend of mine named Paul Waite found his last-name-only greeting often followed by a very long pause!)

Use of "How may I help you?" (or a similar phrase) following your name tells your caller whom they are speaking to and indicates that you are ready to converse with them. When answering another person's telephone, be sure to identify both that other person and yourself, for instance, "Michelle Theron's office. This is Shelly Sampson. May I help you?"

Of course, receptionists would never need to ask who is calling if *callers* would use good business etiquette. Good manners dictate that when we call people, we identify ourselves immediately, for example, "Good morning, Barry Adamson calling. Is Sharon Silverstein there?" Get in the habit of doing this, and you will set a good example for others who may realize the advantage of such courtesy.

> As a caller, use good business etiquette by identifying yourself immediately.

Action Tip 5: Use Courtesy Titles

While referring to yourself as *Mr.* or *Ms.* may sound stuffy, don't assume that a caller prefers to be addressed by his or her first name. Use proper titles for the people with whom you communicate. If in doubt about whether to use a first name, call the person by the more formal *Mr.* or *Ms.* If they prefer the more informal first name, they will say so. It is better to be a little too formal than overly familiar.

Titles and formality can create credibility. If you refer to other professionals, refer to them formally. You'd be a bit thrown off if a medical doctor introduced himself like this: "Hi, I'm Larry, your brain surgeon." Even if your organization has an informal culture, don't assume that others do.

Action Tip 6: Thank People for Calling

"Thank you" is the most powerful phrase in human relations. Express appreciation regularly. Some companies use it as a greeting: "Thank you for calling Avis." A "thanks for calling" at the end of a conversation is also a strong customer satisfaction booster. It reassures customers that you are interested in serving and that their calls are not an intrusion.

A "thank you for visiting" note on a Web site can convey the same appreciation, especially if the site visit was a good one.

Action Tip 7: Keep Your Conversation Tactful and Businesslike

Nothing turns off a customer or caller like poor wording. I've had experiences where, upon telling people my name, they say, "Who?" rather abruptly. Few things make a caller feel less appreciated. If you didn't catch the name, ask politely: "I'm sorry, I didn't get your name, sir. Would you repeat it?"

Keep your comments positive and oriented toward solving the caller's problem or concern. Don't just toss the ball back when you can't immediately help. Avoid saying anything that makes people or your organization look unprofessional or uncaring.

Here are some other dos and don'ts:

Don't Say	Do Say
Who is this?	May I ask who's calling?
What's your name?	May I have your name?
What do you need?	How can I help you?
Speak up, please.	I'm sorry, I can't hear you. Could you repeat that?
Well, I wasn't the one you talked to.	I'm sorry, Ms. James, someone else must have spoken to you.
He's out to lunch.	Mr. Barringer is away from the office for about one hour. Can I ask him to call you back?
You'll need to call our billing office.	That information is available in our billing office.
Sorry, I can't help you with that.	I don't have that information here. May I have someone from our quality service department give you a call?
There's nothing I can do about that.	I'll put that on my calendar for next Tuesday, and I'll check on your request again then. Then I'll call you back.

Action Tip 8: Speak Clearly and Distinctly

Hold the telephone mouthpiece about a half-inch from your lips. Whether you answer with your name, the company name, or the department name, speak clearly and distinctly. For example, carefully say, "Good morning, Primo Computer Service," "Hello, this is KJQQ radio," or "Scheduling department," followed by your name. Separate the words with tiny pauses.

Even if you say these words a hundred times a day, resist the temptation to get lazy or to repeat the greeting in a mechanical, unfriendly manner. Remember that each caller hears your greeting just once, even though you have said it many times. Make it fresh and sincere.

Action Tip 9: Speak Naturally and Comfortably

Talk to your caller as you would to a friend. Use warm, friendly voice tones and natural, spontaneous reactions. If a caller says something humorous, laugh. If his or her tone of voice suggests tension or even anger, it may be appropriate to comment on that: "You sound upset; is there something I can do to help?"

A strong, clear voice is a tremendous asset. It conveys confidence and high credibility. But even if a person is not gifted with the voice of a professional broadcaster, he or she can use the voice to create and hold listener interest.

The key to holding interest is *variation* in the voice. People cannot pay attention to something that does not change. But we do perk up when speakers adjust their voice. The three things any speaker can vary are pitch, loudness, and rate.

Pitch is an almost musical quality, the place on a musical scale where the voice would be. Male speakers tend to have more trouble varying pitch than females. The problem, of course, is that too little variation in pitch sounds like a monotone. In a word, it is boring.

Another problem occurs when people try to force the voice into a different pitch. By artificially speaking too low or too high, we create a stage voice that sounds phony. Use your natural range, but experiment with broadening that range, too.

Some speakers do not want to risk much variation. They fear sounding silly. But failing to vary pitch is like throwing away one of your most useful tools for effective communication. Listen carefully to good radio or TV announcers, comedians, or other entertainers. You will find that they vary their pitch a lot. Try pushing your range of pitch outward a bit. Go a little higher and a little lower than you typically do, and you will find listeners more interested in what you have to say.

Action Tip 10: Do Not Allow "Dead Air"

Broadcasters call those awkward gaps when nothing is being broadcast "dead air." Listeners have no idea what is going on and often change stations if the silence persists. The same can happen with a telephone call.

If you need to transfer a caller, look up some information, or read some material, *tell the caller what you are doing.* Remember, he or she cannot see you. Use statements such as these to reassure your caller that you are still with him or her:

> "I will transfer you to Mr. Kovak now. He can get you that information. One moment, please."

> "I understand your concern. Ms. Jessop in our billing department can best help you with that. May I put you on hold for a moment? I will see if she is in."

> "I'm reviewing your account now, Mr. Jenson. Let me just check a few figures, and I can give you that information in a moment."

Putting callers on hold can be annoying to them, but you can reduce this annoyance by telling them what you are doing and why.

Always acknowledge comments audibly. Be sure to react to your callers' conversation. Since your callers can't see you and don't receive visual feedback from you, they must rely on your spoken feedback—what you say—to determine whether you understand what they are saying. By frequently saying "yes" or "I see" or "uh-huh" or "I agree," you are providing the needed feedback. Don't let caller comments go unacknowledged.

The Web page equivalent of dead air happens when material loads too slowly. Keep current by letting the latest technology give you a quick-moving, efficient Web site. Stamp out dead air.

Action Tip 11: Take Messages Cheerfully and Accurately

Be willing to take messages for others. Keep a notepad handy to record key words and phrases. Read the message back to the caller to be sure it is accurate. Then remember to pass the message to the right person. Most organizations use message forms such as the pink quarter-page slips used in many offices. Fill out such forms completely and legibly.

As you fill out a message slip, be complete. To avoid possible communication problems, it is especially important to do all of the following:

1. *Get the full name and correct spelling.*   If you don't understand the name clearly, ask the caller to spell it for you. Let him or her know why you are asking for the spelling by saying something like "I want to make sure your message is accurate. Will you spell your name?"

2. *Ask for the name of the person's organization if appropriate.*   This information may give the message receiver a hint as to the nature of the call. It can also be helpful if there is a mistake with the number.

3. *Get the full telephone number, including the area code if it's long distance.*   If the caller says, "She has my number," you can say politely, "I know she can get back to you even faster if I jot your number down with your message."

4. *Ask for additional information.*   If the caller doesn't volunteer any specific message, it will help on the callback if you ask, "Is there any information you would like to leave that may be helpful to Ms. Jones when she calls you back?"

5. *Say, "thank you," and tell the caller that you will give the person the message as soon as he or she is available.*   Say this with assurance.

6. *Note the time and date the message was taken, and add your initials in case there are any questions.*

Action Tip 12: Smile

Picture the person you are talking with, and treat him or her as though you were face-to-face with a friend. Be pleasant, concerned, and helpful. Physically smiling somehow travels through the telephone line via your voice tones.

Keep a mirror by the telephone to remind yourself to smile. It really does come through to the caller.

Action Tip 13: Be Sure the Conversation Is Finished Before You Hang Up

If you initiated the call, take the responsibility for ending it. Use conclusion words such as "Thank you for your help" or "That is just what I needed."

If you received the call, be sure the caller is finished. In our earlier story (p. 125), Garth was about to ask the salesperson if the dealership had any other sports cars available but was cut off before he could pose this question.

Action Tip 14: Make Your Greeting Message Efficient

When you are not available, use an answering machine or voice mail to capture messages. Keep your greeting message current and not too long or too clever. Messages like the following usually work well:

> "You have reached 555–1131. We cannot take your call now. Please leave a message at the tone." (Note: This message does not identify who you are and may provide privacy and security.)

> "This is Acme Manufacturing's warehouse. Our business hours are from 8 a.m. to 6 p.m. Monday through Friday. Please leave a message."

> "Thank you for calling NuHousing, Inc.—your mobile home leader. Please leave a message at the tone, and we will get back to you as soon as we can. Thank you."

Recorded messages may also ask for specific information from callers ("If you have your account number available, please leave it so we can respond to your request more quickly."). Do not, however, ask for too much. Also, assure the caller that you will return the call.

When you leave a message on another person's machine, be sure to state the following:

- your name (spoken clearly and spelled if necessary)
- time and day of your call

- a brief explanation of why you are calling
- your phone number
- when you can be reached

Here are two examples of effective caller messages:

"This is Jim Steadman calling. It's 7 p.m. Friday. I have a question about your new Wave Runners. Please call me at 555–3077 after 10 a.m. Saturday."

"This is Raul Sanchez—that is spelled S-A-N-C-H-E-Z. I am interested in your job opening for an experienced night programmer and would like to arrange an interview. I have six years' experience with a company like yours. Please call me at 555–0819 after 6 p.m. today, Thursday the 4th. Thank you."

Action Tip 15: Learn to Use Your Phone's Features

The wonderful world of telephone technology is constantly coming up with new features. Unfortunately, like the 80 percent of people who have no idea how to program a VCR, many businesspeople haven't learned to use the many tricks available through their phone system.

Customer dissatisfaction with the way a firm handles phone calls stems from two general factors:

1. inability of employees to use the features of telephone and voice mail systems
2. shortcomings in treating customers with the highest degree of courtesy

Customer-focused companies respond to these concerns by providing appropriate training for all employees. Such training boosts customer satisfaction with a company's telephone responsiveness dramatically.

If you are uncertain about your telephone system's features, take time to read the user's guide or call the service provider. They will be happy to have a representative teach you how to use the system. After all, it is in their best interest to have you utilizing the equipment fully—so that they have a satisfied customer.

Action Tip 16: Keep a Constant Flow of Information

If you spend a sizable percentage of your day on the phone, consider getting a headset rather than having to hold the receiver to your ear. Likewise, if you find that you frequently have to step away from the phone for information while the caller holds, consider using a cordless phone that allows you to continue talking while you move about.

Also, use the hold button carefully. What may seem to you like a brief hold can seem awfully long to a caller. Even if your phone system plays music, callers get pretty upset after 30 seconds or so. Try timing the next instance you are put on hold. A minute can seem like an eternity. Keep voice contact or pick up every 15 to 20 seconds to let the caller know that you haven't forgotten him or her. If you anticipate a fairly long hold time, offer to call back or at least prepare the caller by saying that this will require several minutes to complete. Then give him or her the option of holding or awaiting a callback.

Action Tip 17: Plan Your Outgoing Calls for Efficiency

Although small talk is sometimes useful to create a good relationship with callers, strive to make business calls concise without being curt or abrupt. This can be especially important when using cellular telephones because both the receiver of the call and the caller may be billed for "airtime"—the time you use the cellular network. Even for local calls, charges can run 50 cents per minute or more, depending on the time of day.

When placing a business call, plan what you will say, preferably in writing. Jot down some notes that include:

1. the purpose of your call
2. a list of information you need to get or give

Be sure to identify yourself and the reason for your call early in the conversation. Businesspeople do not like playing "guess who" or "guess what." Here are examples of good phone call openers:

"Hello. This is Tina Watson calling from Unicorn Corporation. Is Marilyn Smith in?"

Once connected with Ms. Smith, say,

"Hello, Ms. Smith. This is Tina Watson with Unicorn Corporation. I need to get some information about your recent catalog order. Is this a good time for you to talk?"

Notice that the caller here identifies herself, previews what she needs to discuss, and also asks about the person's readiness to talk. If the person is busy and cannot give your call full attention, this gives him or her a chance to offer to call you back.

When you need to return calls to people who have called you, schedule them at times the people are likely to be in. Be aware of probable lunch hours and long-distance time differences. If you do not, you are likely to play that dreaded game: telephone tag. You keep returning calls and just missing the person who is trying to call you.

Time your return calls for efficiency. Be specific about when you plan to call a person back. Vague statements like "I'll get back to you on that" may create unrealistic expectations. The caller may expect to hear from you within 15 minutes, while you meant two or three hours. Instead, say, "I can call you back between 1 and 2 this afternoon." And, of course, do call during that time frame.

Action Tip 18: Don't Let the Telephone Interrupt an Important Live Conversation

One of the pet peeves of many customers is having their discussion with a businessperson interrupted by a phone call. If you are talking live to someone, do not assume that the phone call is more important or should be accorded priority.

If you must take the call, always excuse yourself and, when you determine what the call is about, inform the caller that you have someone with you now and will be happy to return the phone call in a specified time.

Action Tip 19: Keep Callers on Track

If a caller digresses into chitchat or nonessential conversation, use a bridging technique to get back on track. This often calls for some creativity, but give it a try.

If your caller says,

> "I get really sick of this gloomy weather around here. It really gets to you after a while, don't you think?"

you might say,

> "Well, one way we can brighten your day is to get this billing problem straightened out" [or "get that new recliner ordered for you" or "give you the information you've been wanting"].

If your caller says,

> "How about those Buffalo Bills last week? They never looked tougher. I'm thinking this is their year, don't you think?"

you might say,

> "They were good. I hope I can get your *bill*s straightened out for you real soon" [or "which reminds me, we need to be looking long and deep into your financial plan" or "let's tackle this order for you"].

If your caller says,

> "I really appreciate your help with the Special Olympics last weekend. Your company is a big help."

you might say,

> "Well, thank you, Ms. Knowaki. I hope I can help you find that widgit you called about, too. Let's see. Here it is . . . "

If your caller wants to chat on and on, take charge: "Mrs. Customer, let me summarize what you've said and then if there is anything else you need to tell me, you can fill in."

If your caller is exceptionally upset, let them get it all out before you attempt to interrupt. An interruption will just make the person angrier. As the caller describes his or her anger, offer sympathetic comments that show that you are still listening: "I see" or "Wow, that doesn't sound like we treated you very well" or "I know how upsetting that can be."

Action Tip 20: Handle the Upset Caller with Tact and Skill

We discussed customer recovery in Chapter 3. Here are some additional tips for recovering upset callers. First, recognize that there are two phases to handling upset or difficult people.

Step one is to understand why they are upset or difficult. The three common root causes of anger/frustration arise from people's feelings that:

1. they are not valued or important
2. they are helpless
3. "it" just isn't fair

We have all experienced these feelings at some time. Express empathy and recognize that these feelings don't make the caller a bad person but rather a person who is having an unpleasant experience. Try to put yourself in that person's position.

Step two involves diffusing the anger or frustration with statements or questions such as these:

1. *Help me to understand.*   This will encourage customers to explain why they are upset. Don't try to defend or argue with their perceptions— they know what they feel, even if it doesn't make a lot of sense to you. Then, let them know that you empathize by saying,
2. *I can understand why you would feel that way.*   Do not say, "I know *exactly* what you mean," because you probably don't. Instead, convey that you have an idea of what he or she might be feeling. Then ask,

3. *What would be a good solution from your point of view?*   This begins to shift the conversation away from the venting of emotion toward solution seeking.

Strive to have the caller share the responsibility for finding a reasonable solution to the problem at hand. When he or she has made a proposal or suggested an idea that might work, you can begin a negotiating process that can lead to a reconciliation with—and cooling off of—the caller.

Self-Analysis | Critique This Call

The following situation describes a fairly commonplace business telephone conversation. In the space provided at the right, critique what is going on, noting both effective and ineffective techniques used by each speaker. Then answer the probe questions at the end of this exercise.

The Story	*My Critique*
Diane: Good morning. Marketing department. This is Diane. May I help you?	
Bobbi: Hi, is this marketing? Oh, good. I need to find out some information about your future seminar schedule. Let me see now . . . [pause] There are several cities where our people might want to attend. [pause] I've got a list here somewhere. I know Cleveland is one . . .	
Diane: We do have seminars scheduled for Cleveland, but which programs are you interested in?	
Bobbi: I'm not real sure. My boss just asked me to get a schedule from you. Don't you have a secretary training class?	
Diane: Yes. In fact we have three professional secretaries' programs. One is for the new employee, and the others are for more advanced secretaries—those with two years' experience or more. And there is one that focuses on desktop publishing.	

Self-Analysis | Critique This Call   *continued*

The Story   *My Critique*

Bobbi: Oh, good. Oh, here it is. I found my
list of cities. The Cleveland, Buffalo,
Denver, and Biloxi offices all seem interested. They said they saw a
brochure about your company.

Diane: Have you seen our Web site?

Bobbi: No, I haven't seen it.

Diane: Okay. Here's what I think we should do.
Go online to www.quickanswerseminars.
com and you'll see a list of cities and dates
for our seminars. Let's see. We will be in
Cleveland, Buffalo, and Denver in the next
two months, but not Biloxi. Perhaps there
is a nearby city your Biloxi people
could go to. You can handle the registration
online or by phone or fax. Will this be satisfactory?

Bobbi: Great. Sounds perfect. Your site
includes pricing and everything, I assume?

Diane: It sure does. And I know your people
will love the seminars. They're really neat.
Now, can I get your email address?
I'll put you on our email list.

Probes

1. What was accomplished by Diane's greeting?

2. What did Bobbi fail to do in her opening remarks?

3. What information did Bobbi need to make this a successful conversation?

4. How well did Diane handle the call?

5. What would you do differently if you were Bobbi? if you were Diane?

6. Did you notice the ways Diane reassured the customer? Why is that important?

7. How was the overall efficiency of this call?

Action Tip 21: Bring the Conversation to a Pleasant but Efficient Close

It can be tempting to talk on with friendly people, but others may be waiting to talk to you and other work awaits. Try some of these techniques for tactfully closing a conversation, even when the caller seems to want to go on:

1. *Summarize the call and what has been decided.* Say, "Let me go over what we decided to do" or "Let me summarize the process for you." Spell out what has been accomplished: "I closed that account and transferred $1,000 to your new fund" or "That is all you need to do for now. It has been taken care of."

2. *Speak in the past tense:* "As we discussed . . . " or "That was all the information I needed" or "I'm glad that you called."

3. *Say "thank you for calling."* This is a universal clue that the conversation is over.

4. *End the call positively.* You might say, "I've enjoyed talking with you, Mr. Blanko."

Action Tip 22: Always Ask, "Is This a Convenient Time to Talk?"

Too many callers burst into their message as soon as the person being called answers. Ask if this is a good time to talk before you begin.

If you are asked that question and it really isn't a good time, let the caller know and arrange another time to talk that would be more convenient.

This tip also holds true if you don't have information you may need to answer a caller's questions. Be honest and tell him or her so. Then arrange a callback.

Action Tip 23: Consistently Work to Improve Your Telephone Communications

Good telephone skills are essential for career success in almost every field. Make it an ongoing effort to get feedback about your telephone skill level. Take the opportunity to attend seminars or view training videos that teach new and specialized skills.

If you supervise other people, don't hesitate to critique their telephone skills. Be frank with them if some things they are doing are inconsistent with the tips in this book. Remind them of the critical importance—to the company and to their professionalism—of good telephone skills.

Be observant. Listen carefully to both the spoken and unspoken messages that may be sent to your callers. Remember that when you use the telephone, your communication channel is limited. There are no visual cues being sent—your callers can't see you. So help them "see" you in the best possible light by using winning telephone techniques.

A FINAL THOUGHT

More and more customers are using electronic media to access businesses. Telephone and e-mail usage is increasingly important to modern organizations. (I'll provide additional tips for effective e-mail use in Chapter 8.) People need to be aware of the advantages as well as the limitations of these media. Customers who have a poor experience with your company over the phone or Net are highly unlikely to become loyal customers.

Clearly, poor telephone use can have a dramatic impact on a company's success. Winning techniques build stronger relationships with customers and other people important to the organization. And employees who master such techniques are particularly valuable to the company.

Summary of Key Ideas

- Understanding our own attitudes toward telephone use and courtesy can help us become more effective in dealing with customers via electronic media.
- Ineffective telephone mannerisms can lead to poor first impressions and customer dissatisfaction.
- Application of 23 techniques will improve your overall telephone effectiveness.
- Web sites and Internet contact must run efficiently and be constantly reassessed to maintain excellent customer contact and responsiveness.

Key Concepts

call screening   phone attitudes
courtesy titles   visual cues (lack of)
dead air   voice pitch

Self-Test Questions

1. Compare and contrast the benefits of phone communication versus face-to-face contact with customers.

2. How do attitudes toward using the phone affect one's telephone techniques?

3. What is call screening? When is its use appropriate? When should it be avoided?

4. What three elements can speakers vary in their voices to better hold listener attention?

5. What is dead air, and how can it impact customer relationships?

6. What information should people have on their answering machine greeting messages? What should be avoided?

7. What are the two important factors required to effectively handle irate customers on the phone?

Application Activity 1: Identify the Errors in Garth's Call

1. Reread the story of Garth's call to the car dealership on page 125. Then describe four or more telephone use problems that probably led to Garth's irritation and his decision not to do business with that dealer.

   Problem 1:

   Problem 2:

   Problem 3:

   Problem 4:

2. Most people who hear of this incident quickly identify the unspoken but loud and clear message projected by the dealership: this caller (and potential customer) isn't particularly important. Perhaps this is because the car in question isn't for sale (and the shortsighted salesperson can't see any advantage to be gained by being polite), or perhaps it is because their telephone usage is completely rude and unprofessional. They've forgotten or have never learned the basics of telephone courtesy.

3. Whatever the reason, the outcome is the same: a caller who has been treated poorly and will harbor some resentment against this business.

Application Activity 2: Try Rewording for a Better Tone

1. Imagine that you are answering the phone and replying to a caller's request. Rephrase the following statements to make your wording positive and tactful. Also strive to solve the caller's concern as efficiently as possible.

   1. Bill is out playing golf again. I doubt that he'll be back in the office today.

   2. Sarah went to the restroom and then is going to lunch for about an hour or so.

   3. Who did you say you were?

   4. You say you've been trying to get through? When did you try?

   5. Who are you holding for?

   6. This is Bobby. What do you need?

   7. Hey, sorry about that. I got backed up and couldn't call you back.

   8. We don't do that kind of work here.

   9. Try again after 5, okay?

   10. Sally used to work here, but we let her go. Maybe I can help.

Application Activity 3: Hear the Difference

1. Try this simple exercise to demonstrate how voice inflection can change the meaning of what you say. Say out loud the following sentence, first just using your normal voice:

   "Henry didn't show up for work today."

Now restate the same sentence with surprise in your voice. Next, make it sound like a secret. Finally, turn it into a question.

2. Next, try saying the following sentence with the emphasis on a different word each time:

"I think Doris can do that."

Notice that when you emphasize the word "I," the unspoken message may be "I think she can do it, although maybe no one else thinks so." When you emphasize the word "think," you convey an unspoken message of uncertainty.

3. Listen for the possible unspoken messages as you emphasized "Doris," "can," "do," and "that." Notice how these subtle changes in voice and emphasis can communicate widely different meanings.

Notes

1. S. Gale. "Three Ways to Train for Call-Center Success." *Workforce.* [Online]. Available http://www.workforce.com/section/11/feature/23/17/89/ index.html. March 5, 2000.

2. Transmitted online *Internet Daily* sponsored by CBS MarketWatch. September 1, 1999.

3. Many of the ideas in this chapter are adapted from the author's videotape training program and book *Winning Telephone Techniques* (Chicago: JWA Video, 1997). This program can be purchased through JWA Video by calling 312–829–5100.

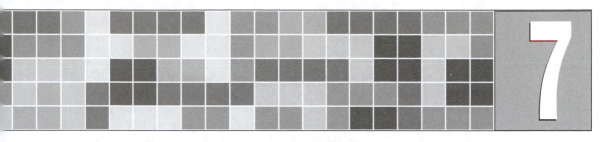

Use Web Sites to Build Customer Loyalty

Tap into the Miracle of the Internet[1]

Unless your business is exclusively local, customers have come to expect a Web presence. This will become increasingly true as Internet use continues to grow.

WHAT YOU'LL LEARN IN THIS CHAPTER

- Internet Web sites play an important role in building customer loyalty.
- Key Web technologies are revolutionizing customer service in the new economy.
- There are both advantages and disadvantages in providing Web-based customer service.
- It is important to know the common mistakes to avoid when moving the customer service function to the Web.
- Your business can establish an A-plus presence on the Web.

THE WAY IT IS . . .
Web Pages Provide Information Customers Need and Want[2]

Remember Crayolas? You know, crayons—those colored waxy sticks you used to create art masterpieces. Like most budding artists you probably started with the basic medium of coloring books but, like many kids, soon graduated to something on a much larger scale, like creating wall murals that showed promise well beyond your years.

Speaking of walls "decorated" with love, did you ever wonder how to restore the wall surface to its original condition—be it paint, wallpaper, or marble? If so, you're not alone. Binney & Smith, best known for the Crayola brand of crayons, often received customer inquiries about just that topic: how do I remove crayon markings from a wall? Until recently, Binney & Smith handled those type of inquiries through a call center. In 1997, e-mail was added to handle additional volume. That helped for a little while. But by 2000, the phone and e-mail volume outpaced the 12 customer service reps assigned. One-third of the inquiries originated from e-mail alone. The response time needed to get back to a customer exceeded three days—a lifetime in the world of electronic commerce.

Today, Binney & Smith uses the Web to allow customers to find for themselves answers to common questions. A knowledge base of over 200 frequently asked questions (FAQs) has reduced the need to provide personalized customer assistance to less than 2 percent of inquiries. At the same time, Binney & Smith has turned the online customer service experience into an adventure that's fun for the whole family. Check the site out at www.crayola.com. Once you figure out how to remove the crayon from the walls, the site offers you a virtual trip to the Crayola factory at Easton, Pennsylvania. It's all there on the Net: answers, a virtual trip, and more.

WHAT IS WEB-BASED CUSTOMER SERVICE?

> The Web is emerging as a channel for delivering customer assistance.

> Studies show that 67 percent of customers stop doing business with a company because of poor access to service and information.[4]

Listening to World Wide Web gurus talk, you'd think the Internet was made for customer service. Not only is the Web a "perfect" sales channel, it's the perfect channel for presale and postsale customer support. Today the Web is home to $33 billion in retail shopping in the United States alone.[3]

The Web is not just for selling. According to a survey conducted by Purdue University, over 30 billion customers are expected to contact North American businesses for some type of support. While the phone will still be the dominant way people contact businesses, Web sites are expected to handle 25 percent of such contacts. E-mail will account for the remaining 20 percent.[5] Clearly, Web-based customer service is on the rise.

UNDERSTAND THE CATEGORIES OF WEB-ENABLED CUSTOMER SERVICE

Let's look at some key characteristics of Web-based customer service. For one thing, the customer isn't physically present. And second, there's usually some kind of Internet communication software between the company and the customer. Given these conditions, customer contact can occur in several ways and for several purposes.

Self-Serve Common Answers

From the company's perspective, "low interaction–delayed communication" is the nirvana of online customer service. Here customers take care of themselves using knowledge bases, which are databases of answers to frequently asked questions (FAQs).

Knowledge bases may be structured or unstructured. Structured knowledge bases are organized into a question-and-answer format. Unstructured knowledge bases are repositories of customer interaction, such as e-mail correspondence with customer service or postings on an electronic bulletin board. Such repositories are indexed by keyword.

Providing such basic information is often the starting point for organizations moving some of their customer support to the Web. Typically, the organization will create and host a static (unchanging) Web page, something like an electronic version of a marketing brochure. Information usually includes organizational contact information such as name, address, phone number, and little more.

Characteristically, FAQs include key product questions with short answers, such as:

- Are your coffee-flavored ice creams caffeine free?
- What can I do about wind noise from my mountain bike rack accessory?
- How do I use my personal digital assistant (PDA) to read my e-mail?

Often the questions are listed at the top of the Web page and hyperlinked to the answers further down the page. (Hyperlinks are those words or phrases that you can click on to get to another place.) Questions would be sorted alphabetically or by the frequency in which they are asked. For common questions, FAQs are both efficient and effective. And for many sites, FAQs are still the norm.

The problem with such static Web pages is that, in order to get an answer, customers have to wade through a list of the top 100 or so questions hoping to find one that matches or comes close. This is kind of like forcing them to read an encyclopedia from beginning to end to satisfy their query. Again, this is relatively easy for the organization hosting the FAQs but not efficient for the self-serve customer, except computer-savvy "Web-heads" who know the tricks. For example, Web-heads know that you can do a keyword search on any Web page just by holding down the Control key while pressing the letter F on the keyboard. This brings up the "Find" dialogue box, offering the option to search up or down by whole word. This is useful if the customer's question can be distilled into a single keyword.

> *Online knowledge bases make it possible for customers to answer their own questions. Self-learning knowledge bases constantly update themselves based on customer inquiries.*

More sophisticated Web sites can do multi-word searches of the frequently asked questions. Some offer a searchable, self-learning knowledge database. A knowledge database is an online repository of information—the collective wisdom regarding the product or service. And unlike static FAQs, this knowledge base is dynamic, ever-changing, and self-learning. This means that it is automatically updated based on customer inquiries. In this way, the repository evolves with each new question. Customers can search knowledge bases, not just by single keywords but by phrases.

Delayed Answers

> *High-volume e-mail usually indicates that customers logging on to your service site are having trouble finding answers on their own.*

When customers can't get the answers they need from self-serve sites, they often turn to e-mail. Using manual knowledge bases and e-mail management software, customer assistance reps take turns responding to customer-initiated inquiries. Most Web customers expect a 24-hour turnaround, but all too often the response time is no better than snail mail, if there is a response at all. And because e-mail relies on one-way communication, the possibility of miscues and misunderstanding is high. This delayed communication is neither very effective nor efficient—to the extent that some experts discourage companies from trying it. According to leading customer service consultants, "large volumes of e-mail result from customers NOT being able to find answers they need on your Web site."[6] Rather than representing an effective customer care solution, handling a lot of e-mail can be a symptom of an ineffective Web page.

Live Answers

> *Web chat allows two or more people to carry on a two-way conversation using text.*

High-assistance service can be provided by such things as Web chat or live chat, a relative newcomer on the customer service scene. When customers began to complain about the slow response times of e-mail queries, several companies responded with online chat. This is an adaptation of the "chat rooms" popular with online services such as AOL (America Online). With live chat, the customer service representative communicates live (in "real time") with the customer who needs assistance. All messaging is text-based—both parties type questions and responses. Often, a complete transcript of the chat session is available to the customer for review.

Self-Serve Personalized Answers

Personalized service—customized real-time data about the customer's specific problem—is the ideal technology-assisted service a company can offer. For example, you just ordered the perfect gift for your mom three days before Mother's Day. You received multiple assurances that the gift would arrive before that special Sunday morning. Now you want to know where your order stands. Has it been filled? If so, where is it? Has it left the loading dock? Is it on a UPS or FedEx truck? These kinds of customer inquiries are simple for Web-enabled tracking systems. The customer enters the tracking number and seconds later knows just where the package is.

Personalized self-serve solutions rely on real-time tailoring of Web content to the customer's individual needs. Web pages are dynamically adjusted (frequently changed) based on customer profiles. For instance, when a Platinum-level frequent flyer checks her itinerary on the Web, she'll see flight status, the in-flight meal menu, and an airport map showing her where the Platinum Club lounge is located in relation to her arriving gate. Economy-class flyers, on the other hand, would see only flight status. Such personalization provides A-plus information for frequent flyers, engendering an almost-religious loyalty among those valuable business travelers.

> *Personalized service information exceeds customer expectations, providing an A-plus experience.*

RECOGNIZE THE BUSINESS CASE FOR "WEBIFYING" CUSTOMER SERVICE

Using the Web to communicate can be very cost effective. Based on a recent study by Gartner, the average cost per transaction for self-service Web assistance was just 24 cents. Compare this with telephone customer care ($5.50 per incident), and it's easy to make a case for moving the customer service function to the Web. Of course, as we've discussed earlier, Web self-service is only one component in a customer service contact portfolio. A complete Internet-based customer service strategy would ordinarily include e-mail ($5 per incident) and possibly Web chat ($7 per incident). Nevertheless, the economics of self-serve Web are dramatically superior to other forms of customer contact (see Table 7.1).

> *Web self-service has the lowest average cost per transaction of all customer service contact options.*

TABLE 7.1   Cost per customer service channel.

Service Channel	Average Cost Per Transaction
Web self-service	$0.24
Interactive Voice Response (IVR) self-service	$0.45
E-mail	$5.00
Telephone	$5.50
Web chat	$7.00

Source: Gartner, Stamford, CT[7]

Advantages of Web-Based e-Service

Aside from cost savings, are there other benefits to migrating Web-based customer self-service from traditional channels? Definitely! For one, self-service is often faster than representative-assisted service. Rather than having to hop in the car to drive to the customer service counter or wade through levels and levels of telephone voice-response menus only to be put on hold, customers with access to the Web can get immediate answers to their most frequently asked questions. Quick answers often translate into increased customer loyalty—A-plus experiences in the areas of information and speed. Better yet, a satisfying Web experience builds customer bonds. Increasingly, the customer comes to view your site as a "window" into a shared community.

> *Web portals provide a centralized access point for a broad array of Internet resources and services.*

Consider this example: TIAA-CREF, a leading pension and mutual fund manager for educators, not only provides customer account access via the Web but offers daily financial market updates and news. Initially, customers use the site to view their fund balances or make portfolio changes. Soon, however, they find their relationship with TIAA-CREF expanding beyond customer service. Before long, customers are accessing the site regularly to check the stock market or read financial news analyses of particular interest to them. What started out as a customer service site has become a portal for selling additional services and products.

> *The key benefits of e-service are quicker answers, increased customer bonding, and global 24/7 assistance.*

One last benefit of Web-based service is global coverage. In a world increasingly attuned to the demands of a 24/7 economy spanning across nations and time zones, a self-service Web presence provides some form of assistance anytime, anywhere. And, for unique customer needs, people will always have e-mail. With e-service, the customer never has to wait to begin the inquiry process and may find most answers immediately.

Disadvantages of Web-Based e-Service

E-service alone is not a 100 percent, surefire strategy for handling all customer contacts. It is a helpful "platform" for several cost-effective channels—self-service Web, company information, e-mail, and live chat—but e-service is not a substitute for old-fashioned phone calls and direct contact with customer care representatives. (Review Chapter 6 for a discussion of effective telephone service.) E-service, then, is "in addition"—another set of channels for communicating with customers. As such, e-service is just one more assistance approach that must be designed, implemented, and maintained. Installing an e-service solution is no small undertaking. It is costly and highly dependent on available technology.

The Internet, like most information technologies, is a moving target. The hardware used has a life cycle averaging five years before it becomes obsolete. Software life cycles are even shorter, with minor product updates appearing every few months and major updates every 18 months. As some experts caution, "The leading edge can often be the bleeding edge." The wrong technology can end up "bleeding" a company's human resources and capital.

Finally, the rush to migrate customer service to the Web has produced its share of failed sites and frustrated customers, prompting a not necessarily undeserved reputation akin to the voice-response runaround, where the customer sits on hold listening to tinny elevator music. Poor e-service delivery can substitute one negative stereotype for another. Ignoring the human side of customer service can turn what looks like a low-cost service alternative into a costly mistake. But it doesn't have to be that way.

> *Poorly managed e-service systems can cost more than they were expected to save and often result in a reputation for bad service.*

APPLY THE TOP 10 ACTION TIPS FOR AVOIDING E-SERVICE PROBLEMS

While the Web offers great potential for building customer loyalty, it also can lead to frustration and failure if not done right. By putting the following actions into practice, a company can be well on its way to establishing an A-plus presence on the Web. Here is the list. I'll describe each tip in more detail in the following pages.

1. Be there and be quick
2. Make site navigation simple
3. Respond quickly
4. Provide communication alternatives
5. Pay attention to form *and* function
6. Track customer traffic
7. Benchmark service levels

8. Teach your site to learn
9. Build an ongoing e-relationship
10. End high for better loyalty

Action Tip 1: Be There and Be Quick

Did you ever log on to your favorite bank or credit union site to do a little online banking only to find the site down? It's like showing up at the bank during business hours only to find the doors locked. For e-tailers (electronic retailers, including online banks), when the site's down they are closed for business. And to make matters worse, a competitor is only a click away. For customers looking for assistance (who are likely to already be frustrated), an inaccessible or slow site can be extremely annoying. Instead of a customer being able to help herself online, the situation usually escalates. Now your company has to deal with three problems: an inoperable site, a frazzled customer, and the customer's original concern.

Or, have you ever found yourself frustrated because a Web site seemed to take forever to open pages? Keystone Systems, an organization that measures Internet speed and reliability for Web site clients, claims that if a page takes longer than *eight seconds* to load, most visitors won't stick around.[8]

> *In an Internet world, a competitor is only a click away. If a site is inaccessible or if the pages load too slowly, customers let their mouse do the walking.*

Therefore, the first rule of successful e-service is to be there and be quick. When the customer hits your company's Web page, they want it to be up. Many companies go to great effort to offer stable, redundant Web servers. (*Redundant* means having backup to ensure that if one aspect of the service goes down, others take over to keep it running.) The goal is 99.999 percent uptime and rapid page-loading times.

Action Tip 2: Make Site Navigation Simple

Web customer service should be only one click away. Once customers connect to a home page, they should be able to get to the customer assistance page with a single click. And they shouldn't have to scour the home page to find the button, tab, or hyperlink.

> *Navigating a Web site should not be an exercise in traversing a maze.*

Site navigation should be simple and obvious, with a consistent scheme for going from page to page. The customer should always have a way to get back to a specific page or be able to press the back button on their browser to escape. Forcing the customer to stay in a site doesn't build loyalty, especially since, for most customers, the only way out is to shut down the browser and relaunch it.

Action Tip 3: Respond Quickly

Today's Nintendo generation expects immediate response from their game consoles, desktop computers, and sports cars. Waiting more than two to three seconds for a computer screen to refresh is unacceptable.

Web users have a need for speed. Successful customer service sites respond quickly to each customer inquiry.

Web site performance is only one dimension of quick response. Even more important is quick turnaround on customer questions. Average response times should be tied to your customer contact profile. For e-mail, I recommend a response time of 24 hours or less. For something as dynamic as Web chat, the communication should have the pace of a live conversation. Long pauses on the order of five minutes or more may confuse the customer into thinking the chat has been abandoned. Before long, the customer is typing "Are you still there?" in the chat window.

Allegiance Technologies, the providers of the Active Listening System I described in Chapter 2, tracks the amount of time it takes to respond to a customer's complaint, questions, comments, or compliments. Managers receive reports showing response times and can work to minimize these to create A-plus service.

Action Tip 4: Provide Communication Alternatives

The more high-tech the world becomes, the more some people crave *high touch* service. In the realm of customer care, the Internet is almost a synonym for high-tech. Unfortunately, except for the automated personalization discussed earlier, today's Internet is anything but "high touch." At some point, customers may become frustrated with the various self-serve options and seek human contact. The solution may be to provide several communication alternatives such as e-mail, Web chat, two-way interactive video, or even something as low-tech as the telephone. Some customers just need the human touch and should be given such options.

Here's a quick example: Erika Wilde runs a Web site selling floor mats to businesses. Her site, StopDirt.com, is easily available for people needing a wide variety of industrial mats and matting products. When a customer contacts Erika's Web site to get information or to describe a problem, she immediately

For low-tech customers, good service is personalized, synchronous "hand-holding."

calls them back on the phone. This provides immediate, synchronous, and very personalized service. It also helps to create "hand-holding" relationships with her customers, who are invariably impressed by the level of personal service they receive. She thus offers A-plus information and personality.

Action Tip 5: Pay Attention to Form and Function

Just because technology can give a company animation, 256 type fonts, and 16 million colors doesn't mean its Web site has to use it all. Customer care sites should be functional and visually pleasing, but they need not be elaborate or incorporate every possible bell and whistle.

Web users want substance and form. Don't distract them with technology just for technology's sake.

Successful sites, like modern video games, are the result of a team effort. Graphic designers, usability engineers, database administrators, content experts, and programmers all play a part. Form should support function, avoiding jazzy technology for technology's sake. The most customer-friendly sites avoid unnecessary clutter, instead keeping the site simple and functional.

Action Tip 6: Track Customer Traffic

Web user traffic patterns can be tracked to provide continuous quality improvement in customer care.

The best thing about the Web may be that companies can track anything using available software. They can determine the "click path" the customer took to get to the site and whether the customer is a first-time visitor. They can track service resolution and abandonment rates, average site connect time, and frequent requests. If companies want to know where to spend their time to better serve customers, they should track customer paths and then use the data to systematically improve the site.

Action Tip 7: Benchmark Service Levels

You can't "expect" unless you "inspect." As with most things, with e-service you get what you measure.

Web sites with successful customer care benchmark and compare against themselves and against their best competitors. Benchmarking means keeping careful statistics about existing service levels. These statistics can then be used to set targets for the future. Typical services monitored include site uptime, average response rate per page request, average time to respond to e-mail inquiries, average time to respond to Web chat inquiries, and number of resolved and unresolved inquiries per day.

Action Tip 8: Teach Your Site to Learn

If the content of a Web site remains the same today as it was last week, chances are it will be able to satisfy only last week's customers. Successful e-service requires learning such things as:

- what doesn't work and what content is missing
- what click paths end in dissatisfied customers
- what new questions your customers are asking

Web infrastructure should include mechanisms for identifying fruitless Web paths as well as new concerns. Some commercial software scours Web activity and automatically updates a company's knowledge base with new content. Whether a company chooses to have its site "learn" via such software or whether it has the content updated by staff, adaptive sites let customers know the organization is listening and responding to their needs.

> *A learning customer service site like a learning organization readily adapts to the challenges of a dynamic world.*

Action Tip 9: Build an Ongoing e-Relationship

Successful human relationships are usually two-sided. Sometimes people initiate communication or behaviors that build the relationship; sometimes they reciprocate to others. Traditional customer service, however, tends to be 100 percent customer-initiated and thus 100 percent reactive. Yet e-service offers companies the opportunity to take the initiative—to be proactive. To build an e-relationship, companies can simply offer e-mail notifications to customers. "Notify-on-change" puts the customer's e-mailbox to use. With each change in product, catalog, or content area, the company can automatically fire off an appropriate e-mail to its customer base. Of course, they should be sure to get permission from customers first. "Spamming," the practice of sending unwanted e-mail, can damage a relationship rather than enhance it. If customers do agree to accept notifications, the company should always give them the option with each e-mail to have their name removed from the notification list.

> *Organizations can use proactive technology to make the customer's e-mailbox an extension of the company's Web site.*

Action Tip 10: End High for Better Loyalty

One common model for providing traditional in-person customer service suggests apologizing for any inconvenience (expressing caring), solving the problem (showing competence), and offering a peace token (providing comfort) such as additional points in a customer loyalty program. This last step is designed to leave the customer on a high note, thinking positively (or at least neutrally) about the company. With Web-based customer service, even though the focus is on helping the customer help him- or herself, it still makes sense to make peace.

Before customers log off from a Web site, the company should always thank them for visiting. To rebuild the goodwill (if the customer has had a problem), offer some kind of token—a discount on their next purchase, free shipping, or some kind of additional service coverage. This provides A-plus service by giving some add-on.

> *Peace tokens, or A-plus add-ons, work just as well online as they do off-line.*

Another Look | What's Your Company's SQ?

Now that you've had a chance to explore the role of the Internet in building customer loyalty, it's time to see how well your organization is doing. E-service guru Greg Gianforte has developed a short "SQ" (service quotient) test for assessing the health of an organization's Web-mediated customer service.[9] If you are currently working in an organization with a Web site, take a minute and complete the following customer service quotient survey. If you do not work in such an organization, select the Web site of a company you have visited, put yourself in the role of one of the company's leaders, and answer as many of the questions as you can.

SQ Test	Yes	No	Don't Know
Can your customers quickly find answers to their most frequently asked questions on your Web site?			
Can they easily check on the status of the response they previously requested?			
Do you respond to all customer e-mails within one business day?			
Does the e-service content on your site change automatically based on customer input?			
Are the most useful and/or commonly requested knowledge items presented first?			
Do customers have an easy way to get to a human support staffer?			
Do your customers consistently return to your site to get information? Do you have any way of determining whether or not they do?			
Are you tracking activity that has taken place on your site on a week-by-week basis? Do those reports help you determine the return on investment (ROI) of the site?			
Do you give visitors the option to have updates sent to them automatically by e-mail?			
Are you consistently using your Web site to capture and publish useful information that's currently only in the heads of your best staff?			
Does your call center only handle queries that couldn't be handled automatically on your Web site?			

Another Look | **What's Your Company's SQ?** *continued*

SQ Test	Yes	No	Don't Know
Do customers ever praise your company because they found your site especially helpful?			
Can you view both the e-mail and call history of any given incident from a single interface?			
Are the answers you give your customers on the phone the same as the ones you give them on your Web site?			

SCORING:

According to Gianforte, a "Yes" answer on 10 or more items indicates that your organization's e-service health is excellent. Anything less should prompt you to reexamine some of your on-line customer service strategies.

A FINAL THOUGHT

Today's Web-mediated customer service offers a low-cost approach for run-of-the-mill customer transactions. Getting answers to frequently asked questions, checking the status of an order, or even researching the details of an invoice are easy tasks for Internet-enabled customer care service centers. The Web has made building and maintaining customer relationships simpler. We would expect that of technology. But there's the dark side—some Web sites are more complicated and difficult to navigate than a video arcade game.

In the near future, customers will abandon the mouse and keyboard as input devices and will turn to voice recognition. Getting to a customer care site will require nothing more than speaking commands. Problem resolution will involve speaking with an "avatar"—a digital, on-screen representation of a live customer service agent. Using artificial intelligence, Web avatars will guide the customer through the Internet experience, displaying appropriate Web pages and making necessary customer account adjustments. In such a scenario, virtual service replaces self-service, providing a personalized solution to every customer concern.

While many companies are not yet this sophisticated with their technology, even simple Web sites can be useful in building customer loyalty if they provide good information, are easy to use, and convey to the customer that the company is accessible and cares.

Summary of Key Ideas

- The Internet has provided a new avenue for delivering customer assistance.
- Migration of the customer service process to the Web remains in its infancy. Experts foresee that soon the Web will handle almost half of all customer contacts.
- Online knowledge bases make it possible for customers to answer their own questions. The best of such knowledge bases are dynamic and keep "learning" as they process customer input.
- E-mail provides delayed answers to customer inquiries. A rule of thumb for A-plus customer service is to acknowledge all customer e-mail and respond to it within 24 hours or less.
- Web chat is an adaptation of Internet chat room technology that allows customers and service representatives to carry on two-way communication.
- Personalized self-service relies on customer profiles to provide information tailored to the individual's needs.
- Web self-service has a significant cost advantage over traditional customer service channels, such as talking to a live agent on the telephone.
- E-services are not only cost effective, but they often provide additional benefits such as improved customer relationships. However, poorly managed e-services can eliminate any potential cost savings and result in lost customers.
- Successful e-service delivery requires attention to several factors: Web site uptime, navigation ease, server speed, personal touch, appropriate site design, benchmarking, traffic monitoring, adaptive knowledge bases, proactive communication, and customer loyalty programs.
- Future customer service delivery may involve the use of virtual customer assistance representatives.

Key Concepts

benchmarking

cost per transaction

e-service

e-tailer

FAQs (frequently asked questions)

knowledge base

portal

service channel

Web chat

Webify

WWW (World Wide Web, or Web for short)

Self-Test Questions

1. Describe in your own words the categories of Web-enabled customer service as discussed in this chapter.

2. How important is it for businesses to "webify" their customer service? Is this equally important for all types of businesses?

3. Summarize the advantages and disadvantages of Web-based e-service.

Application Activity: Explore the World of e-Service

1. Pick three of your favorite companies or organizations, locate the home page for each of these organizations, and investigate the online customer service they provide. Do they include most e-service channels such as FAQs, e-mail, and chat? What additional online services are provided?

2. Imagine that you have purchased a new scanner for your computer. You take it home, hook it up, and find you can't get any of your photos to scan properly. Select a major scanner vendor, and connect to its customer service Web site. Perform a navigation analysis of the site. How many links did you have to follow to get your problem resolved? Were you able to "serve yourself," or did you have to contact a customer assistance representative? If you were assisted, was it easy to contact customer service? Did you use e-mail? Web chat? Telephone?

3. If you currently work in a company that uses Web-based e-service, review the e-service quotient survey (pages 156–157), and perform an SQ test on your company's site. What was your score? What service areas do you need to reexamine? What suggestions would you make to management in order to improve your SQ?

4. Log on to the customer service site of an established Internet retailing company (e.g., www.amazon.com, www.overstock.com, www.proflowers.com) and the site of a relatively new entrant to the Web (e.g., a local business such as a martial arts studio or an auto repair shop). Record how long it takes to move from Web page to Web page. Send an e-mail, and see how long it takes to receive a reply. Compare the performance (speed) of the two e-service providers. Did these organizations meet your need for speed?

5. Find a business or an organization that doesn't have a customer service Web presence. Develop a plan to create Web-assisted e-service capability. Outline what steps would be necessary. You need not flesh out every detail, just the major decisions and steps involved in the organization in moving some of its customer assistance processes to the Internet.

Notes

1. Some material in this chapter is adapted from P. R. Timm and C. G. Jones, *Technology and Customer Loyalty* (Upper Saddle River, NJ: Prentice Hall, 2005).

2. Adapted from RightNow Technologies. Binney & Smith Properties, Inc. "Service as Easy as Child's Play." 2002. [Online]. Available http://www.rightnow.com/resource/casestudy.php?id=807. February 2, 2002.

3. M. Pastore. "U.S. E-Commerce Spikes in Q4 2001." CyberAtlas. February 20, 2002. [Online]. Available http://cyberatlas.internet.com/markets/retailing/print/0,,6061_977751,00.html. May 15, 2002.

4. S. Fletcher. "Technology: Coming to a Contact Center Near You." *CRM Community News* 2002. [Online]. Available http://www.crmcommunity.com/news/article.cfm?oid=0E7FBBC3-45D7-4878-AAD33919DBD2FA72. February 2, 2002.

5. Ibid.

6. G. Gianforte. "The Insider's Guide to Next-Generation Web Customer Service. RightNow Technologies." 2000. [Online]. Available http://www.rightnow.com/resource/whitepaper.html. February 18, 2002.

7. B. Read. "Special Report: Making CRM Work in Uncertain Times." *Call Center Magazine*. November 5, 2001. [Online]. Available http://www.callcentermagazine.com/article/CCM20011026S0004. May 15, 2002.

8. C. Y. Chen and G. Lindsay. "How to Lose a Customer in a Matter of Seconds." *Fortune*, June 12, 2000, p. 326.

9. G. Gianforte. "The Insider's Guide to Customer Service on the Web: Eight Secrets for Successful e-Service." 1999. [Online]. Available http://www.rightnow.com/resource/whitepaper.html. May 13, 2002. Reprinted with permission.

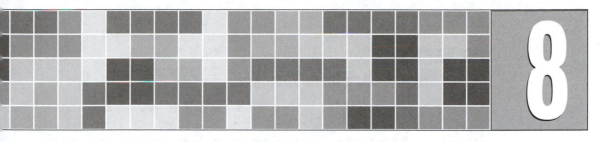

Use Written Messages to Boost Customer Satisfaction and Loyalty

Writing Can Create Valuable Ties

Because written messages are used less frequently now than in times past, businesses can surprise customers with well-written messages, thus creating an A-plus experience.

WHAT YOU'LL LEARN IN THIS CHAPTER

- Written media and e-mail messages can build stronger customer loyalty.
- Build customer loyalty with unexpected thank-you notes and goodwill messages.
- Use written media to get publicity and foster customer awareness.
- Effectively share information with customers in written documents and e-mail.

THE WAY IT IS . . .
Follow-up Notes Are Good Business

Several months after getting my first job out of college as a manager trainee, I sent a letter to the college recruiter who had hired me. The letter was brief—I simply said how much I enjoyed working for the company and thanked him for helping me get started with the company. A few days later, I received a call from him. He thanked me for the letter and commented that of all his trainees he had worked with, I was the only one who had written to him in this way.

Interestingly, a short while later he was instrumental in my getting promoted to a better position. My letter had helped me make an impression that proved very helpful in my career. For an investment of the few minutes necessary to write that message, I created an A-plus experience for my "customer"—this recruiter.

Best-selling author Harvey Mackay talks about "short notes [that] yield long results" in his book *Swim with the Sharks Without Being Eaten Alive*.[1] He comments on how few people send follow-up notes to customers—even those who have made a major purchase, like a car. Another glaring omission of many people interviewing for a job is the follow-up thank-you note to the interviewer.

Mackay cites many successful people who constantly send out short but effective notes with messages like "I want you to know how much I enjoyed our meeting/interview/your gift/your hospitality" or "Congratulations on your new house/car/tennis trophy."

The moral of the story: Don't hesitate to let people know that you appreciate them, and *do it in writing*. Don't worry about formality or business protocol. Often, a handwritten note, worded conversationally, works fine.[2]

A professor friend of mine recently asked members of an executive education business class this question: "How many of you have written a business document for your job within the past 24 hours? The past week?" The answer was surprising. Out of the 62 working professionals in the class, only 1 had written within the past day and 4 within the past week. The professor's point is that business communication, with its many media choices, is quite different than it has been in the past and that many managers seldom, if ever, write a paper document. The other point, however, is that when we do put forth the effort to write a document, it has the potential to become noteworthy in the mind of the reader. The idea that someone would take the time and effort to write can have a dramatic effect on people.

Thank-you letters are routinely sent to customers by businesses that sell high-price items like cars, trucks, appliances, furniture, and the like. But companies are increasingly recognizing the value of the thank-you note to buyers of even lower-priced products. I recently received a note of appreciation from the owner of the athletic shoe store where I'd just purchased some jogging shoes.

E-mail messages are being used more frequently than ever to convey some of the same goodwill. Their impact may be somewhat less than a "hard copy" letter, but they are certainly better than no follow-up at all. If personalized and genuine, and if customers value e-mail communications, these can accomplish much of what a written letter or note might.

Why write at all? Because such correspondence can pleasantly surprise customers and form the beginning of ongoing business relationships. Such messages tell customers that they are important to you and that you are available to serve them further. Written notes to customers are an often-overlooked way to create that all-important one-to-one relationship.

In this chapter, we will consider the power of such letters, notes, and e-mails, which are called goodwill messages. When you have finished this chapter, you should be comfortable preparing effective one-to-one relationship-building messages with ease.

APPLY THESE ACTION TIPS WHEN USING GOODWILL MESSAGES

Goodwill messages are defined as messages people write even though they don't have to. They reflect a sense of interest in and courtesy toward others and can be powerful in strengthening relationships and social networks. Many people, by failing to send goodwill messages, overlook an excellent opportunity to promote good feelings toward and within their organization. Applying the power of written communication can quickly set one organization apart from most others. Here are two valuable tips for writing goodwill messages.

Action Tip 1: Just Do It

Few things make an employee (an internal customer) feel better than to receive a brief letter of appreciation, congratulations, sympathy, or concern from the boss or a coworker. It only takes the writer a minute, yet it can help to develop good employee relations. Likewise, external customers who receive sincere, personal messages from people they do business with will likely harbor more favorable feelings toward that person and organization.

A manager friend of mine makes it a point to send short letters to the homes of employees whose work was exemplary. Such a simple action has several payoffs:

1. Employees know the manager recognizes and appreciates their good work.

2. By sending letters home, the manager lets employees' families share in the praise.

3. Letters become a part of employees' personnel files and can be used when preparing performance reviews.

4. By noting that copies have been sent to higher levels of management (cc: the boss), employees know they are getting additional attention.

Opportunities for goodwill notes come up almost daily. Besides on-the-job performance, personal and family accomplishments can be acknowledged. A daughter's wedding, an impressive bowling score, and outstanding community service can all be opportunities to show you care.[3]

> *Look for opportunities to send goodwill messages—then, just do it.*

If you can't think of a reason to send a note to a customer or friend, perhaps you can clip a story or an article out of a magazine that you know would interest him or her. Send that with a brief note acknowledging that you are aware of their interest.

Action Tip 2: Be Original

There was a time when sending Christmas cards was an effective way to plant your company's name before current and prospective customers. But there is only so much warmth to go around at the holiday season. So many companies now send cards at traditional seasons that yours can get lost in the shuffle. That's why some companies and individuals have added other, less traditional card-sending holidays to mailing rosters: Thanksgiving, St. Patrick's Day, Veterans Day, and the Fourth of July, for example, in the U.S. (other state and local holidays can also work). Break through the expected clutter of typical holiday cards and show some uniqueness.

> *Look for opportunities to send a variety of written messages to customers, internal and external. Make these greetings unique and personalized.*

Originality means paying attention to detail, as well. Some people have cards designed specifically so they're different from the run-of-the-mill variety. Custom stationery can be a much more personal way to reach customers.

USE SALES FOLLOW-UP LETTERS AND E-MAILS

The letter below is sent to customers who buy automobiles from a Chevy dealer. As you'll see, it combines goodwill with some useful instructions.

Christensen
Chevrolet/Buick/GMC

Jan 6, 2005

Paul R. Timm
81 E. Cyprus St.
Orem UT 84058

Dear Paul:

We appreciate your business and the opportunity to work with you. Below is some information you will find helpful.

We normally receive your license plates about four weeks after all the paperwork from the sale is completed. We will send you a postcard when the plates are ready to be picked up here at our Cashier's window.

The title is issued by the state government and will be sent directly to the firm that loaned the money for the vehicle. If you paid cash, the title should reach you about two months following the completion of the paperwork from the sale.

Our Service and Parts Departments are open Monday through Friday for regular service. A courtesy bus is available at no charge in the Provo-Orem area Monday–Friday. Please call when your car needs servicing to make an appointment in order to minimize delays.

Chevrolet, Buick and GMC all send out important survey forms to a percentage of our customers during the first month after the sale and again at 5 months. We strive to make our customers *very satisfied*. If you are not, please let us know first. When you receive a survey form, please take the time to fill it out and return it in the envelope provided.

We care about you as our customer and look forward to a continued business relationship. Our goal is to be deserving of your future business.

Sincerely yours,

Mike Echevarria

Mike Echevarria
General Manager

Self-Analysis   Critique the Letter

You can learn a lot from the examples of others. Get into the habit of critiquing business letters you receive. Create a list of your likes and dislikes. Start with the follow-up letter from the Chevy dealer. List five likes and dislikes, and then summarize what you'd do differently if you were to write such a letter.

Likes	Dislikes

Please remember that there is no magic formula or absolute *right* way to create such a message. When it comes to communicating, there are no answers, only choices. We can choose to convey certain information in certain ways, but ultimately the effectiveness of our message depends upon the receiver's interpretation. The best bet is to be authentic, be friendly, and express a sense of caring.

USE ROUTINE INFORMATIVE MESSAGES

Routine letters, memos, and e-mails are essential to almost any business. For many companies, they represent the bulk of business writing. Some common forms of routine writing include announcements, inquiries about products or services, letters granting a request, and letters of introduction. Customers appreciate well-written, effective routine messages and get frustrated by unclear or poorly written ones.

Routine messages answer questions (sometimes before they are asked), and the recipient of such a message is likely to be happy to get it. Routine messages also present opportunities for relationship building.

Below is an example of an announcement letter—a message that tells customers about some change and thus makes them feel connected to the organization.

Routine informative messages answer questions and provide opportunities for relationship building.

Bronson Security Systems

Keeping an Eye on Your Assets

Mr. Blaine Wilson, President
NuWay Technology
12777 Highway 50
Orlando, FL 27002

March 18, 2005

Dear Mr. Wilson:

At Bronson Security Systems, we're always looking for better ways to serve your needs for plant security. I think we've found another in Arnold (Bucky) Corridini.

Bucky has joined us as Coordinator of Surveillance Services. He will help us maintain and improve the high standard of quality service you've come to expect from Bronson.

Of all the candidates we considered for this position, we found Bucky offered the best combination of ability, enthusiasm, and professionalism. Most important, he is the kind of person we want working on your account at NuWay Technology—the best.

I'm confident you'll see this valuable addition to our staff as further evidence that we are committed to our clients. I've asked Bucky to personally introduce himself to you within the next week. If there's anything he or I can do for you, please call.

Thank you for doing business with us.

Sincerely,

Guido Lambini, President
BRONSON SECURITY SYSTEMS

The samples above give you a feel for the types of written messages that can be used to build customer relationships. Think about how you might change their tone or content to better fit your personal communication style. Remember, just because these appear in print in a book does not mean they are perfect for all occasions and audiences. Your personal touch can dramatically improve these, we suspect. Communication is an art, and you are the artist.

> *Get into the habit of critiquing the letters you receive. Then develop your own style.*

FOLLOW THREE GENERAL GUIDELINES FOR ROUTINE MESSAGES

Writers should apply the following principles when writing routine letters: be direct, be complete, and be friendly. A writer can do little to destroy the effectiveness of a blatant good-news message. When the intent is to tell readers something they are glad to hear or, at worst, are neutral toward, those readers will appreciate directness and value efficiency of communication. Keep goodwill letters brief and to the point, although not curt. Start with phrases such as "thank you" or "congratulations" to get to the point in a manner that people will appreciate.

Service Snapshot	The Ultimate Electronics Difference

Bill decided to buy his compact disc player at Ultimate Electronics. He'd heard positive things about the store and decided to give it a try. He had this to say of the experience:

> I personally get very frustrated when I go into a store and I have to find someone to help me. Fortunately, I was attended to at Ultimate Electronics. I learned what I needed to about the different models and then purchased the one that fit my needs. About a week later, I got a letter addressed to me with no return address. When I pulled out the small card inside the envelope and read it, I was pleasantly surprised. The Ultimate Electronics salesperson who helped me had sent a handwritten card to me thanking me for the recent purchase. Writing the card probably took the salesperson about two minutes, and the postage cost was minimal. However, this is a very small fee to win over a current customer for a lifetime. The thank-you card helped me have a personal experience with the company. I felt the employees at Ultimate Electronics actually cared I had come into the business. Ultimately, they cared I had helped them stay in business.

WRITE APPRECIATION MESSAGES

A note or letter expressing appreciation is always a treat for the recipient, and opportunities for these are almost unlimited. The format of such a message is less important than the tone. In fact, you can often be casual and creative in such messages so long as you project a pleasant tone. Handwritten notes can work as well as formally typed messages; personal notepaper can be used rather than letterhead.

The following ideas will make a note of appreciation stronger:

- *Mention or describe the specific actions, attitudes, or characteristics that you appreciate.*   Just saying "I appreciate you," is nice. But saying "I appreciate the way you are open to new ideas" or "I appreciate your help in providing me with . . . " is likely to have more impact.
- *Use the person's name in the body of the message.*   Don't overdo it—which may sound patronizing—but do personalize the message. Address the reader as you would when talking to him or her. Use the

person's first name, nickname, or a more formal address as appropriate. Don't call the reader "Bill" if you would normally call him "Mr. Kosinski." With customers, it is better to err on the side of being too formal, rather than too familiar (unless you know the customer well).

- *Be conversational.*   A goodwill letter should sound the way you would talk. Stuffiness or formality can damage the tone. Contractions ("*I'm*," "*we'd*," etc.) are fine, and even terms that are grammatically incorrect can create a chatty, pleasant tone ("Way-ta-go!" or "Ya made my day!" or "Lookin' forward to meeting your needs"). Of course, in some situations, more formal phrasing would be more appropriate. For example, a letter thanking a major client for a substantial purchase might necessitate careful or formal wording.

> *It never hurts to spread a little goodwill. In doing so, be personal and conversational.*

WRITE CONGRATULATIONS OR RECOGNITION MESSAGES

You can surprise customers and convey A-plus personality by sending unexpected notes of congratulations. Congratulations messages should generally follow the same guidelines as the appreciation note, although they may be slightly more formal. Be sure to include the following elements:

- description of the specific actions you are congratulating the reader for (graduation from the company's advance training program, promotion to a new position, bowling a 300 game, a son's advancement to Eagle Scout, etc.)
- expressions suggesting that you understand the effort that went into the achievement ("I know this reflects many hours of hard work," etc.)
- expressions of pride and support as appropriate ("I'm proud to have worked with you and want you to know you'll have my continued support in your new position")

EXPRESS SYMPATHY OR CONDOLENCES IN WRITING

You can strengthen goodwill when you are faced with the experience of sharing grief. Although unpleasant to consider, we inevitably will confront the need to communicate with those who are mourning. It is useful to understand something of the psychology of mourning.

Mourning involves the psychological task of breaking the bonds with that which has been lost and eventually reinvesting that attachment in living people and things. Society's death-related rituals, including the letter of condolence, play a significant role in repairing and restoring the emotional and social damage caused by death.

Well-meaning family and friends sometimes interfere with the grieving process by avoiding mention of the loss at the very time the bereaved need to confront it. By doing so, people prevent the bereaved from experiencing the reality of death and the full range of emotions necessary to accomplish a healthy resolution. Working through grief is the process of consciously admitting and accepting the loss—intellectually and emotionally. The ultimate goal of grief work is to be able to remember the loss without emotional pain and to direct emotions to the future.

The psychologically sound letter of condolence should help the bereaved person work through grief. You can accomplish this by following these guidelines:

- Acknowledge how you learned about and reacted to the death.
- Avoid euphemisms relating to death and to the deceased person. Refer to him or her by name, not "the dearly departed"; say "died," not "expired."
- Maintain a sincere, positive tone by focusing on the contributions of the deceased person. Perhaps relate a specific example of how he or she influenced your life.
- Avoid quoting poetry, rhetorical writing, or scripture unless you are certain that it will bring comfort. Your original thoughts are far more valued.
- Make a specific offer of assistance, if possible. Offer to help with child care or to house visiting relatives as appropriate. Anticipate your reader's needs, and try to be of service.

ADHERE TO A GENERAL PATTERN IN GOODWILL MESSAGES

A get-right-to-the-point approach usually works best in goodwill messages. Often the first words will be "thank you," "congratulations," "I appreciate," or "I am sorry to hear . . ." The pattern, format, or even the grammar of a goodwill message is less important than the fact that it was sent and reflects a sense of caring. Typically, a goodwill message will take only a few minutes to produce but will offer a great return in improved relationships.

Opportunities for goodwill notes come up almost daily. Write them often, and you take advantage of the opportunity to A-plus your "customers" by showing that you care about them.

CREATE GOODWILL FOR THE ORGANIZATION THROUGH NEWS RELEASES

The public version of a goodwill message may take the form of a news release. The intent is to convey good news or to shed light on some positive aspect of an organization via a message broadcast through print or electronic media. Although not personalized, such messages can help create a positive image for the company and attract customers.

Get Appropriate Publicity with News Releases

A well-written news release can be critical to any customer awareness campaign or image-building effort. While sending out news releases is an obvious part of getting mentioned in the media, creating real news about your product or service is actually the first step. The next step is identifying and contacting the appropriate media

> *Follow up any news releases you send to the media.*

to receive your news release. To get the best results, send your releases only to those media whose audiences are very likely to be interested in what you have to say. Then, follow up to improve the likelihood that the message will be broadcast or appear in print.

The follow-up often gets overlooked, but it is crucial to any publicity campaign. Make follow-up phone calls to the media contacts to make sure they received your release, but don't try to pressure them into running it. If they use it, be sure to thank them. If they don't, don't call and complain. If you think your news releases would be of interest to a certain medium's audience, keep sending them new information and following up. The more releases you send, the more likely one of them will eventually be run. Don't get discouraged; just keep trying. If your releases are newsworthy, with enough patience and persistence you'll get them placed.

Write the News Release

The basic tool for generating publicity (i.e., public goodwill) is the news release. With it companies can get free publicity from newspapers, magazines, radio, and television. Much of the news in newspapers and magazines comes from news releases sent out by companies, government agencies, associations, and various individuals and groups. News releases have obvious value as free ad-

> *News releases can be ways to convey A-plus information or personality.*

vertising but can also create A-plus information and A-plus personality possibilities.

You can use a common, easy-to-follow format for most successful news releases. It has several key elements: the originator (you), the release date, the contact, a headline, and the double-spaced text copy itself.

If you send the news release on your company stationery, that will take care of the originator. All you have to do is type "NEWS" or "NEWS RELEASE" in capital letters at the top of the letterhead.

The release date is the date you want the story released. In many cases, it can say "FOR IMMEDIATE RELEASE." This is probably best, unless there is some overriding reason why the story can't be released before a certain date. Other necessary information includes the name, email, and telephone number of a person to contact for further information.

The headline should appear in capital letters, six spaces below the contact line. It should be as clever and catchy as possible so it captures the attention and arouses the interest of the editor or producer. Newspaper headlines can be used as models of how to write news release headlines. Try for a headline that compels the reader to read the entire release.

Eight spaces below the headline, you should begin the body of the release. It should be double-spaced and written like a newspaper article, with the most important information in the first paragraph, the supporting information next, and the least important information last. A news release can be any length, but a one-page release is probably best. If you do use more than one page, place the word "MORE" in the bottom center of the first page.

You can use news releases to announce the start of your company, new products and services, speaking engagements, appearances on radio or television shows, or any other event connected with your company that has potential news value. Well-written, conversational releases can strengthen relationships with readers and customers.

Who you address your news releases to is extremely important. Newspapers and magazines have specialized editors, while each radio and television talk show has a specific producer. Your best chance for getting the publicity you desire is to direct your release to the appropriate editor or producer.

Because your release may be reprinted verbatim in some newspapers or organizational newsletters, spend ample time to compose clever, readable releases. In some cases, your release may even be used as the basis for a feature story.

> A press release (or news release) can be a great way to inform customers and potential customers about the goings-on in your company.

A good idea for your news release is to end with a "For more information" paragraph. Use this to give your company's contact information and to offer a free brochure or some other kind of promotional material. Doing this encourages people to go to your Web site or contact your business, giving you new prospects and an opportunity to gauge the relative impact of that particular coverage.

A FINAL THOUGHT

Written communication is often overlooked as a customer service tool. Many people are uncomfortable writing, but, by applying some simple techniques such as those discussed in this chapter, you can use the power of written messages to build customer relationships. Comedian Woody Allen's oft-quoted line "80 percent of all success is just showing up" applies to using written messages for customer service. Eighty percent of your success will be in simply doing it! Don't be overly worried about the "correctness" of your writing; just write the way you'd talk and let the customer know that you care enough to send a written message.

Writing principles apply to both paper documents and electronic ones (e.g., e-mail). Whenever a company creates a dialogue with its customers and other interested readers, it faces an opportunity for creating A-plus service. Written documents often convey A-plus information and always offer the potential for A-plus personality. Strong companies find ways to systematically and regularly use written messages to supplement their other customer service efforts.

Summary of Key Ideas

- Written messages (paper documents or e-mails) are often-overlooked tools for enhancing customer satisfaction and loyalty.
- Goodwill notes are those you send even though you don't have to. Their power arises from customers' surprise at receiving them.
- Originality helps boost the power of goodwill messages. Almost everybody sends Christmas cards; be more creative, and you'll get greater impact.
- Be direct and straightforward in routine messages. Get right to the point.
- Create goodwill via news releases about the organization. These can provide A-plus opportunities in both information and personality.

Key Concepts

appreciation messages

congratulations or recognition
  messages

follow-up letters or e-mails

goodwill

news release

routine informative messages

sympathy messages

Self-Test Questions

1. Summarize some key tips to apply when writing goodwill messages to customers.
2. Describe several situations in which a sales follow-up letter would be seen as an A-plus.
3. What is a routine message in business? Give an example.
4. What are three important steps to writing an appreciation letter?
5. What actions can improve your chances of getting a news release published?

Application Activity 1: Prepare a Generic Customer Thank-You Note

1. Using the guidelines in this chapter, draft a thank-you note that could be used for immediate follow-up with your customers. (Use an imaginary business if you are not currently employed.) Leave blank spaces where others in your organization could fill in details as they use the same format for their own thank-you notes. Suggest ideas for filling in those blanks.

Application Activity 2: Prepare a Practice News Release

1. Using the guidelines in this chapter, write a brief news release from "You, Inc." Announce a significant achievement or bit of information about you. (Don't worry too much about newsworthiness at this point—the purpose here is to practice following the news release format.)

Notes

1. H. Mackay. *Swim with the Sharks without Being Eaten Alive* (New York: William Morrow, 1988), p. 68.
2. P. R. Timm and J. A. Stead. *Communication Skills for Business and the Professions* (Upper Saddle River, NJ: Prentice Hall, 1996), p. 259.
3. S. Bienvenu and P. R. Timm. *Business Communication: Discovering Strategy, Developing Skills* (Upper Saddle River, NJ: Prentice Hall, 2002), p. 126.

Get Others to Give Great Service

Roles of the Supervisor, Manager, or Leader

If you want a good indication of the quality of your people management, ask your customers how they are being treated by your employees.

—Ken Blanchard[1]

WHAT YOU'LL LEARN IN THIS CHAPTER

- The central thread running through all management functions is communication, and organizations suffer when communication is ineffective.
- Lead people in articulating an effective customer service credo or theme.
- Set objectives and develop an effective customer satisfaction strategy.
- Some potentially disquieting, yet penetrating, questions can readily point to customer service problems.
- Manage the service process with questions.
- Instruct and motivate employees to provide quality customer service.
- Seven critical tasks can initiate and sustain an A-plus customer loyalty strategy.

THE WAY IT IS . . .
What Level of Service Do Managers Allow?

A recent national news magazine carried a letter from a reader responding to a story that was critical of the poor service given by a large retailer. This retailer had seen its profits fall dramatically. The reader wrote:

> I found [the story] extremely timely and on the mark. Having spent the past 20 years in sales and marketing, 10 of them in discount and upscale retail management, I still can't decide if the [company's] posture has been one of "you snooze, you lose" or simple corporate arrogance. Perhaps [the company] may just now be waking up to the fact that you can no longer abuse your customers and get away with it. Your article spoke of [an] example where only four checkout lanes out of 12 were open. We also see four checkout lanes open, with a dozen customers in each lane, the manager on duty and head cashier standing with arms crossed at the service desk surveying the chaos. On one trip, when I asked the manager why he didn't either open a register himself or bag items for the checkers, he responded that it wasn't his job.
>
> My heart goes out for the well-being of the quality folks who work at the stores. Regardless of their efforts, they can only raise the level of quality up to that point "allowed" by the corporate structure and support mechanisms.[2]

Is this reader fair in placing the blame for poor service on management? This chapter will consider that question as we examine the roles of managers and leaders in providing customer service.

DO THE WORK OF MANAGEMENT

As a reader of this book, you are very likely preparing for or currently working in a management position in an organization. By management position, I am referring to any situation in which a person supervises, coordinates, or leads the efforts of other people. The manager's job calls for an ability to get others to do the right things in addition to doing the right things oneself. The ability to multiply one's efforts explains why managers are typically paid more and why skilled managers are always in demand. Their impact on an organization can be dramatic. Employees tend to live up to—or down to—their manager's expectations of them.

UNDERSTAND THE KEY FUNCTIONS OF MANAGEMENT

Traditionally, the job of a manager is seen as consisting of four key functions: planning, organizing, coordinating, and controlling. Although this list may oversimplify a bit, it provides a good start for looking at the management process. Let's consider each function as it relates to customer service.

1. *Planning* is a thinking process—a sort of internal communication within one's mind. The manager looks ahead at what must be done to maintain and improve performance, to solve problems, and to develop employee competence. To plan, a manager sets objectives in each area that are to be pursued this week, this month, this year. Having set these objectives, the manager then thinks through such questions as:

- What has to be done to reach these objectives?
- How will these activities be carried out?
- Who will do them?
- When will these activities take place?
- Where will this work be done?
- What resources will be needed?

Done well, such planning requires asking questions of customers, both internal and external, and determining what to do in the future based on the input received.

> *Effective planning involves gathering information and projecting future outcomes.*

2. *Organizing* involves arranging the work sequence and assigning areas of responsibility and authority. Having decided the objectives and activities of the work unit, the manager must:

- assign these responsibilities to employees
- give employees the supporting authority to fulfill their responsibilities

Done well, this management work will reduce potential systems turnoffs caused by ineffective staffing, poor training, inefficient work layout, and so on. Remember that "systems" involve anything having to do with the delivery of products or services to the customer. (Review Chapter 2 to refresh your memory about customer turnoffs.) Constantly organizing and improving systems is a major leadership responsibility.

> *The management responsibility to reduce systems turnoffs often involves organizing.*

3. *Coordinating* is often summed up in the term *leading*. The manager leads by enabling the organization to achieve its objectives. To do this, he or she:

- shows (by example) what subordinates should do
- generates the energy (motivation) that subordinates should feel
- provides the needed resources to accomplish the tasks

What leaders do in an organization sets the tone for motivation throughout. Motivation can be simply defined as "providing motives for action." Leaders provide motives or reasons why people should act in particular ways.

Controlling is a process of following up to be certain that planned-for actions are, in fact, being carried out. Managers inspect what they expect.

4. *Controlling* is the function of ensuring that employees are working toward the selected objectives. It involves comparing actual results to expected or planned-for results so as to identify any needed deviation from plan. Typically, any deviation calls for using different motivation attempts, adjusting activities to close the gap, or changing the objectives to be more realistic.

The essence of the manager's job is to accomplish work with and through other people.

The common thread in each of these management functions is that they involve *people*. Herein lies the universal characteristic of the manager's job: only when managers *accomplish work with and through other people* are they doing the job correctly.

RECOGNIZE HOW GOOD MANAGEMENT REQUIRES GOOD COMMUNICATION

To ensure the smooth functioning of any organization, managers must maintain an ongoing flow of appropriate communication. Communication is crucial to all management functions.

Organizations fail to maximize their effectiveness and create customer service problems when too little communication takes place, too much communication is attempted, or ineffective communication is widespread. Let's consider each of these conditions.

Too Little Communication

Crumbling relationships and dysfunctional families often result from too little communication. Countless marriages fail primarily because couples withhold expressions of appreciation, concern, or ideas. Husbands and wives who cannot express their feelings to each other in marriage seldom succeed as a family organization.

Keeping people informed and getting a constant flow of information from stakeholders are strategies of strong organizations.

Likewise, businesses in which customers are not asked about their needs, employees have insufficient product knowledge, or employees don't know what behaviors are appropriate run a huge risk of internal confusion and poor service success. Good organizations keep their people well trained and fully informed. Great organizations constantly solicit information from stakeholders (all people who share an interest in the company's success) and act upon it.

Too Much Communication

Going to the opposite extreme can be a problem, too. People who find themselves bombarded with too much information, much of it irrelevant, may collapse under the load. This is the organizational equivalent of the old quip "I asked him what time it was, and he told me how to build a watch." Smart companies keep people in-

> *Communication overload can cripple an organization and damage employee productivity.*

formed of things they need to know or may want to know, but don't bombard them with trivia or too much detail. The problem of spam on the Internet is a classic and growing symptom of overcommunication.

Widespread Ineffective Communication

Widespread ineffective communication also results in organizational failure for several reasons. Among the most common are unclear direction or coordination, inadequate processing of important data, and missed organizational opportunities. Some examples of ineffective communication with customers may be unclear or burdensome company policies, poorly planned product information meetings, failure to publicize accomplishments, poor telephone or Web site techniques, or ineffective writing.

RECOGNIZE THAT CUSTOMERS LIKE ORGANIZATIONS THAT COMMUNICATE WELL

I've asked thousands of people at training sessions to think about places they regularly do business; I then asked for specific reasons why they kept going back. In every group I'd get responses like these:

- The servers (or proprietors or clerks) are really friendly. They call me by name and seem genuinely interested in me.
- Sudha always knows how I like my food cooked.
- Old Phil at the gas station waves when I drive by.
- Mike the butcher listens to me when I ask for a special cut of meat.
- Sarah's so friendly—she's always willing to help.
- Dr. Chan's nurses are really nice. They seem to take a real interest in the kids.
- The call center people are always friendly and helpful.

The words in these responses are different, but the theme is almost always the same: the organization, through its people, *communicates* a sense of caring. Conversely, researchers for the Forum Corporation interviewed customers

> *The greatest cause of lost customers: they feel badly treated.*

> *A lack of caring is clearly communicated, even if not in words.*

lost in business-to-business relationships (one business buying from another). The research concluded that 69 percent of those business customers who stopped buying were lost not because of product quality or cost, but because they felt badly treated.[3] Good communication goes a long way to reduce such feelings.

When I have asked people what organizations they "hate to do business with," respondents cite organizations whose people convey a sense that "you [the customer] are an intrusion," "we really don't care whether you are satisfied or not," "I hate my job and it's partly your fault," or "I can't be bothered with you now." Employees don't say these things out loud, of course, but they do convey these impressions.

An obvious and significant challenge for managers is to be sensitive to the ways their employees communicate to the world around them—especially customers. If communication processes are not being handled well, managers need to provide training, hire people with better attitudes, or initiate some reward system that encourages better communication.

REMEMBER THAT THE CUSTOMER DETERMINES COMMUNICATION SUCCESS

Having said that managers need to encourage good communication, we need to also recognize the limitations of such efforts. A critical point about

> *Although we cannot ultimately control communication, we can learn effective ways to influence it.*

the nature of communication is important to note: *we really can't control communication.* We can, and must, seek to influence it, but ultimately it is the customer who determines the meaning of any messages we send. This inconvenient reality is frustrating to people who naively think they can control 100 percent of their communication outcomes. It's not that simple.

Communicating with another person is not a science; it is an art. No magic checklist of precise and exacting procedures exists. Specific, sound principles and themes can be learned, but there are thousands of variations on these themes. When it comes to communicating, there are no answers, only choices. Managers need to encourage people to make good choices about interacting with customers.

Developing the art of communication often means letting go of old assumptions—getting out of the comfortable rut of communicating as usual. Improvement has little to do with talking more loudly, more emphatically, more earnestly. It may have little to do with increasing the amount of information we give others. It has little to do with making the message sound better. It has everything to do with *developing more under-standing.* This means looking at the world through the eyes of others, walking the proverbial mile in another's moccasins. Most of us are hesitant to do this, but it is exactly this kind of thinking that leads to meaningful improvement in communication.

EMPLOY SPECIFIC MANAGEMENT FUNCTIONS FOR CUSTOMER SERVICE

Let's take a closer look at key management functions as they apply to customer service. Several specific actions we can take to work with and through other people can make a dramatic impact on customer satisfaction and loyalty. Below, these are described as action tips for managers.

Action Tip 1: Articulate a Service Theme

The manager's planning function includes efforts to articulate a vision forecasting where the organization would like to go. One idea found useful for many organizations is to develop a service theme, credo, or mission statement.

As I consult with organizations, I typically ask if they have a customer service theme or credo. Fairly often I get answers something like this: "Oh, yes, we have 13 points to excellent customer service." I'd reply, "Oh, really? What's point 11?" and the manager would say, "Well, I don't know exactly." Then I'd ask, "Well, how about point 6? Which one's that?" And again the typical answer is, "I'm not sure; I actually haven't memorized all these things, but every employee has a copy and we post our mission statement throughout the company."

Unfortunately, if the credo is too complex, it doesn't do much good. To articulate a theme means to come up with a succinct, clear statement of what the organization is about and how it could be seen as unique in the eyes of the customer.

Let's go through that one more time. An effective service theme must be:

- succinct
- clear
- descriptive of uniqueness

Someone once said that one criterion for a good mission statement or theme is that "you could repeat it at gunpoint!"[4]

The reason you want it succinct and clear is so that all employees can remember and "buy into" this as a guiding statement that will shape their actions and help them make decisions.

Let's look at a couple of examples.

Federal Express, the package delivery service, has a simple, clear theme. They express it in three words: "Absolutely, positively overnight." They will get the packages there absolutely, positively overnight, and they're 99.8 percent successful at doing that. The direct marketing clothier Lands' End has a simple motto/credo with just two words: "Guaranteed. Period." Both of these themes communicate the company's highest customer service priority.

A *Harvard Business Review*[5] article told of a Seattle restaurant staff who wrestled with this idea of a simple, clear theme. After carefully looking at the company through the eyes of the customer—just what does our restaurant guest want from us?—they came up with this theme: "Your enjoyment guaranteed. Always." That is exactly what they offer their guests, enjoyment.

A neat thing about this simple theme was that people could buy into it, and in fact they made it into an acronym: YEGA. While YEGA may not mean anything to most of us, it became a catchword for their organization. They developed YEGA promotions and YEGA bucks and YEGA pins and hats to get their employees involved in the spirit of YEGA. It was fun, it was interesting, and it reminded the employees constantly of that simple four-word theme: "Your enjoyment guaranteed. Always."

Here is what managers can do to articulate a good theme:

- Commit to work on the process of identifying a theme that is *succinct, clear, and descriptive of your uniqueness.*

- *Gather ideas from your customers (internal and external).* Ask them, "As customers, what five things do you want in doing business with us?" Ask them to respond quickly off the top of their heads, and look at the language they use.

- *Similarly, gather ideas from your own people in the organization.* Ask them, "If you were our customer, what five things would you like to get from a company like ours?" Ask employees to respond quickly. Jot down the language, and then collect all of the words. Front-line people know the customers best and can give you great ideas. Never overlook the ideas of this group of experts.

> *Listen for keywords from customers and customer-contact employees as you develop a theme.*

As you gather perceptions from customers and employees, you'll notice that some terms come up over and over again. These typically are the kinds of words that will reassure your customer. These are good words to put into your customer service theme.

As you draft a theme for your organization, remember:

- Participation and input from customers and employees are very important. The customers can best tell you what they're looking for in an organization like yours, and the employees' participation will ensure that they will accept and, hopefully, live by the intention of the theme.

- Write several rough drafts of the theme; don't be too quick to come up with the finished version. Phrase the final version in 10 words or fewer.
- If possible, try to make the theme into an acronym, in which the first letters of each word form a word in themselves. The YEGA example given earlier represents such an acronym.

When you've devised a statement of uniqueness, ask yourself the question, would everyone in the organization choose roughly the same words you chose to describe this distinctiveness? A simple way to verify this is to grab some of your employees and ask them to describe the organization's theme. Especially invite an employee who's been with the organization for 10 days or less to identify the theme.

What good does it do just to be able to repeat such a phrase? The answer is that it's a start. Repeating some words may seem meaningless at first, but most organizations fall far short of even that level of agreement. Focusing your people on a common theme can be well worth the effort.

One final note: A theme is not necessarily forever. As an organization changes directions, or as markets or economic conditions change, a theme may be modified. Some organizations may want to use a theme statement for a limited period of time, much the way advertisers use a slogan for only a few years. Modifying the theme should not, however, be done without careful thought. Consistency of direction is in itself valuable.

> *Be sure to involve employees and customers in developing a service theme.*

Remember this important fact: by having employees participate in clarifying a theme, they will feel more committed to it. Participation leads to buy-in. This has been shown time and again since the earliest studies in human relations.

Action Tip 2: Set Objectives and Develop a Service Strategy

The next management planning function involves determining desired service end results and deciding how and when to achieve service goals. Goal setting has long been recognized as a powerful tool for focusing effort. Be sure that targeted improvements are measurable and reasonable. Changes in organizational behaviors and results take time. Don't rush the process. Goal setting helps establish the priorities, sequence, and timing of strategy steps. You can't fix everything at once, so look for the kinds of results that can give you the most impact relative to the effort involved. Pick the low-hanging fruit first. Handling obvious shortcomings can motivate the troops to tackle the more difficult problems later.

Managers typically need to budget for improvements. Many changes, especially those that attack systems or value turnoffs, require the expenditure of money or other resources. Once better methods are developed, establish them as policy—as standing decisions on how the organization is to work. Later in this chapter you'll find a seven-step process for creating an ongoing strategy.

Action Tip 3: Organize People and Delegate Authority

The organizing function of management involves such actions as clarifying the organizational structure, assigning certain responsibilities, and giving authority to organization members. People at all levels need to know the scope and range of their job. Employees need to understand what they can or cannot do for the customer.

Among companies giving legendary service, people at all levels are given a lot of latitude. Nordstrom employees know they can do almost anything to meet a customer's needs. They have been known to send clothing to customers using overnight delivery (regardless of the additional cost) and to give customers an add-on to make up for any customer disappointment. Ritz-Carlton hotel employees are encouraged to take personal "ownership" for any problem a guest may have. If a guest's need comes to their attention, they drop what they are doing and solve the problem or meet the guest's request. Bellhops have been known to rush out of the hotel to buy a foreign newspaper for a guest who was disappointed that the publication wasn't available in the hotel's gift shop. No questions asked, managers have given bellhops the authority to do whatever it takes. This may be one reason that Ritz-Carlton won the prestigious Malcolm Baldrige National Quality Award for corporate excellence.

Action Tip 4: Staff with Quality Employees

Managers are responsible for recruiting qualified people for each employee position, orienting new people to the company's service expectations, and providing training so that people become proficient by instruction and practice.

Some successful managers recruit by stealing good employees from other companies. (That may be stated a bit indelicately, but the principle works.) As managers come across people with great attitudes and excellent customer service skills, they might try to hire them away or at least recommend them to company recruiters.

One owner of a chain of fast-food restaurants solved his problem of getting quality people in a high-turnover industry by giving his business card to employees of other companies who wait on him. He'd say something like, "Thank you for your great service. You did a nice job. If you are ever interested in changing jobs, I'd appreciate it if you'd call me personally. I'm sure I could find a place for you in my organization."

Managers can recruit good people by inviting employees who give great service to join their company.

An ongoing process should be to keep a file of people you'd like to have working for you; when an opening occurs, contact them. Don't worry if they are working in a totally different type of business. The specifics of your organization can be taught. Great attitudes cannot.

Once new employees are hired, managers need to be sure that they have ample opportunity to develop their knowledge, attitudes, and skills. The best jobs are those that allow people to grow.

Action Tip 5: Direct the Company's Efforts

Managers fulfill their directing functions by delegating. This means assigning responsibility and accountability for service results to the people they manage. They also need to motivate by persuading and inspiring people to take desired action. Other directing functions include coordinating desired efforts in the most efficient combination, managing differences, resolving conflicts, and stimulating creativity and innovation in achieving service goals. All these duties should be performed with an eye to how they will affect customers.

Action Tip 6: Control the Organization

Managers need to determine what critical service data are needed to track important results. They can then benchmark (measure and track) key results and compare them with the original goals or standards. Control also involves taking corrective action by coaching people to help them attain standards or by adjusting the plan as needed.

Gathering customer feedback data as discussed in Chapter 2 is critical. Online systems like Allegiance Technologies' Active Listening System can provide managers with metrics that capture customer input and time the company's responsiveness to the customer. The more quickly a company responds, the better. Measure responsiveness—it is critical to customer loyalty.

Action Tip 7: Manage the Reward System

Finally, providing rewards is a crucial part of controlling and motivating. Managers should be very precise about which behaviors and actions they reward and which they do not (or maybe even punish). Unfortunately, sometimes reward systems do exactly what they should not do—they tend to reinforce the wrong behaviors. For example, if managers encourage salespeople to work as teams to meet customer needs, but then give a bonus to only one person, the reward defeats its intention. If companies pay people by the hour, they are rewarding people for using up time, without regard for what they accomplish in that

> *Managers need to be very careful to reward actions that benefit customers and not reward the wrong things.*

time. If managers reward department heads for not getting any complaints, the system may be stifling valuable customer feedback. (Critical feedback is a *good* thing!) Management approaches that reward people for accomplishing work that is crucial to the organization (and do not reward counterproductive actions) may require some creativity on the part of managers.

Self-Analysis   Some Potentially Disquieting Questions

A starting point for determining how well an organization is doing with customer service may be to answer questions like the ones below. A positive response to one or more of these may not be devastating, but if you answer "yes" to most of them, your organization is likely to face an uphill battle to substantially improve customer service.

Does your company, organization, or department

1. Talk about customer service but pay front-line people a low, flat wage?
2. Offer little or no training in appropriate customer service behaviors for customer contact people?
3. Offer no special incentives for taking exceptional care of the customer?
4. Punish or reprimand employees for poor customer service but take good service for granted?
5. Place greater emphasis on winning new customers than retaining ones it already has?
6. Offer no awards or recognition for behind-the-scene staff's efforts to indirectly serve customers?
7. Hold "be nice to the customer" programs or campaigns that last for a few weeks or months but are soon forgotten?
8. Have top managers who rarely if ever devote time working on the front line, listening to customers, and helping them solve problems?
9. Make no effort to carefully measure service quality as perceived by customers?
10. Make no attempt to hold managers at all levels accountable for service and reward them on the basis of service?
11. Punish departments for receiving customer comments (including complaints) that may be useful feedback?
12. Give lip service to teamwork on behalf of the customer but really reward individual competitiveness that may work against the customer?
13. Have a service slogan or motto that no one really thinks about? One that is too complicated to remember? One that gives lip service but has little impact on daily decision making?

Most managers would have to answer "yes" to several of the above questions. That, in itself, is not an indicator of poor service policies, but it could point to some potential problem areas. And the process of asking lots of penetrating questions can be a valuable management activity.

MANAGE WITH QUESTIONS

Author Bill Maynard agrees that the art of management often involves asking lots of questions. He recommends that as managers interact with people throughout the organization as well as with customers, they ask questions like these:

What made you mad today?
What took too long?
What caused complaints today?
What was misunderstood today?
What costs too much?
What was too complicated?
What was just plain silly?
What job involved too many people?
What job involved too many actions?
What was wasted?[6]

An effective manager would be wise to commit these questions to memory and ask them often. Then, of course, it is crucial that managers act on the answers people give as best as possible.

Self-Analysis   Understand Your Feedback Receptiveness Attitude

Think back to the last time you received criticism from someone else. Recall a specific event or situation, and describe it in a few sentences. Now, mentally review the situation. To what degree did you:

1. hold back on defending or explaining yourself until the criticism was fully expressed?

2. work to understand the criticizer's point of view as best you could?

3. ask for elaboration or clarification without being overly defensive?

4. express an honest reaction?

5. thank the person for the feedback?

For most people, *giving* criticism (even in a constructive way) is risky. When people first offer such feedback, they watch closely to gauge the receiver's responses. The reaction they receive will usually determine whether they will offer feedback again. This means that *you* have the opportunity to avoid turning off future feedback that could be valuable to you.

Overall, how would you rate your feedback attitude in the above situation? What might you change, if anything?

SPEND TIME TO INSTRUCT AND MOTIVATE EMPLOYEES

"Management by walking around" has, in recent years, been seen as an increasingly important function of the manager. Doing so increases opportunities for giving recognition and gaining insights from the people "on the firing line." The payoff goes beyond mere pleasant interpersonal relations; it shows up in better motivation and clearer communication among organization members.

A manager can have a profound effect on his or her employees by simply thanking or complimenting them. It sounds simplistic, but the fact remains that, as Robert Townsend said in *Up the Organization*, "Thanks [are] a really neglected form of compensation."[7]

EXPRESS APPROVAL TO CREATE WORKER MOTIVATION

Management consultants have applied systematic approaches to expressing verbal approval that have demonstrated remarkable results. What is a *systematic* approach to expressing verbal approval? The most common one is based on a psychological strategy called *behavior modification*.

Managers typically implement such a systematic program by first holding a series of meetings in which managers and employees discuss mutual needs and problems as well as potential solutions. Key data are benchmarked to measure a starting point. These diagnostic sessions provide a base for determining job performance standards and how they will be met. The meetings also identify rewards that managers may use to "modify" the employees' behavior.

The second step is to arrange for worker performance to be observed with a reliable follow-up; the third is to give feedback often, immediately letting employees know how their current level of performance compares with the level desired. For example, in one early attempt, an airline company with five telephone reservation offices employing about 1,800 people kept track of the percentage of calls in which callers made flight reservations. Then they fed back the results daily to each employee. At the same time, supervisors were instructed to praise employees for asking callers for their reservations. Within a few months, the ratio of sales to calls soared from one in four to one in two.[8] It was as simple as counting how often employees asked for the customer's business.

> *The objective of a systematic approval program is to reward systematically—to tie the reward to specific performance.*

USE THE PSYCHOLOGY OF CHANGE

At the heart of any performance improvement is the premise that *future behavior is influenced by the outcomes of past behavior*. If the outcome immediately following an act is in some way rewarding, people are likely to repeat the behavior. If the response is punishing, people are likely to not do it again. Managers, then, can provide three types of communicated responses to employee behaviors. The normal effects of each response on employee behavior are shown below.

Manager's Response to Employee Behavior	Effects of Response
Positive reinforcement . . .	encourages employee to repeat the behavior
Negative reinforcement . . .	encourages employee to avoid the behavior in the future
No observable response at all . . .	usually causes the employee to extinguish the behavior (no incentive for continuing is given)

Some people question just how far we can go with verbal approval as a motivator. Theoretically, it should work indefinitely so long as appropriate *schedules of reinforcement* are used. The two main reinforcement schedules are *continuous* and *intermittent*. Continuous reinforcement means the individual receives reinforcement (a compliment or supportive statement) every time he or she engages in the desired behavior. This approach is useful when the person is being taught a new behavior and needs to be shored up to develop confidence in this new ability. People learn very quickly, at least initially, under continuous reinforcement.

> *Continuous reinforcement gets quick performance results initially.*

You can readily see the results of continuous reinforcement when teaching a small child how to do something like catching a ball. If you praise the child each time the ball is caught, the child will develop this skill very quickly. The principle generally holds true for employees working on unfamiliar tasks.

Yet the use of continuous reinforcement poses at least three problems:

1. It takes too much time and therefore costs a great deal in terms of supervisory effort. It is just not feasible always to be there complimenting each job done—managers might as well do the job themselves!

2. It can diminish in effectiveness because of "inflation." Verbal approval can be cheapened by overuse.

3. Once continuous reinforcement is expected, it is tough to wean people away from it without certain risks. If we suddenly drop continuous reinforcement—that is, we no longer express verbal approval for each good behavior—the message to our worker may be that the behavior is no longer appropriate and should be stopped. In short, we may extinguish the desired behavior.

The drawbacks to continuous reinforcement are largely overcome by shifting to *intermittent reinforcement*. Here, instead of expressing approval of every act, managers use another system to allocate compliments. They may decide to express approval at intervals, or each time a particular type of task is completed—say, a difficult customer is recovered.

Random, intermittent reinforcement can lead to longer-term motivation.

Another intermittent reinforcement approach is to provide rewards at completely random times. Much of the lure of slot machine gambling comes from the anticipated random windfall. The anticipation or hope of a sudden big reward keeps the players engaged in the "desired behavior"—putting money in the slot. Random rewarding with unexpected bonuses can have this effect.

Under random, intermittent reinforcement, the worker doesn't know exactly when he or she will be rewarded. So long as the employee holds hope of eventually receiving a reward such as verbal approval, extinction of the desired behavior is delayed. If the rewards are too far apart, of course, the worker will not continue to produce unless he or she is particularly good at working hard today for some far-off but certain-to-be-worthwhile reward. Relatively few workers these days are content to "get their reward in heaven."

The best approach is to use continuous reinforcement when new behaviors are being developed and then gradually move to an intermittent schedule so the desired performance won't be inadvertently extinguished. In other words, shift employees' expectations so that longer intervals between reinforcement are seen as normal.

USE APPROPRIATE PRAISE AND CRITICISM

Sometimes praise is downright embarrassing and so-called constructive criticism just plain makes you mad. Morrison and O'Hearne have developed an explanation of why praise and criticism seem to have such an on-again, off-again value.[9] These authors suggest that both praise and criticism can be broken down into two types. Type 1 praise consists of those statements that have little effect on the performance of the receiver. They are accepted like water off a duck's back. Type 2 praise consists of those statements that *might* have a positive effect on performance under certain circumstances. There are no guarantees, but these kinds of "attaboys" and "attagirls" might motivate or at least build stronger relationships between the giver and the receiver. Some examples of Type 1 and Type 2 praise are offered in Figure 9.1.[10] A similar classification of criticism is illustrated in Figure 9.2.[11] Type 1 criticism results in defensiveness and deterioration of performance, while Type 2 criticism is at least potentially constructive in that it *might* result in improved future performance.

GIVE CLEAR INSTRUCTIONS

Two-way methods of giving instructions work best.

Often the most frequent communication managers have with employees is giving orders, directions, or instructions. Although some bosses think of this as one-way, boss-to-subordinate communication, a two-way format is usually far more appropriate.

Type 1 praise—Has little effect on performance of the receiver.	Type 2 praise—May have a positive effect on performance and build an authentic relationship.
1. Generalized praise such as, "You're doing a good job, Charlie." This is meaningless and it generally rolls off the back of the individual without effect.	1. Specific praise—such as, "Charlie, you did a great job handling that unpleasant customer with a complaint this afternoon." This communicates to the receiver that the boss has actually observed or heard about the praised action.
2. Praise with no further meaning. There is no analysis of why a praised behavior is being commended. This discounts the persons being praised by assuming they will react with higher productivity and better morale merely as a response.	2. Continuing with, "The reason I think it was such a good job is because you acted interested, asked questions, wrote down the facts, asked the customer what she thought we should do to make it right." Analysis of this kind permits the employee to internalize the learning experience.
3. Praise for expected performance, when such praise may be questioned. Mabel, who always gets in on time and is met one morning with, "Mabel, you're sure on time today, you're doing great," from her boss, may wonder what's really going on.	3. Praise for better-than-expected results, for coming in over quota, exceeding the target, putting out extra effort.
4. The "sandwich" system—praise is given first to make the person be receptive to criticism (the real reason for the transaction), which is then followed by another piece of praise, hoping thereby to encourage the person to try harder next time, and feel better about the criticism.	4. Praise, when deserved, is believable when it is given by itself; when mixed with critique it is suspect. Authentic relations develop better when people talk straight. When positive conditional recognition is in order, give it; when critique is deserved, give that. Don't mix the two.
5. Praise perceived by the receiver as given in the nature of a "carrot," mainly to encourage the receiver to work even harder in the future.	5. Praise that is primarily to commend and recognize, and does not seek to put a mortgage on the future.
6. Praise handed out lavishly only when the brass or higher-ups are present. Employees soon recognize the boss is trying to impress superiors with what a good human being he or she really is in dealing with subordinates.	6. Praise given when it is deserved, not just on special occasions, or when it seems to build the image of the praiser to some third party.

FIGURE 9.1   Ineffective versus effective praise. (From Morrison, James H., and O'Hearne, John J., *Practical Transactional Analysis in Management*. Reading, MA: Addisson-Wesley, 1977. Reprinted with permission.)

Type 1 criticism—Tends to produce a defensive reaction in the receiver and worsen performance.	Type 2 criticism—A type of constructive criticism that may improve performance.
1. Criticism that involves use of the personal "you," e.g., "You're having too many accidents on the lift truck, Bill. What's the matter with you anyway?" It is almost always seen as a discount or put-down by the receiver.	1. Criticism using a situational description, e.g., "Bill, we're experiencing an increase in lift-truck accidents. What's going on?" This indicates the manager is open to looking at all the facts leading to the unfavorable result.
2. Criticism that is unanalyzed. The subordinate then tends to rationalize the criticism as a personal opinion of the manager. Or, the manager is viewed as unable to analyze the problems effectively.	2. Discussion of cause and effect with the unfavorable condition perceived by both as the result of one or more causal factors, one of which might even be the manager!
3. If the situation has been properly assessed, some managers are at a loss to provide coaching necessary for the subordinate to improve. This may be the result of ignorance or lack of competency in deciding on the corrective steps.	3. If steps 1 and 2 above have been properly accomplished, it is important for solutions to be outlined and agreed on. If the subordinate can't do this, the manager must provide, or arrange for, a resource that can develop corrective measures.
4. Critique of an individual in public is not only regarded as humiliating by the subordinate involved, but sometimes even more so by other members of the organization.	4. Individual criticism given in private is usually more acceptable. Saving face is almost as important in Western cultures as it is in the Orient.
5. Criticism given *only* in the interests of the boss (to get the boss recognition, promotion, or raise) or the organization (more profit or status in the marketplace). These may all be legitimate interests, but *authentic* relationships are not likely to develop.	5. Criticism given *also*, or even chiefly, in the interests of the employee (to provide greater competencies, future achievements, or a more secure future with the organization).
6. The manager does all the critiquing, which sets the stage for a Parent-Child [relationship].	6. The subordinate participates in the critiques, even to the point of taking the lead role in defining the unsatisfactory condition, analyzing causes, and suggesting corrective steps.
7. Criticism used as a [calculated] game to justify withholding raises or promotions.	7. Game-free criticism leading toward candor and [authentic interactions].

FIGURE 9.2 Destructive versus constructive criticism. (From Morrison, James H., and O'Hearne, John J., *Practical Transactional Analysis in Management.* Reading, MA: Addisson-Wesley, 1977. Reprinted with permission.)

As managers, we need to know exactly what action we want to result from instructions given. That seems self-evident. Yet this step is occasionally overlooked. When we give an employee instructions to "be more responsive to customers," we may not have a clear picture of exactly what behavior we want to see. Instead we need to mentally clarify our purpose—our reason for giving the order—and then *plan* the best way of creating understanding with the employee.

The phrase "be more responsive" will likely have different meanings for different people. An effective instruction giver will create a clearer picture of what he or she wants by supplying some details, such as, "You need to greet customers within 10 seconds when they come into the store."

> *Use clear, concrete terms when giving instructions.*

Providing sufficient details and repetition are good ways to minimize misunderstandings. The journalist's "who, what, where, when, why, and how" provide a good framework for giving instructions. Be sure you know the answers to each of these questions before directing someone else. And be sure to encourage questions from the message receiver.

Asking, "Do you have any questions?" probably isn't the best technique. That question calls for a "yes" or "no" response, and many people opt for "no" to avoid showing ignorance. By changing the wording to "What questions do you have?" you say to the employee, "It's okay to have questions," and you encourage task clarification. Be sure to pause long enough to let your listeners know you are serious about taking questions from them.

INITIATE AND SUSTAIN AN A-PLUS CUSTOMER LOYALTY STRATEGY

Managers can "operationalize" good intentions into a workable A-plus strategy by implementing the seven key tasks described briefly below.[12] These need not always be done in the order presented, but several will be done concurrently.

Task #1: Orient All Employees

Take steps to ensure that all employees clearly understand the need for cultivating customer loyalty. Teach them about the cost of lost customers, how lost customers lead to lost jobs, why poor service givers pay a psychological price, and why it is in their best interest to develop customer service professionalism. This step is typically done via a series of training sessions.

Also, through training, strive to get employees speaking the same language. Be sure they know the importance of little things and service attitudes, such as A-plus and turn-off categories, for example.

Task #2: Build Momentum

Conduct regular follow-up departmental meetings after the initial training. Teach basic creativity and group problem-solving skills; schedule and conduct regular brainstorming sessions to discuss possible new A-plus ideas. Show individuals and work groups how to set departmental or team goals.

Coordinate a reward system so that the most useful activities get the best rewards. Create a reward committee to decide special bonuses, determine budget, and define the criteria whereby people can win the rewards. Then develop data-gathering forms/processes that give credit for good works. Distribute "attaboy, attagirl" cards or small rewards to recognize success immediately.

Task #3: Monitor Customer Expectations and Employee Behavior

Teach "naive listening" techniques to employees. Recognize the value of unhappy customers as sources of improvement ideas. Install an active listening system. Schedule focus groups regularly on the calendar. Record, digest, and keep data and trends analyses.

At the same time, conduct regular shopper surveys to determine the kinds of services people are getting from employees. These should typically be done by independent "shopper services" that provide immediate and specific feedback to employees.

Task #4: Establish Systematic Customer Retention/ Follow-up Efforts

Develop creative customer follow-up techniques. Schedule regular follow-ups with mail-outs, phone calls, announcements, and special incentives. Try other loyalty builders such as customer photos or letters posted on display. Perhaps establish a "Customer of the Month " recognition.

Task #5: Provide Continuation Training for Employees

Schedule repeat "basic" training for new employees. Also schedule regular continuation training sessions, where employees can receive instruction on tasks such as writing customer correspondence, handling difficult people, improving telephone techniques, and mastering time and task management.

Task #6: Conduct Ongoing Systems Reviews

Create a task force to review systems. Employ explorer groups to visit competitors or similar businesses that have good ideas. Create a suggestion program to improve systems by announcing and publicizing the program, budgeting award money, creating forms, and forming a review committee to evaluate suggestions submitted.

Task #7: Recruit, Develop, and Retain Excellent Employees

Attract and select exceptional service personnel by developing aptitude/attitude testing and interviewing procedures. Proactively invite promising employees from other businesses to join you.

Once they've been hired, be sure to clarify promotion criteria and tie these criteria to the customer service reward system. In short, base employee advancement on service attitudes and skills. As part of this process, be sure to conduct meaningful performance reviews in which service criteria are measured and factored.

Another Look	Peer Coaching: How to Manage when Managers Are Few and Far Between[13]

Once upon a time not very long ago, the average supervisor had responsibility for 5 to 15 people. In today's world of downsized, re-engineered organizations, that figure is closer to 30. The result is, as one frustrated service manager expressed to me: "We don't do management—we do crowd control."

Yet the need for coaching to achieve high-quality service is greater than ever. The solution of choice: peer coaching. Employees of the same level, without the traditional leverage of a boss-subordinate relationship, are being asked to coach one another on substandard and problematic performance.

How's it working? It has its enthusiasts and skeptics.

The negatives are easy to imagine. If you've ever been approached by someone offering to "give you a little feedback," you know the potential problems. On the positive side, peers well trained in the nuances of effective interpersonal communication can be an asset. If you've ever had a colleague pull you aside to warn you the boss is on a tear so you shouldn't bring up the Johnson account, or simply to let you know something was unzipped or stuck between your teeth, you know how valuable peer feedback can be.

Peer coaching—some people prefer to call it peer support—succeeds when the conditions are right and the ground rules clear. Specifically, a successful peer coaching venture requires a supportive environment, awareness of the limits of peer coaching, and tolerance for clumsy communication.

SUPPORTIVE ENVIRONMENT

If your organization has a history of interdepartmental warfare—marketing and operations only speak through their UN ambassadors, manager-to-manager relations are characterized by jealousy

(continued)

Another Look	**Peer Coaching: How to Manage when Managers Are Few and Far Between** *continued*

[and] back-biting and nasty barbs at 20 paces, and employees only hear "well done" when they are ordering steak—then peer coaching will fail in your organization in about 2.5 minutes.

If your organization tolerates mistakes as learning opportunities, not time for punishment, peer coaching has a good chance for success.

AWARENESS OF THE LIMIT

Peer coaching is not a panacea. Rather, it is a way of leveraging your skill as a coach by investing some of it in others. It is a supplement rather than a substitute for the coaching you provide. And it definitely is not a way to get out from under the responsibility of dealing directly with employees who have chronic performance problems. That is never a peer responsibility. Peer coaching—all coaching—is about working together with people to build individual and team success.

There are three fundamental axioms to swear allegiance to:

1. *Peer coaching is not back-seat driving.* Peer coaching is about giving direct, clear feedback and advice, and only doing so with permission or when solicited.

2. *Peer coaching is not group therapy.* No one in the workplace has a right to probe anyone else's psyche or motivations. The peer coaching process is about "The facts, Ma'am, just the facts." And a limited set of facts—observable, amenable work behavior.

3. *Helping out is the spirit of peer coaching.* Peer coaching is not a license to blow off steam or give a colleague a piece of your mind. The onus is on the giver to answer three questions before offering Charlie a little help:

   - Is Charlie having trouble with a customer, colleague, or situation, or are you uncomfortable with the way Charlie does things?

   - Is the problem clearly Charlie's—as opposed to a problem Charlie is involved in but not one he owns?

   - If you don't offer to intercede, will the situation cause an irreparable problem for the organization—or for Charlie?

If the answers to all three questions are "yes," you have an obligation to offer help. Peer coaches respect the "Rule of Once" and the "Right of Refusal":

The Rule of Once: You get to give your feedback and advice once. And only once. The assumption has to be that Charlie heard and understood you. Beyond that, he is free to accept, disregard, or hold your input in abeyance.

| Another Look | **Peer Coaching: How to Manage when Managers Are Few and Far Between** *continued* |

The Right of Refusal: You and we and Charlie have a right to say "thank you" and ignore peer input. We even have the right to not listen to peer input.

TOLERANCE FOR CLUMSINESS

Giving counsel and advice to a subordinate is a sweaty-palms situation for many a seasoned manager. Doing it with a peer is even more tense. So a little tolerance goes a long way in creating a climate in which peers can learn to help each other focus their efforts to create a service edge in their organization.

A FINAL THOUGHT

Managing an organization's customer service is a complex task requiring constant vigilance and effort. Managers can accomplish their objectives only when working with and through the efforts of other people. To do so requires tact and skill in communication and motivation. A key to managerial success is to ask pertinent questions and be open to feedback. Seven steps to ongoing service improvement provide a way to translate good intentions into a strategy that works.

Summary of Key Ideas

- Basic management functions all play a role in creating and sustaining a customer service strategy.
- Communication plays a central role in all management processes. Problems arise when people receive too little, too much, or poorly expressed information.
- Managing functions that can apply to customer service include developing a service theme, setting service goals, delegating responsibility and authority, recruiting good staff, directing actions, controlling by checking results against goals, and establishing a reward system.
- Managing by asking tough questions can point to weaknesses in any system.

- Employee motivation can be stimulated by systematically rewarding appropriate behaviors. Among the most powerful motivators is simple thanks for work well done.
- Praise and criticism must be given judiciously and worded carefully.
- Instructions should be given clearly and repeatedly.
- Seven tasks can effectively translate a slogan into a strategy.

Key Concepts

behavior modification

controlling

coordinating

disquieting questions

organizing

planning

poor communication (Types 1 and 2)

reward system

service theme

Self-Test Questions

1. What are the four key functions of management, and how do they relate to customer service and loyalty?
2. What are the three types of poor communication affecting organizations?
3. How can a manager make the most of a service theme?
4. What are the seven key tasks that managers can use to turn good intentions into a workable strategy for building customer loyalty?

Application Activity: Look at Feedback Receptiveness

1. Take a moment to answer this short self-quiz. Circle a 5 if the statement is almost always true, a 1 if it's almost never true, and some number in between if you prefer to waffle.

    A. I feel embarrassed when people point out my mistakes.   5 4 3 2 1

    B. I resent people telling me what they think of my shortcomings.   5 4 3 2 1

    C. I regularly ask friends and associates I trust to comment on how I am doing.   5 4 3 2 1

    d. I know how to offer constructive criticism to others
       in a sensitive way.   5 4 3 2 1

    e. I like having people tell me their reactions to my
       activities because it helps me adapt my future behavior. 5 4 3 2 1

2. If you scored 4 or 5 on items A and B, you may be putting up some resistance that could deter you from getting useful feedback. We are normally uncomfortable when we receive harsh or insensitive feedback, but even that can be useful if we wring out the emotion and look at the criticizer's perspective. Even our worst critic can provide a gift of good advice if we do not allow emotion to blind us. Successful communicators learn to look for helpful advice even when it's buried under a lot of worthless noise.

3. If you answered 4 or 5 to items C and D, you are creating a climate where helpful feedback is expected and accepted. People and organizations who foster such openness can benefit from others' advice.

4. If you answered 4 or 5 to item E, you are probably a little unusual. But you are on the right track.

5. Remember, being open to feedback does not mean that you necessarily agree with it. But if you get little or no feedback, you have nothing to sort out, apply, or learn from.

Notes

1. K. Blanchard and N. V. Peale. *The Power of Ethical Management* (New York: William Morrow, 1988), p. 121.

2. S. Nushart. Letter to the editor. *U.S. News and World Report,* December 11, 1995, p. 6.

3. R. C. Whiteley. *The Customer Driven Company: Moving from Talk to Action* (Reading, MA: Addison Wesley Publishing, 1991), p. 27.

4. L. B. Jones. *The Path: Creating Your Mission Statement* (New York: Hyperion, 1996), p. 4.

5. T. W. Firnstahl. "My Employees Are My Service Guarantee." *Harvard Business Review,* July–August 1989, pp. 28–32.

6. B. Maynard. "How to Manage with Questions." *TeleProfessional,* 209 W.5th Street, Waterloo, IA 50701–5420.

7. This principle is frequently stated in different ways, Townsend potently reminds managers in his book—one of the first management books to be a best-seller. R. Townsend. *Up the Organization* (New York: Alfred A. Knopf, 1970), p. 184.

8. "Productivity Gains from a Pat on the Back." *Business Week*, January 23, 1978, pp. 57–58.

9. J. H. Morrison and J. H. O'Hearne. *Practical Transactional Analysis in Management* (Reading, MA: Addison-Wesley, 1977), pp. 118–121.

10. Ibid., pp. 118–119. Reprinted with permission.

11. Ibid., pp. 120–121. Reprinted with permission.

12. This 7-Step Process is © 2003 Paul R. Timm, Ph.D. May not be reproduced without written permission. For further information, contact the author via e-mail at DrTimm@aol.com.

13. R. Zemke. "Peer Coaching: How to Manage When Managers Are Few and Far Between." *The Service Edge*, July 1996, p. 6. Reprinted with permission of Lakewood Publications.

Understand the Future of Customer Loyalty

Changing Conventions in Customer Service

The key to achieving financial success today, or success in any field for that matter, is being able to learn new things. . . . Things change so quickly that the most successful people in virtually every field are the people who learn new things fastest.

—economist Paul Zane Pilzer[1]

The customer and the business together are now redefining what it means to participate in a commercial relationship. It is becoming a collaborative, interactive world. The new dynamic of competition is based on doing battle for one customer at a time.

—Jim Sterne[2]

WHAT YOU'LL LEARN IN THIS CHAPTER

- Certain paradigm shifts are transforming marketing and customer service.
- One-to-one marketing and personalized service are changing the face of commerce.
- Technological changes are having a great impact on people in all segments of society.
- Technological trends will be applied to enhance customer loyalty.
- Businesspeople need to know some important facts about relationship marketing and service.

THE WAY IT IS . . .
Back from the Future[3]

In late 1991 the telegraph industry's life was taken, suddenly and brutally, by the facsimile machine. For more than 150 years, the telegram stood for immediacy and importance. It was an icon for urgency. But now, Western Union has closed down its telegraph service around the world. The fax was a new technology the telegram could not survive.

The shift from teletype and telegram to facsimile transmission represents one aspect of what some business consultants term a "paradigm shift"—a discontinuity in the otherwise steady march of business progress.

The automobile was another discontinuity, one that radically transformed both the economy and society. When the automobile first appeared, it seemed to be merely a horseless version of the well-known carriage. Predicting the consequences of the automobile's introduction would have been nearly impossible. Who would have imagined that a noisy, smelly, unreliable machine would eventually be responsible for the creation of suburbs; the fractionalization of families; and the growth of supermarkets, malls, and the interstate highway system?

Today companies worldwide are passing through a new and technologically assisted shift of epic proportions. The old paradigm, a system of mass production, mass media, and mass marketing, is being replaced by a totally new paradigm, a one-to-one economic system.

> *Successful businesses of the future will focus not on market share as much as share of the customer.*

The one-to-one future is increasingly being characterized by customized production (sometimes called mass customization), individually addressable messages, individualized accommodation of customer needs and wants, and one-to-one personalized marketing. Customers are no longer seen as some amorphous mass of beings; each is new viewed as an individual. This shift is totally changing the rules of business competition and growth. Instead of market share, the goal of most business competition will be share of the customer. Companies will compete for the loyalty of each customer, one at a time.

Having the size necessary to produce, advertise, and distribute vast quantities of standardized products will no longer be a precondition for success. Instead, products will be increasingly tailored to individual tastes, electronic media will be inexpensively addressed to individual consumers, and many products ordered over the phone or Internet will be delivered to the home in eight hours or less.

In the one-to-one future, businesses will focus . . . on the kinds of profits that can be realized from long-term customer retention and lifetime values—on customer loyalty.[4]

In customer service, massive levels of communication on the Internet will greatly multiply the ripple-effect problem we discussed in Chapter 1. Jeff Bezos, president of Amazon.com, says, "If you have an unhappy customer on the internet, he doesn't tell his six friends, he tells his 6,000 friends."[5]

UNDERSTAND THE TECHNOLOGY SHIFTS FOR THE NEW FUTURE

The demise of the telegraph industry is, of course, only one of countless examples of so-called paradigm shifts—new ways of thinking about and doing business. The list of obsolete products and services replaced by new, previously unimagined ones is long. And the pace of these changes seems ever-increasing. Yet many of us forget today's commonplace devices that were not yet used as recently as 1980. For example, there were no automatic teller machines, laser printers, or cellular phones. But even more incredible, "the number of televisions with remote control devices was statistically insignificant. There were no compact discs or DVDs, almost no videocassette recorders, and no video rental stores. Only restaurants had microwave ovens. Facsimile machines cost several thousand dollars each, took five minutes or more to transmit a single page, and were found only in very large companies. No one had a personal computer."[6]

> *Technology has changed our lives dramatically in the past few decades.*

And we haven't even touched on the Internet, with its astronomical impact on commerce and customer relationships. E-commerce will soon account for trillions of dollars as it becomes commonplace throughout the world. Already, the increase in products purchased via the Net doubles and triples each year. Whole books are addressing customer service in e-commerce. The following is from the preface to one such book, *Customer Service on the Internet*, by Jim Sterne:[7]

> Until recently, the computer's impact on business was measured almost exclusively in terms of speed and convenience. That is, a business kept working the way it always had, but it worked faster, and it worked with fewer people. In other words, many businesses have harnessed computers to become more competitive in operations. But continually declining information processing costs and rising computational power now mandate a transformation in the way businesses actually compete for customers.
>
> The astounding capabilities of the microchip have dramatically changed the business landscape—not just boosting the speed and reducing the cost of doing business, but changing the actual dimension of competition, too. Instead of centering on products and brands, this new form of business competition centers on customers and customer relationships—at the individual level.

In essence, computers have now made it possible to create an individual "customer feedback loop," integrating the production and service delivery processes into the research and promotion processes. The customer database allows a business to tell its customers apart and remember them individually. With interactivity, customers can talk to businesses—businesses are no longer limited to talking at their customers. And, with mass customization technology more and more businesses can actually make and deliver a single, customized product or service—cost efficiently—to an individual customer.

This feedback loop renders obsolete nearly every traditional marketing principle any business used to hold sacred. No longer is the marketer confined to dealing with awareness levels, or attitudes and brand preferences, or even competitive product comparisons. No longer must he project the results of sample surveys to a larger population.

Instead, the customer and the business together are now redefining what it means to participate in a commercial relationship. It is becoming a collaborative, interactive world. The new dynamic of competition is based on doing battle for one customer at a time.

There are many things a business should do to cope with this shift in the competitive ground. First and foremost, it should realize that its most valuable, most indispensable asset is not the product it sells, and not the service it renders. A business's only truly irreplaceable asset is the customer it serves, and the relationship it enjoys with that customer. Developing relationships with individual customers, differentiating one customer from the next, and treating each one as a separate, identifiable participant in the commercial relationship—these are the competitive activities of the most successful businesses today.

Second, a business should try to increase the level of interaction with its customers, across all media. If a business values its customers as its principal asset it will want to interact with those customers at every conceivable opportunity. Interactivity can occur in a wide variety of ways, from the touch-tone phone, to the ATM, to the cashier's station at the store, to the Internet.

> *Today's customer and the business together are increasingly redefining what it means to participate in a commercial relationship.*

Third, a business should be trying to customize whatever it can to the individually expressed needs of individual customers. This might mean tailoring a manufactured product, or it might simply mean invoicing a customer not on the seller's billing cycle but on the customer's paying cycle. The point is, in order to center the business around individual customers, the firm must learn to change its behavior with respect to the feedback it gets from each.

Let's look more specifically at some of the technology changes that are or will soon be impacting customer loyalty for businesses.

RECOGNIZE EMERGING TRENDS IN CUSTOMER SERVICE TECHNOLOGY[8]

Skim through any recent customer service trade publication, and you'll find articles with catchy titles like "World-Class Call Centers: The Next Generation," "Help Desks of the Future," or "Customer Service on the Cutting Edge." Predictions about technology abound, from concepts that resemble science fiction to more down-to-

> *Several technical and operational trends will reshape the customer care landscape of tomorrow.*

earth technological applications like ones working today. Experts do agree on some common themes that will transform the way we deliver technical customer service. The computing and communication landscape of the future will be affected by two categories of trends—technical and operational. *Technical trends* include unified messaging, seamless Internet integration, near-infinite bandwidth, and natural language processing. *Operational trends* include virtual call centers, global outsourcing, and teleprofessionals.

Technical Trend 1: Unified Messaging

Today's contact centers host customer conversations through a variety of channels. Most of these customer dialogues are electronically mediated, offering one- and two-way communication of voice, text, or image content. Lamentably, more often than not each communication channel is freestanding. Voice mail is a separate system from e-mail; fax is separate from Internet chat. Discrete hardware and software systems manage customer messages as independent from one another, unlinked to any common conversational thread. In fact, according to the latest research, only 27 percent of organizations had fully integrated phone, Web, and e-mail systems.[9] What is being done to remedy this?

Unified messaging attempts to integrate all customer communication. Using a single computer-telephony interface, unified messaging provides the customer service representative (CSR) with one source for all customer contact. Rather than switching between applications to pick up voice mail, e-mail, fax, or Web-based communication, the CSR receives and responds to all messages from the same computer screen. In such a system, all in-

> *Unified messaging uses a single message store linking disparate message systems to provide users common access to mixed media.*

coming messages are centrally stored and tracked until they can be handled. None of these messages will drop through the cracks. According to a recent study, a single messaging interface can save between 50 and 60 percent of the agent's time in checking messages.[10] By providing the CSR with an integrated message system, inbound contacts can be efficiently handled

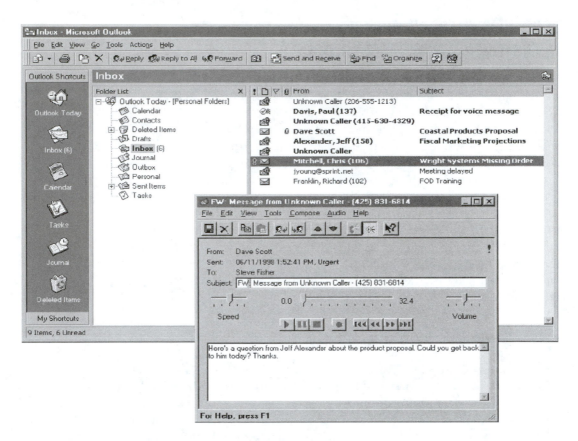

FIGURE 10.1   Sample unified messaging inbox with combined e-mail and voice mail (courtesy of the Information Technology Support Center).

regardless of the media. Figure 10.1 depicts an inbox that manages both e-mail and voice-mail messages.

Technical Trend 2: Internet Integration

In a recent survey of over 4,000 call centers, Purdue University researchers found that contact integration (especially Web integration) was the most popular technology improvement for enhancing customer service.[11] Web integration, as defined by the study, included Web chat, Web callback, and collaborative browsing. Web chat, which is growing in popularity for Internet users everywhere, allows real-time two-way text messaging between the customer and the customer service representative.

> Internet integration is much more than "live chat."

Web callback enables online customers to use a button push or hypertext link to request a return call by an agent on a separate phone line. The

CSR receiving the callback request can then phone the Web-page visitor in order to answer questions, provide assistance, or complete a transaction.

Collaborative browsing (also referred to as co-browsing) is considerably more involved than Web chat or Web callback. With collaborative browsing, the customer service representative can take control of the customer's Internet browser in order to demonstrate how to use the company's Web pages. For example, if a customer is having trouble completing an online service repair order, the CSR, using collaborative browsing, could walk the customer through the Web form, providing the appropriate mouse clicks and keystrokes needed to complete the order.

Technical Trend 3: Near-Infinite Bandwidth

When people first started using the Internet, connection speeds over telephone lines were abysmally slow (9,600 to 14,400 baud), leading to the humorous characterization of the World Wide Web as the "world wide wait." Even today, the vast majority (60 percent) of Internet users log in with landline speeds of 56 kilobytes per second (kbs) or less.[12] Using such a low-speed line can be annoyingly slow. This will all change. Near-infinite bandwidth is around the corner.

What does this mean for technical customer service? With infinite bandwidth, full Internet integration is possible. Customers no longer have to hang up a connection to toggle between browsing and talking to a customer service rep. Instead of static Web pages, customers can watch videos on new products, listen to Web wizards that guide them through online form completion, or even connect their defective or malfunctioning products to the Internet allowing the CSR to provide remote diagnosis and repair.

In the new economy, bandwidth replaces computer power as the driving force of technological advance. And bandwidth is exploding. Its abundance is the most important social and economic fact of our time.[13]

> *Cheap bandwidth will replace cheap computer power as the engine of the twenty-first-century economy.*

Technical Trend 4: Natural Language Processing

Some experts criticize today's computers as too hard to use, characterizing PC users as servants to the same machines that are supposed to make life easier, more productive, and simpler. One solution posed is to create human-centric machines that rely on natural interaction.

"You were born with ears, a mouth, eyes, and the ability to listen, speak and see," says Michael Dertouzos, director of the Laboratory for Computer Science at MIT. Human-centric computing lets you use these natural human capabilities to communicate with your machines so you won't have to learn new, complicated approaches to do what you already know how to do effortlessly.[14]

Natural language processing relies on speech for human-machine interaction rather than the mechanical substitutes of keyboards and pointing devices.

In the not too distant future, natural language processing will replace keyboards and mice for most human-computer interaction.

Natural language systems include automatic speech recognition, speaker verification, and speech synthesis. Speech recognition will move beyond discrete natural language processing (where the speaker must pause between words) to completely continuous speech. Regional accents and speech-distorting illnesses such as the common cold will no longer hamper recognition accuracy as they do today. Customers can speak interactive voice response options rather than keying them in on their touch-tone phones. CSRs could speak desktop commands to their PCs rather than typing or pointing with a mouse.

Speaker verification uses voiceprint technology to provide enhanced security for customer information and customer accounts. Rather than keying in a personal identification number (PIN) on a touch-tone phone, the customer pronounces his or her name or a password phrase. Speaker verification then matches the customer against a database of pre-verified voice recordings. Such an approach provides a "hands-free" way to access secure data and guarantees that the customer talking on the phone is, in fact, who he or she purports to be. This minimizes identity theft since it is much harder to steal a voiceprint than it is a customer account and PIN.

In addition to the technology advances I've mentioned, companies also face new options in terms of their operations—how they do business.

Operational Trend 1: Virtual Call Centers

Customer service call centers sometimes cannot handle the volume of calls received. As the volume of incoming or outgoing traffic increases, physical space may limit adding more agents. Worse yet, the supply of qualified customer service representatives may be exhausted, making it impossible to hire additional personnel. To address these constraints, companies often set up multiple call center sites in various geographic locations. This solves the capacity problem at the risk of confusing customers with multiple contact points when they have a problem. A better approach is often to have a single contact point. *Virtual call centers* (VCC) address this need.

Virtual call centers provide a single point of contact even when the actual call centers may be continents apart.

Organizations can link two or more geographically dispersed call centers into a single virtual call center using sophisticated telephony. All incoming calls are handled by a central telephone switch and then routed to the next available CSR, regardless of where the CSR is located. From the customer's perspective, it appears that a single site is handling the call—even when agents are working in call centers scattered throughout the world or operating out of their homes.

Operational Trend 2: Global Outsourcing

Similar to the virtual call center is the use of outsourcing call centers and help desk functions. Outsourcing means the company hires another company to fulfill some key functions such as its call centers or help desks. The trend is to use more *global outsourcing*—outside suppliers in geographically dispersed regions of the world that provide low-cost, continuous support. By strategically sourcing call center and help desk personnel from

> In "follow-the-sun" service, as the sun sets on one contact center, the next center, eight hours removed, comes on line to assist customers.

key time zones spaced eight hours apart, it is possible to offer 24/7 service to any place in the world. Global outsourcing enables anytime, anywhere customer assistance from agents working normal business hours, unhampered by the fatigue associated with swing or graveyard shifts. Alert CSRs provide a better customer experience. Look for global outsourcing to equalize call center/help desk staffing around the globe so that the "follow-the-sun" approach to customer service becomes the norm.

Operational Trend 3: Teleprofessionals

Teleprofessionals work by logging in from remote offices, often located in their own homes. Such jobs offer advantages to people wishing to work at home, and they reduce office costs for companies. InStat, a market research firm, estimated the number of U.S. workers operating away from the office increased from 30 million in 2001 to 40 million in 2004. That's a whopping 28 percent of the U.S. workforce.[15]

> Teleprofessionals telecommute to work by logging in from remote offices, often located in their own homes.

Telecommuting is win-win. Homes outfitted with high-speed Internet access provide the perfect venue for agents who prefer to work from the house. For agents who have taken leave to raise a family, this can be a godsend. For disabled workers, telecommuting provides an opportunity to join the ranks of the employed. Call centers win because telecommuting allows a company to retain employees who move or take family leave. Call centers can also use work-at-home agents to cover peak periods or provide essential coverage when a disaster closes roads or shuts down the call center. With virtual call center technology, customers need never know that the agent who so ably assists them is in reality sitting behind a desktop display in her pajamas. And all of this benefits customers who want immediate access to the companies they do business with.

These are some of the technology trends that are affecting customer service today and into the future.

RECOGNIZE THE SOCIAL AND ECONOMIC SHIFTS FOR THE NEW FUTURE

Aside from technology, other noteworthy changes affect business and customer relationships today. On the social and economic scene, we see substantial demographic shifts. Workforces are increasingly diverse—made up of people from a wide range of economic circumstances, cultures, and religions, as well as from both genders. Today's workforce consists of many two-income families and single parents with the associated family responsibilities this poses. We have an increasingly educated workforce, and its people are less tolerant of mindless, repetitive work. Today people expect to be more involved in organizational decisions, to have their input considered.

All these people are, of course, customers. Their shifting social conditions have stimulated demand for new and different products and services. Working couples have come to value shopping efficiency, convenience, and expanded business hours. Ethnically diverse neighborhoods have created markets for restaurants serving many kinds of food. Fast-food and take-home cuisine has become the mainstay of some busy families.

Politically, organizations face increasing government regulations, most of which reflect levels of social awareness previously not considered in the business world. Equal employment opportunities for people of all backgrounds, for persons with disabilities, and both genders are among the more notable changes of recent years. Likewise, a concern for the environment, employees' health and safety, and even employees' emotional well-being has become a hallmark of today's successful businesses. Caring companies attract and keep better employees (internal customers) and ultimately succeed in the marketplace. Most companies are aware of "green" issues: recycling and ecologically friendly packaging. In short, customers have come to expect different kinds of satisfaction.

USE THE NEW MEDIA FOR A ONE-TO-ONE FUTURE

Media changes have made big differences in the ways organizations communicate among their own members and with customers. In addition to the obvious speed and efficiency advantages of today's media, there are other considerations that have an impact on customer relationships. One of the most significant trends is the increasing ability to efficiently generate personalized, one-to-one messages tailored to the needs and wants of individuals, especially customers, coworkers, and associates.

> *One-to-one, individually tailored messages can now be sent to huge audiences.*

We should not underestimate the power of customized messages in business and professional communication. Today's organizations are seeing a shift from mass marketing—sending the same messages to a massive number of people in hopes that some of them will respond favorably—to individualized marketing in which a unique individualized message is sent to each person. This personalization began with word processing, which gave us the ability to produce "merge" letters that include personalized sections interspersed with the generic message.

Today, mass mailers routinely take advantage of this ability to personalize sales letters, sweepstakes entry forms, and even the envelopes they are sent in. But today's media is letting us go far beyond what has been done to now include past buying information and personal preferences to convey a sense that company knows and understands its reader.

> *Today's media systems go beyond the simple merging of names and addresses.*

EXPLORE CUSTOMER RELATIONSHIP MANAGEMENT (CRM) AND CUSTOMER STRATEGY SOLUTIONS

The acronym CRM has different meanings to different people. It has been applied to something as simple as keeping track of customer contact information to something as sophisticated as using intelligent systems to merge all kinds of customer data and customize marketing approaches.

According to the experts, *customer relationship management* (CRM) is ". . . a business strategy to select and manage the most valuable customer relationships. CRM requires a **customer-centric** business philosophy and culture to support effective marketing, sales, and service processes. CRM applications can enable effective customer relationship management, provided that an enterprise has the right leadership, strategy, and culture."[16] The definition may be a little long, but all the elements are there—*strategy, relationship, processes,* and *customer-centricity.* Of course, if you're like me, the shorter the definition, the better. Here's a one-liner from the *Harvard Business Review*: "CRM aligns *business* processes with customer strategies to build customer loyalty and increase profits over time."[17]

Notice something interesting in these two definitions? The term *software* is completely missing. The term *technology* isn't even mentioned. That's because CRM is not about software—it's about Creating Relationships (CR) that you want to Cost Manage (CM).

> *CRM employs technology to facilitate the alignment of business processes with your customer strategy.*

With the help of CRM technology, we are progressively moving toward one-to-one marketing that can create long-term *relationships* with customers and provide for a wide range of their needs. You do this by gathering as much information about customers as possible and responding to their needs, thus earning their loyalty.

> *One-to-one marketing builds relationships that allow businesses to earn a larger share of the customer's business.*

EMPLOY A CUSTOMER STRATEGY

Ever since management guru Peter Drucker proclaimed that "the true business of every company is to make and keep customers,"[18] corporate management has systematically shifted its focus away from pushing products to satisfying buyers—but not necessarily satisfying them all equally. Customer-centricity does not mean all customers are to be treated the same or that they have the identical value to the organization. A successful *customer strategy* involves market segmentation—categorizing customers according to their profit potential. Product and service levels are adjusted accordingly, with the higher-profit customers getting the most attention. For CRM to work, you need to know what business you're in, which customers you would like to find, which you want to keep, and which you want to lose. (Yes, sometimes we do want to "lose" a customer—if that customer is not a viable source of profit for the organization.) Then, and only then, are you ready to develop the processes and the infrastructure to support your business and customer strategy.

USE CONTACT MANAGEMENT SYSTEMS

Although not as sophisticated as CRM, contact management is a good start in the process of building loyalty—if used appropriately. Contact management is the process of managing, tracking, and organizing contacts with your customers and potential customers.

Picture this: You walk into work one morning, and your secretary tells you one of your customers, John, is on the phone. John wants to know if the delivery time of two weeks is still possible. John also forgot the prices and quantities you had quoted him and would like to get them now before he goes into his meeting in five minutes. "Wow," you think to yourself, "which customer is John anyway?" Finally, you find the two different files John's information is in, and you pick up the phone to call him back. Just then a customer walks into your office and says to you, "Where were you? You were supposed to come to my office and present your product to the board of trustees this morning. I'm sorry, but I don't think you will be good enough to get the contract."

With better contact management, this unfortunate scenario can be resolved. The idea of contact management is to record every important detail of any communication with the customer. This information may include price quotes, date of last contact, dates of future meetings, promises made, reminders of any special information, letters or advertisements sent, and so on. This information must be organized and filed in a way that it is readily available. Today, companies are using computerized contact management software to do this.

The software allows you to file away great amounts of information that can be brought up in seconds. For example, if the phone rings and John is on the phone, you can open any file with the name John and see exactly who he is, what you have promised him, when you are supposed to contact him next, and what you should be talking to him about. Most software programs allow you to search all customers for general information as well. For example, if you like to be proactive and contact your customers on a regular basis, contact management software can search for those customers who have not been called for at least two weeks.

> *Contact management software can be of tremendous value to virtually any business.*

Because you can readily access information about your customer, you can build a stronger relationship. For instance, if a customer mentions that she is going out to dinner (say, at Chuck E. Cheese pizza place) for her daughter's birthday, you can add a note in your contact management software. The next time you talk with this customer, you can ask, "How was your daughter's birthday dinner?" Questions like this will get a customer thinking about you as a concerned friend, not just another person trying to sell her something.

Although large companies may use highly specialized, custom contact management software, most of us can use software that is sold at any local electronics store. There is no reason for a small company to spend thousands of dollars having contact management software or database software custom-made. Check any office-supply store or online retailer for contact management software.

USE INTERACTIVITY OPTIONS NOW AVAILABLE

It is today's technology that facilitates this one-to-one CRM process. In the past, keeping track of customer names and addresses, sales data, and personal preferences was a complex and time-consuming process. Many people have kept such customer data on 3- × 5-inch cards in a file box. As the number of customers grew, the task became

> *Technology allows more sophisticated collection and processing of customer data.*

impractical. Yet today's computers and point-of-sale electronic data-gathering devices make it easy. We can now track individual preferences, poll customers about their needs, and customize services and products to meet those needs. Many stores are now offering specialized discount coupons to the customer at the checkout counter. If the customer buys a six-pack of Pepsi, the scanner generates a coupon for 50 cents off on Frito-Lay potato chips. (Frito-Lay is a division of PepsiCo.) People can also get coupons for the products they buy on the Net.

The one-to-one principle applies to internal customer relationships, too. Managers who keep closely attuned to their employees' preferences, talents, and wants build long-term relationships that can be mutually beneficial to the company. A fully utilized employee is the counterpart to the fully served customer.

On the social friendship level, knowing about and addressing the interests, needs, and wants of friends have always been major factors in building

Interactivity is the key to effective relationship building.

rapport and lifelong relationships. Interactivity—the two-way flow of information—is the key.

Many effective "networkers" keep reminder data on friends and acquaintances. I know a highly successful business entrepreneur who, from the earliest days of his career, kept index cards on each person he met. On the cards he would jot notes about the person's family, interests, pets, birth dates and anniversaries, accomplishments—even favorite jokes. Then, each time he spoke on the phone, he'd pull out the person's card and use ideas from it in the conversation. That's one-to-one communication. And today's media can magnify this ability.

USE MEDIA BREAKTHROUGHS TO ALLOW BETTER ONE-TO-ONE COMMUNICATION

Today's communication media typically utilize the power of computers to allow one-to-one relationship building on a larger scale. These media systems have the following characteristics:

1. They are *individually addressable and highly adaptive* to unique needs. They permit messages to be fully tailored to each customer, not just superficially modify versions of a form letter.
2. They are *interactive*, creating two-way, not one-way, communication. They make it easy for customers to give their feedback and reactions to messages.
3. They are *affordable and powerful.*

Are such media available to the typical businessperson or professional? More than any time in history, the answer is an unqualified "yes." Even the smallest business or individual proprietorship can afford much of today's technology. We are steadily moving toward more effective one-to-one service in business and the professions, supported by electronic media that can individualize messages.

APPLY RELATIONSHIP MARKETING: THE ONLY WAY TO SURVIVE IN THE FUTURE

Companies may argue they have the best-quality product at great prices. The fact is, customers have gotten used to having quality products at reasonable prices. These things are givens. They alone cannot readily distinguish one business from the competition.

But customers don't yet expect great service. They continue to expect less than marginal service. Why? Because that is what they've been getting in the past. Can you see the enormous opportunity that exists for building a strong competitive advantage through excellent A-plus service?

Think back to when you were a child. Do you remember a corner grocer or a candy store manager? Did he know who you were or who your parents were? A typical comment from the grocer might have been, "Hi, Billy; it's good to see you. Did you have a good vacation to the Grand Canyon?" Or from the candy store manager, you might hear, "Hello, Susie. Last time you were here you bought a half-pound of licorice. Can I get you the same thing, or would you like to try something different?" This is relationship marketing— having a one-to-one relationship with your customers. Every company—from a Fortune 500 business to a local baby-sitter—can utilize relationship marketing with just a bit of training. In fact, relationship marketing is limited only by the creativity of the people in the company.

> *Customers in a free-market economy expect good products at a reasonable cost. This is a given. What they don't always expect is great service.*

> *Relationship marketing opportunities are limited only by one's imagination.*

With the use of creativity, the opportunity to exceed customers' expectations extends well beyond just calling someone by name. That is a great start, but consider the following example given by Michael Gerber in his book *The E Myth Revisited* to see how far superior service can be taken:

On his way back to his home in San Francisco from a business trip, Michael decided to stop for the night in a little hotel overlooking the Pacific. When he arrived at the reception desk, quickly a well-dressed woman appeared and welcomed him to the hotel. Within three minutes from the greeting, he was ushered into his room by the bellboy. The room was decorated with plush carpeting, white-on-white bedding, natural cedar walls, and a stone fireplace. The fireplace grate had oak logs, rolled paper, and matches waiting to be used.

After changing in his room, Michael walked to the restaurant. The hotel receptionist had made him reservations for the restaurant at the time of his check in. Michael was immediately shown to his table upon arrival— even though others without reservations were waiting. When he got back to his room that night, the pillows were plumped up, the bed was turned down and there was a fire blazing in the fireplace. On the night stand was a glass of brandy and a card that read, "Welcome to your first stay at Venetia. I hope it has been enjoyable. If there is anything I can do for you, day or night, please don't hesitate to call. Kathi."

In the morning Michael woke up to the smell of coffee. When he went into the bathroom he found a perking coffee pot. A card by the pot read, "Your brand of coffee. Enjoy! K." Michael had been asked the night before at the restaurant which brand of coffee he preferred. Now it was bubbling in his room. Michael heard a polite knock on the door. When he opened the door, he saw the *New York Times* laying on the mat. When Michael had checked in, the reservationist had asked him what paper he preferred. Now his preferred paper was at his room for him to read.

Michael explains the service at the hotel has been exactly the same every time he has gone back. But after the first visit, he was never asked his preferences again.[19]

This is a great example of relationship marketing and of customer service. By "learning" his preferences, the hotel management was able to manipulate a common experience into one that was very personal for Michael—exceeding any expectations he might have had. To be a successful relationship marketer, you must become personal with your customers. After having a personalized experience with a business, a customer becomes very loyal. Think about it—would you patronize another hotel in the area after having a similar experience? Why would anyone want to take the chance of getting the "expected" service of another hotel? You can begin to see why relationship marketing is so powerful and so correlated with customer service.

GAIN CUSTOMER SHARE, NOT MARKET SHARE

Let's talk once again about the important concept of customer share. Progressive companies are coming to see the wisdom of focusing on share of customers rather than share of market.[20] Consider the following two competing flower businesses:

- The owners of Flower Company A have worked very hard, with a mass-marketing focus, in order to get a good piece of the market. They calculated that Company A has about 20 percent market share. In other words, for every dollar spent on flowers in the market, Company A gets 20 cents.
- The owners of Flower Company B, on the other hand, have worked very hard to gain a relationship with every one of the top purchasers of flowers (those who buy flowers on the most consistent basis). They estimate that they have a 20 percent customer share. That is, for every 10 customers who buy flowers, 2 of them buy flowers from Company B 100 percent of the time.

Which company is better off in the long run? Remember who Company B focused on, the customers who are frequent buyers—the top customers of the industry. Therefore, Company B enjoys much greater efficiency in their marketing—its customers are the best customers to have. They know them, and they can massage their relationship to gain even more of these people's flower business. They win.

If a company can win over the top customers, then its chance of survival is much better than if it just had a percentage of the market. Managers need to think of the present value of a customer's future business. Here's an example to illustrate what I mean: In the book *Customers for Life*, by Carl

Sewell and Paul B. Brown, Sewell explains the importance of thinking about the present value of future business. Sewell owns one of the largest luxury-car dealerships in the country. He has calculated that every customer has the potential of bringing his dealership $332,000 in sales. If an average car here costs about $25,000, and if people buy on average 12 cars, then the total sale is $300,000. Add service and parts, and each customer of Sewell's dealership is worth about $332,000 in sales.[21]

Mark Grainer, chairman of the Technical Assistance Research Programs Institute (TARP), similarly estimates that a loyal supermarket customer is worth $3,800 annually.[22] Over the course of a lifetime, this could easily add up to more than $150,000 in sales. Furthermore, a businessperson who frequently flies to different parts of the world could easily spend over $50,000 annually on

> *Present value of future business is an estimate of the total a customer could potentially spend with you.*

air travel. This customer could be worth over $1 million in revenue for an airline! This is what we mean by the present value of future business.

With this kind of long-range dollar thinking, who wouldn't give priority to customer share rather than market share? The customer you already have is infinitely more likely to buy from you again, while scrambling for new customers drains your marketing budget and energy. Remember, though, the only way to increase customer share is to build a relationship with your customer and to enhance your customer's satisfaction and loyalty.

Service Snapshot   The Reminder[23]

Thanks to computer databases, Fischer Florist in Atlantic City, New Jersey, is able to collect information and use it for retention of customers. Every day the managers at Fischer Florist send out reminder cards to certain customers. A reminder card may read as follows:

> Dear Mr. Jones: On March 29, last year, you remembered Jenny's birthday by sending her one dozen roses. Enclosed is a catalog of other beautiful flowers we offer. Please call our toll-free telephone number to place an order. We will make sure Jenny has your choice of flowers on that special day. Thank you for your business. We look forward to hearing from you.

When Mr. Jones calls, he must only tell the flower shop what flowers to send. Jenny's address, telephone number, and available times for delivery are already in the computer database. Likewise, Mr. Jones's credit card number is on file and can easily be confirmed and used.

A FINAL THOUGHT

The future looks exciting for businesses, but most companies will either need to make some major changes to be competitive, or consciously decide to keep doing things the old-fashioned, down-home way they do now. The unchanging strategy may appeal to people who don't much care for all this newfangled stuff. But be careful if you choose this approach. People's expectations have changed, and much of the change comes from technological advancement.

Whatever strategy you employ, from using highly sophisticated intelligent system databases to keeping mental notes on customer behaviors and preferences, one-to-one customer service and relationship building must stand as your company's cornerstone.

Summary of Key Ideas

- Today's business world is experiencing important paradigm shifts in the direction of increased personalization of products and services.
- Because of advances in technology, one-to-one customer service will become the standard for businesses in the coming years.
- The business landscape of the future will be affected by *technical trends* including unified messaging, Internet integration, near-infinite bandwidth, and natural language processing, as well as *operational trends* including virtual call centers, global outsourcing, and teleprofessionals.
- Ultimately, customer loyalty will stem from the ability to use relationship marketing to gain a greater share of the customer.
- Customer relationship management (CRM) marries technology and customer service principles to build better relationships and create A-plus experiences for customers.
- Companies that fail to include today's technology run the risk of falling behind customer expectations and losing loyalty.

Key Concepts

collaborative browsing

contact management software

customer relationship management (CRM)

human-centric systems

mass customization

mass marketing

natural language processing

one-to-one marketing

operational trends

paradigm shift

speech recognition

technical trends

virtual call centers (VCC)

voiceprint

Web callback

Web chat

Self-Test Questions

1. What kinds of paradigm shifts are transforming marketing and customer service today?
2. What is meant by one-to-one marketing? How can it build better relationships and enhance customer satisfaction?
3. What are some characteristics of today's one-to-one communication media?
4. Describe some technical trends and operational trends that impact customer loyalty.
5. What is a contact management system? How does this compare with CRM? How can it be used to boost customer loyalty?

Application Activity: Scoping Out the One-to-One Future

1. This chapter's introduction talks of "discontinuity" or paradigm shifts that literally change the world. List three discontinuities you are aware of outside of electronic technology. For each, describe three or more major changes that have resulted.
2. Among the most important determinants of customer satisfaction is the availability of feedback. Describe five ways organizations and individuals can improve their capabilities for gathering useful feedback.
3. Describe one or more examples of how businesses you know are using one-to-one communication to build a stronger relationship with you. (Note: Often these are little things done to build rapport and loyalty.)
4. Do a Web search for customer relationship management (CRM), and report on what you find. What does the number of CRM service providers say about the potential benefit of CRM?

Notes

The author acknowledges with appreciation the work of Clayton Eric Farr, president of Brainstorm, a Utah-based technology training firm, for his help in developing these ideas on the future of customer loyalty.

1. P. Pilzer. *Unlimited Wealth: The Theory and Practice of Economic Alchemy* (New York: Random House, 1991).
2. J. Sterne. *Customer Service on the Internet: Building Relationships, Increasing Loyalty, and Staying Competitive* (New York: John Wiley & Sons, Inc., 1996), p. xxi.

3. Some of this material was adapted from Chapter 1 of P. Timm and J. Stead, *Communication Skills for Business and Professions* (Upper Saddle River, NJ: Prentice Hall, 1996).

4. Adapted from D. Pepper and M. Rogers, *The One to One Future* (New York: Currency-Doubleday, 1993), pp. 3–6.

5. J. Sterne, p. xxi.

6. D. Pepper and M. Rogers, p. 14.

7. J. Sterne, pp. xvii–xviii.

8. The author appreciates the work of Christopher G. Jones, professor of information technology at Utah Valley State College, in drafting this material in the section called "Recognize Emerging Trends in Customer Service Technology."

9. Incoming Calls Management Institute. Industry statistics: Internet/Web. incoming.com. January 2001. [Online]. Available http://www.incoming.com. September 9, 2002.

10. Information Technology Support Center. "White Paper: Unified Messaging." September 2000. [Online]. Available http://www.itsc.state.md.us. September 6, 2002.

11. Information Technology Support Center. "White Paper: The Evolution of the Call Center to 'Customer Contact Center'" February 2001. [Online]. Available http://www.itsc.state.md.us. July 29, 2002.

12. L. Rowan. "Demographics and Statistics for Web Designers." 2000. [Online]. Available http://www.dreamink.com/design5.shtml. September 9, 2002.

13. G. Gilder. *Telecosm: How Infinite Bandwidth Will Revolutionize Our World.* (New York: The Free Press, 2000).

14. M. L. Dertouzos. *The Unfinished Revolution: Human-Centered Computers and What They Can Do for Us* (New York: HarperCollins, 2001).

15. Ibid.

16. B. Thompson. "What Is CRM?" *The Customer Relationship Management Primer.* 2002. [Online]. Available http://www.crmguru.com/members/papers/index.html. May 21, 2002. p. 1.

17. D. Rigby, F. Reichheld, and P. Schefter. "Avoid the Four Perils of CRM." *Harvard Business Review*, February 2002, 80(2), pp. 101–108.

18. P. Drucker. *The Practice of Management* (New York: Harper & Row, 1954).

19. M. E. Gerber. *The E Myth Revisited* (New York: HarperCollins, 1995), pp. 188–92.

20. D. Pepper and M. Rogers, pp. 18–51.

21. C. Sewell and P. B. Brown. *Customers for Life* (New York: Pocket Books, 1990), p. 162.

22. D. Pepper and M. Rogers, pp. 37–38.

23. J. Griffin. *Customer Loyalty: How to Earn It; How to Keep It* (New York: Lexington Books, 1995), p. 125.

Appendix

How to Lead or Participate in an A-Plus Idea-Generating Meeting

Use the Group Process to Boost Customer Satisfaction and Loyalty

In this appendix we will focus on 12 specific tips that will enable you to conduct or participate in meetings designed to generate A-plus ideas. When focused on improved service, such meetings can tap the ideas of the group to provide a gold mine of profitable customer service ideas. Below are 12 action tips for running an effective A-plus meeting.

ACTION TIP 1: MAKE THE MEETING'S PURPOSE ABSOLUTELY CLEAR

Meetings are of two general types: informational and problem solving. Don't confuse them. The most legitimate use of the group process is to bring together a variety of responses to a specific problem or decision. A-plus idea generation requires good group skills. Don't waste time at the meeting just giving out information.

Clarify the specific topic up front so that people come to the meeting with the right mindset. Tell participants that the meeting will seek to generate A-plus ideas from the VISPAC categories, as discussed in Chapters 4 and 5.

ACTION TIP 2: INVITE THE RIGHT PEOPLE

People invited to a meeting should:

1. Have some expertise. Typically customer contact people have the most experience with A-plus opportunities, but others may also have ideas.

2. Have a vested interest in the outcome of the discussion—they should want to improve customer loyalty.

3. Have some skills in group decision making and be able to express themselves reasonably well. Avoid the narrow-minded, inflexible person.

4. Share the overall values of the organization. If participants are antagonistic or in disagreement with the company's goals, it makes no sense to have them participate in decisions affecting those goals.

Be sure, too, to invite the right *number* of people. Have enough to represent a variety of opinions but not so many that the process bogs down. A-plus meetings work best with 4 to 12 participants.

ACTION TIP 3: ASSIGN ADVANCE PREPARATION

Participants should know what the meeting is about and what kinds of information and ideas they may need to gather and bring with them. If the central focus of the meeting will be on generating A-plus ideas to enhance customer *convenience*, telling people in advance will let them think about competitors' tactics, consider creative ideas being used by other companies, and perhaps collect needed data such as sales results others have experienced. Get people thinking on the right wavelength even before the meeting.

ACTION TIP 4: START ON TIME AND USE A REALISTIC SCHEDULE

A major objection of meeting attendees is the failure to start and end on time. Don't wait "a few minutes until the rest of the folks get here," or you'll find yourself doing so every time. Get a reputation for prompt starts, and people will get there on time. Likewise, don't run over. If you've scheduled 90 minutes, stop at or before that deadline. If you really want to shock people, end the meeting early! When the work is done, quit.

Schedule breaks, have refreshments, and encourage people to walk around the room. Do whatever is necessary to make the experience pleasant and satisfying.

ACTION TIP 5: CREATE A POSITIVE CLIMATE

If you are the leader, thank people for coming to the meeting. Let the participants know that they were selected because they can contribute valuable insights and ideas. Set a good psychological climate by example. Let people know that the discussion can be casual and that they are encouraged to be creative.

Also, arrange the meeting room appropriately so that participants:

- can see each other face to face (rather than sitting in rows, auditorium style)
- are provided with writing materials and tables to write on
- use a chalkboard, flip charts, or transparencies to capture ideas
- are encouraged to move around the room freely to relieve tension or fatigue
- are provided with refreshments if the meeting will run more than a few hours

ACTION TIP 6: BE AWARE OF "HIDDEN AGENDAS"

Although we may agree on the discussion topic, people in meetings often have unspoken objectives called "hidden agendas." These may include such things as:

- getting some "exposure" (i.e., favorably impressing others)
- providing a "status arena" where they can assert power or show off their ability
- taking advantage of the chance to socialize with others
- diffusing decision responsibility so that one person won't have to take all the heat if a decision fails
- getting away from unpleasant work duties

When a person's hidden agenda doesn't take away from the effectiveness of the group, don't worry about it. If the ulterior motives of the hidden agenda deter the group from accomplishing its work, talk with participants candidly (perhaps in private) and solicit their cooperation in putting the group's needs above their own.

ACTION TIP 7: REWARD GROUP MEMBER INPUT

Never let a group member's input be met with silence. To do so will quickly extinguish further input from that person—and others. Bear in mind that stating an opinion or idea can be somewhat risky for people. They risk being perceived as wrong, naive, unimaginative, or any of dozens of other possibilities.

By acknowledging contributions, we create a climate where more will be offered. Simple comments such as "good thought" or "you might be onto something there" can go a long way toward drawing out further input. Even if the suggestion doesn't make much sense to you, you can come up with a neutral response like "okay" or "thanks."

ACTION TIP 8: MONITOR PRESSURES TO CENSOR

Problems involving the pressure to censor information are a bit more complex. Two common forms of such pressure are:

- individual dominance
- group-think

Individual dominance occurs when certain individuals will dominate a group discussion by force of their personality, organizational position, or personal status. These people may be particularly charming (and thus disproportionately influential because everybody likes them!) or highly autocratic or hardheaded. Reduce this dominance by drawing other people into the discussion.

Group-think describes a condition of like-mindedness which can arise in groups that are particularly cohesive. While cohesiveness is normally a good condition in groups, it can be carried too far. This can happen when the group members' desire for consensus or harmony becomes stronger than their desire for the best possible decision. Here are seven symptoms of group-think:

1. an overemphasis on team play and getting along harmoniously
2. a "shared stereotype" view that competitors or those in opposition to us are inept, incompetent, and incapable of doing anything well
3. self-censorship by group members, in which personal doubts are suppressed to avoid rocking the group's boat
4. rationalization to comfort one another and reduce any doubts regarding the group's agreed-upon plan
5. self-appointed "mind guards" that function to prevent anyone from undermining the group's apparent unanimity and to "protect" the group from information that differs from their beliefs
6. direct pressure on those who express disagreement
7. an expression of self-righteousness that leads members to believe their actions are moral or ethical, thus letting them disregard objections to their behavior

Each of these symptoms of group-think damages creative or original thinking and effective decisions.

ACTION TIP 9: DON'T ALLOW CONFLICT TO BECOME DESTRUCTIVE

Traditionally, it has been assumed that conflict should be avoided in meetings. The term conjures up images of fistfights or people screaming at each other. In reality, conflict is simply a state of incompatibility. It is neither good nor bad. What creates problems are the participants' reactions to conflict.

We typically respond to conflict in one of several ways:

1. We can attempt to *avoid conflict* by not expressing opposing views and by withholding any disagreement. We keep from rocking the boat, and we minimize the possibility of being subjected to rejection or disagreement from others. (Group-thinkers respond this way.) The drawback here is that some good ideas—ideas that can best solve the group's problems—may be withheld.

2. We get into a *win-lose orientation*, leading to no-holds-barred, open warfare among participants.

3. We *manage conflict* to regulate it but not eliminate confrontation. Recognizing that the abrasive actions of opposing views—like sandpaper or wood—polish the final product, skillful leaders seek free exchange of information without the win-lose destructiveness of unregulated conflict. Accomplishing this calls for communication skills that encourage the generation of information without inhibiting or turning off participants.

This third response, managing conflict, is by far the most useful. Incidentally, a sense of humor helps. Mark McCormack, founder and CEO of a sports management conglomerate, said that "laughter is the most potent, constructive force for diffusing business tension. Humor is what brings back perspective."

ACTION TIP 10: AVOID OVERCENTRALIZED LEADERSHIP

Effective meeting managers work to move the group away from the traditional leader format toward "group-centered leadership" or self-managed teams. The leadership process of guiding and directing the group's activity should shift from person to person within the group rather than be centered in one individual. Having each group member take some leadership role can overcome dominance and conflict problems. The result is what is called group-centered leadership. This is contrasted below with traditional leadership.

Traditional Leadership

1. The leader directs, controls, polices, and leads members to the proper decision. Basically it is the leader's group, and his or her authority and responsibility are acknowledged by members.

2. The leader focuses attention on the task to be accomplished, brings the group back from any digressions, and performs all the functions needed to arrive at the proper decision.

Group-Centered Leadership

1. The group, or meeting, is *owned* by the members, including the leader. All members, with the leader's assistance, contribute to its effectiveness.

2. The group is responsible, with occasional and appropriate help from the leader, for reaching a decision that includes the participation of all and is the product of all. The leader is a servant and helper to the group.

3. The leader sets limits and uses rules of order to keep the discussion within strict limits set by the agenda. He or she controls the time spent on each item lest the group wander fruitlessly.

4. The leader believes that emotions are disruptive to objective, logical thinking and should be discouraged or suppressed.

5. The leader believes that a member's disruptive behavior should be handled by talking to the offender away from the group; it is the leader's task to do so.

6. Because the need to arrive at a task decision is all-important in the eyes of the leader, needs of individual members are considered less important.

3. Members of the group take responsibility for its productivity, its methods of working, its assignments of tasks, and its plans for using the time available.

4. Feelings, emotions, and conflict are recognized by the members and the leader as legitimate factors in the discussion process.

5. The leader believes that any problem in the group must be faced and solved within the group and by the group.

6. With help and encouragement from the leader, the members come to realize that the needs, feelings, and purposes of all members should be considered so that a group awareness forms.

ACTION TIP 11: USE BRAINSTORMING TO GENERATE CREATIVE IDEAS

The term *brainstorming* is sometimes used to mean any kind of creative thinking. But that misuses the word. Brainstorming is a specific technique using explicit rules for idea generation and development. This approach requires a communication climate in which free expression of all kinds of ideas is valued and encouraged—no matter how offbeat or bizarre they may seem. Brainstorming relies on four underlying beliefs:

1. *No idea may be criticized.* No comments; no grunts or groans; no thumbs-down gestures. Just let opinions come out and be recorded.

2. *No idea is too wild.*

3. *The quantity of ideas generated is important.* Push to get as many ideas without regard to whether or not they make sense at this point.

4. *Hitchhiking is important.* Participants should add to or amplify ideas suggested by others.

The climate that has been established by the meeting leader can promote or hamper the use of brainstorming. A climate that encourages humor and informality will work best. Many leaders like to post the four principles where everyone can refer to them.

ACTION TIP 12: ASSIGN SPECIFIC FOLLOW-UP ACTIONS

Be sure that group members have their "marching orders." A brilliant decision will be of no value if it isn't implemented; the people who made the decision are the best ones to direct implementation.

Follow-up assignments typically include informing people of the new action, training people in how to implement it, creating forms or written instructions for implementing it, and communicating to key people about the action and its timing.

A FINAL THOUGHT

Meetings hold the potential for generating good ideas if they are handled well. A meeting aimed at generating A-plus ideas will be more successful if you apply the tips presented in this appendix. Now, let's try on the suggestions and see what great ideas we can generate.

Application Activity: Plan and Run a Brainstorming (A-Plus) Meeting

Select one of the organizations below and run an A-plus meeting in which you come up with at least two ideas for each of the VISPAC categories.

1. the company you are currently working in (After the meeting, prepare a memo describing your ideas and present it to your boss.)
2. your university bookstore
3. a restaurant you frequently patronize
4. your favorite supermarket
5. a video store
6. an upscale clothing shop (boutique)

Try your skills at setting a climate, articulating the topic, running the meeting, capturing ideas, and planning the follow-up necessary to implement ideas your group produces.

If you do not work in an organization or cannot get permission to run the meeting in the company, use your class as the "company" and develop A-plus ideas for making the students (customers) more satisfied with the course.

Index